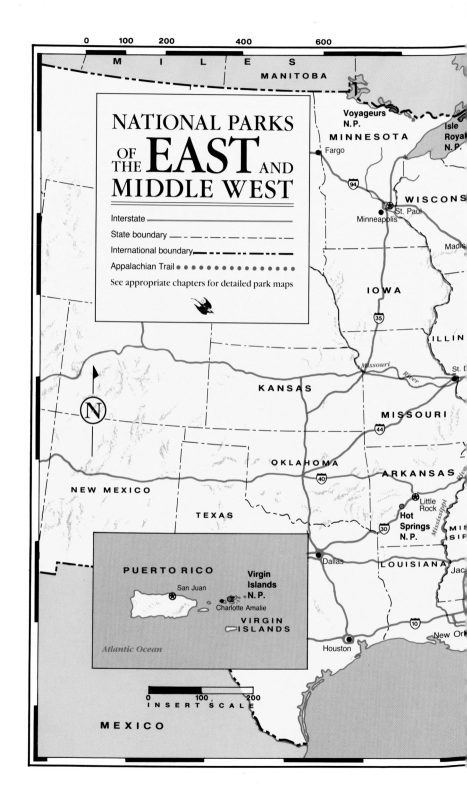

NATIONAL PARKS

OF THE **EAST** AND MIDDLE WEST

Interstate ————————
State boundary — — — — —
International boundary ▪—▪—▪—▪—
Appalachian Trail ● ● ● ● ● ● ● ● ● ● ● ● ●

See appropriate chapters for detailed park maps

INSERT SCALE

0   100   200   400   600

M I L E S

MANITOBA

Voyageurs
N.P.

Isle
Roya
N.P.

MINNESOTA

Fargo

WISCONS

St. Paul
Minneapolis

Madis

IOWA

ILLIN

St.

KANSAS

Missouri River

MISSOURI

OKLAHOMA

ARKANSAS

NEW MEXICO

Little
Rock

Hot
Springs
N.P.

MIS
SIP

TEXAS

Dallas

LOUISIANA

Jac

New Or

Houston

PUERTO RICO

San Juan

Virgin
Islands
N.P.

Charlotte Amalie

VIRGIN
ISLANDS

Atlantic Ocean

0   100   200
INSERT SCALE

MEXICO

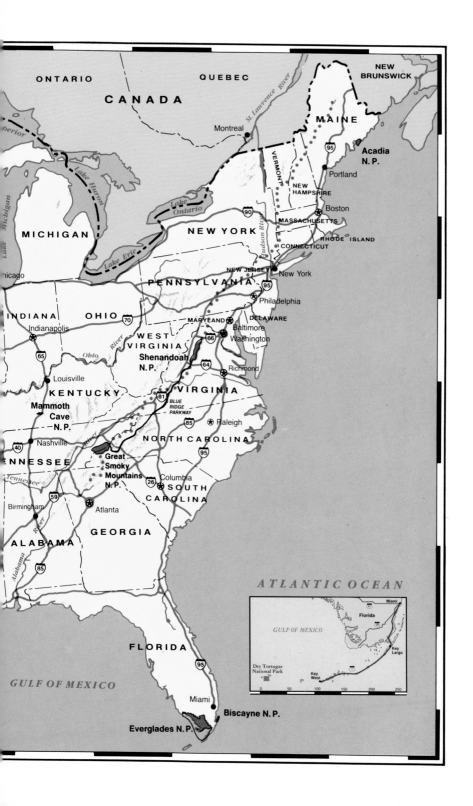

THE SIERRA CLUB GUIDES
TO THE
NATIONAL PARKS
OF THE
EAST
AND
MIDDLE
WEST

Published by
Stewart, Tabori & Chang

Distributed by
R A N D O M H O U S E

Library of Congress Cataloging-in-Publication Data

The Sierra Club guides to the national parks of the East and Middle West /
(text by William Bake . . . et al.). — Rev. and updated.
p.   cm. — (The Sierra Club guides to the national parks)
Includes index.
Cover title: East and Middle West.
ISBN 0-679-76494-1 (alk. paper)
1. National parks and reserves—United States—Guidebooks.
2. National parks and reserves—East (U.S.)—Guidebooks.
3. National parks and reserves—Middle West—Guidebooks. 4. United States—
Guidebooks. 5. East (U.S.)—Guidebooks. 6. Middle West Guidebooks. I. Bake,
William A., 1938-   . II. Sierra Club. III. Title: East and Middle West.
IV. Series.
E160.S54 1996
917.3—dc20
96-11446
CIP

TEXT BY:
William Bake: Great Smoky Mountains
Brian Carey: Biscayne
Hugh Crandall: Shenandoah
Kent and Donna Dannen: Acadia, Hot Springs, Mammoth Cave
Fred Hirschmann: Everglades
Brian McCallen: Voyageurs
Cheryl Koenig Morgan: Dry Tortugas*
Susan Tollefson: Virgin Islands
Bruce Weber: Isle Royale
*New in the revised edition.

Text revisions throughout this edition by the Project Editor.
Photo credits can be found on pp. 392-393.

PROJECT EDITOR: Donald Young
CONSULTING EDITOR: James V. Murfin (First Edition)
IN-HOUSE EDITOR: Joseph Norton (First Edition)
DESIGNER: J. C. Suarès, Gordon Harris, Michelle Siegel
PHOTO EDITOR: Amla Sanghvi
COPY EDITOR: Randy Blunk (Revised Edition)
PRODUCTION: Katherine van Kessel (First Edition)
ART AND PRODUCTION: Alice Wong, Lisa Vaughn, Melanie Random,
Evangeline Yao, Christopher Young (Revised Edition)

Created by Stewart, Tabori & Chang, Inc., 575 Broadway, New York, NY 10012

Printed in Singapore

24689753

Revised Edition

Cover Photographs: Great Smoky Mountains National Park (© Bill Deane);
Atlantis fritillary butterfly and black-eyed Susans (© Mitch Kezar); Squirrelfishes
(© Al Grotell); illustration and map (© Bill Russell). Frontispiece: Dogwood,
Mammoth Cave National Park (© W. Ray Scott) Back Cover Photograph: Black
bear, Great Smoky Mountains National Park (© Bullaty–Lomeo)

P R E F A C E

The fifty-four national parks of the United States contain many glorious natural splendors. Each year, tens of millions of Americans and growing numbers of visitors from around the world contemplate the beauty of snow-capped mountains, cascading waterfalls, groves of soaring trees, glistening surf-kissed beaches, and deep and mysterious red-rock canyons. Herds of large mammals enhance the setting in some parks, and uncounted numbers of other animals, birds, crawly things, and plants occupy their own niches as participants in nature's grand design.

The National Park System contains about 375 units, but the five volumes of *The Sierra Club Guides to the National Parks* feature only those units designated as a "national park" or as a "national park and preserve." An act of Congress is required for the establishment of a park. The world's first national park—Yellowstone— was created in 1872. The list has grown steadily, as the American people, through their elected representatives, demonstrated many times their commitment to preserving parks for the enjoyment of themselves and of generations yet to come. In 1994 alone, three more parks were added to the list.

The Sierra Club was founded in California in 1892 by the naturalist John Muir and some of his friends. One of the oldest and largest conservation organizations, the Club, which now has more than 550,000 members, has been in the forefront of many efforts to create new parks.

This series has been produced with the cooperation of the Sierra Club and with the participation of the National Park Service and Random House. Leading nature writers and photographers have contributed to the guides. This revised edition contains new chapters on the six parks established since the mid-1980s. As well, the chapters on the forty-eight other parks have been thoroughly reviewed and completely updated.

We hope you will enjoy exploring the parks, and we know these guides will enhance your experience.

—Donald Young, Editor

M A P S

C O N T E N T S

ACADIA
NATIONAL PARK

Coastal lands of Acadia were once mountain slopes at much higher elevations.

ACADIA NATIONAL PARK
P.O. BOX 177, BAR HARBOR, MAINE 04609
TEL.: (207) 288-3338

HIGHLIGHTS: Cadillac and Acadia Mountains • Jordan Pond • Park Loop Road • Thunder Hole • The Tarn • Otter Point Intertidal Life Zones • Somes Sound • Carriage Road Bridges • Long Pond • Wonderland • Schoodic Point

ACCESS: Mount Desert Island is reached by Maine 3, Schoodic Peninsula by Maine 186, and Isle au Haut by Maine 15 and passenger ferry.

HOURS: Open year-round, 24 hours daily; 2-mile section of Park Loop Road is plowed in winter.

FEES: For camping and for ferry to Isle au Haut.

PARKING: Ample parking throughout park.

GAS, FOOD, LODGING: Available in nearby towns. Jordan Pond House Restaurant open from May 15 to October 15.

VISITOR CENTER: Acadia National Park Visitor Center, open from May 1 to November 1, offers film on Acadia, cassette-tape tours. Park Headquarters serves as Visitor Center, November to April.

MUSEUM: Islesford Historical Museum and Abbe Museum of Stone Age Antiquities.

GIFT SHOP: At Thunder Hole, Cadillac Mountain, and Jordan Pond.

PETS: Allowed on leashes, except on swimming beaches, at Isle au Haut campground, on trails with rungs or ladders, and inside buildings.

PICNICKING: Numerous picnic sites available.

HIKING: 120 miles of trails and 44 miles of carriage roads.

BACKPACKING: Backcountry camping not permitted.

CAMPGROUNDS: 374 tent and 127 trailer sites in park. Blackwoods Campground open year-round; Seawall Campground open during summer season only; 14-day stay limit in summer. Duck Harbor Campground open from May 15 to October 12; 3-day stay limit in summer. Water available at all campgrounds; no utility hookups.

TOURS: Wide variety of interpretive tours.

OTHER ACTIVITIES: Carriage rides, bicycling, swimming, birdwatching, saltwater fishing (with no permit required), freshwater fishing (with Maine state license), cross-country skiing.

FACILITIES FOR DISABLED: Visitor Centers, some restrooms, and several campsites accessible; contact park for information.

For additional information, see also Sites, Trails, and Trips on pages 30–44 and the map on pages 14–15.

ACADIA NATIONAL PARK PRESENTS A STUDY in the interplay of water and land. Water helped form the park's ancient rocks. Ice in continental glaciers carved its barren peaks, scooped out its lakes, and excavated the trenches that separate its islands from the mainland. The melting of this ice submerged the preglacial mainland up to the park's present coast. Mighty waves tear at Acadia's rugged shore. The land and its creatures invade the sea on many islands, and the sea and its creatures penetrate the land in inlets.

The ebb and flow of the tides sustain Acadia's complex intertidal life zones. Warm and cold ocean currents stir up abundant plankton, which provides the base for an elaborate food web. Over the years, the ocean also has carried people, who first came for the rich wildlife resources and the good harbors excavated by glaciers and later came to delight in the area's incredible beauty—a product of the dynamic convergence of sea and earth.

Bass Harbor Head Light, built in 1858, is maintained by the U.S. Coast Guard.

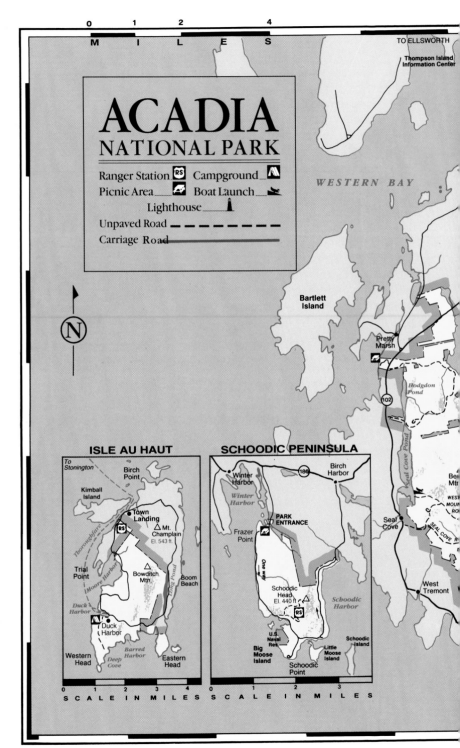

0 1 2 4

M I L E S

TO ELLSWORTH

Thompson Island
Information Center

ACADIA
NATIONAL PARK

Ranger Station **RS**   Campground ⛺

Picnic Area 🅿️   Boat Launch 🚤

Lighthouse 🗼

Unpaved Road — — — — — —

Carriage Road ─────────

WESTERN BAY

Bartlett
Island

Pretty
Marsh

Hodgdon
Pond

102

Seal Cove Pond

ISLE AU HAUT

To
Stonington

Birch
Point

Kimball
Island

Town
Landing

RS

△ Mt.
Champlain
El. 543 ft.

Trial
Point

Bowditch
Mtn.

△

Boom
Beach

Duck
Harbor

🅿️ Duck
Harbor

Moore Harbor

Long Pond

Thoroughfare

Western
Head

Barred
Harbor

Deep
Cove

Eastern
Head

0 1 2 3 4

S C A L E   I N   M I L E S

SCHOODIC PENINSULA

Winter
Harbor

186

Birch
Harbor

Winter
Harbor

**PARK
ENTRANCE**

🅿️

Frazer
Point

One way

Schoodic
Head
El. 440 ft.

△

RS

Schoodic
Harbor

U.S.
Naval
Res.

Big
Moose
Island

Little
Moose
Island

Schoodic
Island

Schoodic
Point

0 1 2 3

S C A L E   I N   M I L E S

Ber
Mtn

WES
MOUN
RO

SEAL COVE R

Seal
Cove

West
Tremont

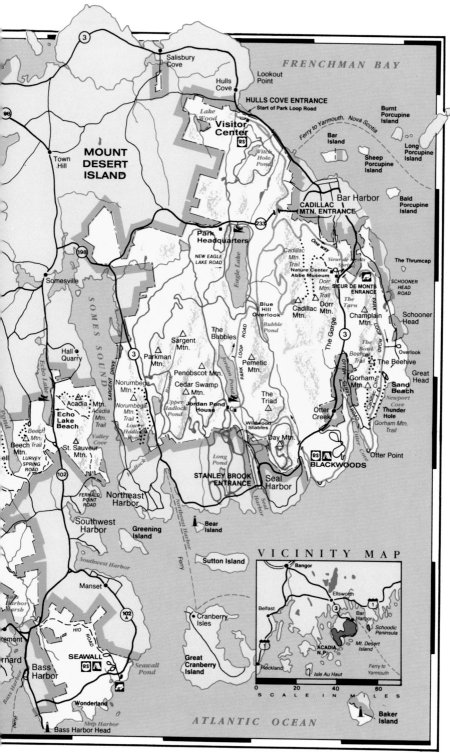

FRENCHMAN BAY

Salisbury Cove

Lookout Point

Hulls Cove

HULLS COVE ENTRANCE
Start of Park Loop Road

Lake Wood

Visitor Center RS

Witch Hole Pond

Burnt Porcupine Island

Bar Island

Long Porcupine Island

Sheep Porcupine Island

Bald Porcupine Island

Bar Harbor

MOUNT DESERT ISLAND

Town Hill

CADILLAC MTN. ENTRANCE

233

Park Headquarters

NEW EAGLE LAKE ROAD

Eagle Lake

Cadillac Mtn. Trail

One way

Sieur de Monts Spring

The Thrumcap

198

Somesville

Nature Center
Abbe Museum

SIEUR DE MONTS ENTRANCE

SCHOONER HEAD ROAD

Blue Hill Overlook

Dorr Mtn. Trail

Schooner Head

Hall Quarry

SOMES SOUND

The Bubbles

Bubble Pond

Cadillac Mtn.

Dorr Mtn.

The Tarn

The Gorge

Champlain Mtn.

Sargent Mtn.

3

Parkman Mtn.

Penobscot Mtn.

JORDAN POND ROAD

PARK LOOP ROAD

Pemetic Mtn.

The Bowl

Beehive Trail

Gorham Mtn.

Overlook

Great Head

The Beehive

Echo Lake

Norumbega Mtn.

Cedar Swamp Mtn.

Upper Hadlock Pond

Norumbega Mtn. Trail

Lower Hadlock Pond

Acadia Mtn.

Echo Lake Beach

Acadia Mtn. Trail

Valley Cove

Beech Mtn. Trail

SARGENT DRIVE

Jordan Pond House

Ca

The Triad

OTTER CLIFFS

Cadillac Cliffs

Sand Beach

Newport Cove

Thunder Hole

Gorham Mtn. Trail

Otter Creek

Beech Mtn.

St. Sauveur Mtn.

LURVEY SPRING ROAD

Hadlock

Wildwood Stables

Day Mtn.

Otter Point

102

FERNALD POINT ROAD

Northeast Harbor

Northeast Harbor

Long Pond

STANLEY BROOK ENTRANCE

Seal Harbor

RS

BLACKWOODS

Otter Cove

OTTER CLIFFS ROAD

Seal Harbor

Southwest Harbor

Greening Island

Bear Island

Ferry

Southwest Harbor

Sutton Island

VICINITY MAP

Manset

102

HIO ROAD

Cranberry Isles

Bangor

Ellsworth

1

Belfast

3

Bar Harbor

Schoodic Peninsula

Harbor Marsh

SEAWALL RS

Seawall Pond

Great Cranberry Island

Rockland

ACADIA N.P.

Mt. Desert Island

Ferry to Yarmouth

Bass Harbor

Wonderland

0   20   40   60

S C A L E   I N   M I L E S

Ship Harbor

Bass Harbor Head

ATLANTIC OCEAN

Baker Island

The First Summer Residents

Indians enjoyed Acadia for some 6,000 years. The most recent, the Abnakis, paddled their birch-bark canoes through these waters for several centuries before the first Europeans arrived. The Abnakis called the mountainous island Pemetic, which means "the sloping land."

In 1604, Samuel Champlain spotted smoke from Abnaki campfires near Otter Point on the southeastern side of the 13- by 16-mile island, which contains most of Acadia's 38,000 acres. When Champlain sailed closer in order to investigate, his ship collided with a shoal. As repairs were being made in placid Otter Cove, Champlain gazed up the broad, green-forested slopes of the mountain later named Cadillac, which looms above a white line of surf disintegrating on shoreline rocks. Wide patches of barren granite glistened on the mountain's 1,530-foot summit—the highest point on the Atlantic shore of the United States. This massive peak is part of a chain of mountains with glacier-smoothed summits on whose bare, wind-swept rock trees cannot grow. Champlain renamed the island *l'Isle des Monts-deserts*, or the "Isle of Bare Mountains." Mount Desert (duh-ZURT) it remains.

Champlain encountered the island while preparing for French exploitation of American wildlife. For the next 150 years, Great Britain and France, each with its Indian allies, fought a series of wars to gain monopolistic control of the lucrative fur trade. Frenchman Bay, on the eastern side of Mount Desert Island, was so named because French warships hid there behind the Porcupine Islands, waiting to plunder English ships and settlements. British warships preferred to anchor behind the Cranberry Isles, on the southeastern side of Mount Desert Island. After Great Britain finally triumphed in 1760 in the French and Indian War, English and (subsequently) American settlers farmed, fished, and logged Mount Desert Island.

By 1850, the island's magnificent beauty was attracting the painters of the Hudson River School. Then tourists came to see the source of the beautiful paintings. Hotels had been built in Bar Harbor by 1880, and millionaires of the Gay Nineties built elegant "cottages"—actually summer mansions. Many mansions burned in the Great Fire of 1947, an inferno whipped across 17,000 acres by October winds. Some cottages did survive, reminders of an era when Mount Desert Island was home to the Astors, Carnegies, Fords, Morgans, Rockefellers, and Vanderbilts.

Establishment of the Park

Beginning in 1901, Boston textile millionaire George Dorr joined with other "summer people" to preserve key parcels of Mount Desert's scenery in a natural state for public use. Years of effort were rewarded in 1916, when President Woodrow Wilson announced the establishment of Sieur de Monts National Monument, and in 1919, when Congress approved a bill creating Lafayette National Park, the first national park east of the Mississippi River. Dorr became superintendent and continued to find more donors of more land. In 1929, the park was renamed Acadia to please the donors of one very large parcel. The name Acadia appears on French maps of 1603 that show the northern North American Atlantic coast and is probably a corruption of Arcadia, a romantic name for ancient Greece.

The most significant donor of lands to the park was John D. Rockefeller, Jr., who eventually contributed more than 11,000 acres, almost one-third its total area. Between 1915 and 1933, Rockefeller also built a delightful system of carriage roads, now used by hikers, bicyclists, horseback riders, and cross-country skiers. Designed to provide an alternative to automobiles, this system includes sixteen massive stone bridges, which enhance rather than intrude upon the natural scene.

George Dorr, a wealthy Bostonian who became the first superintendent of the park.

Tidal pools form wherever the rockbound shore allows shallow waters to collect.

GEOLOGY

Taking Acadia for Granite

From bare summits to wave-battered rock underlying Bass Harbor Head Lighthouse, at the island's southern tip; across Frenchman Bay to Schoodic Peninsula; to Isle au Haut, isolated in Penobscot Bay—Acadia's scenic core is granite. Rivers eroding the land and volcanoes spewing incandescent ash began to lay down sedimentary rock in these ocean waters some 500 million years ago. Time and geologic pressures eventually formed these layers into rocks called Ellsworth Schist, Bar Harbor Series, and Cranberry Island Series. Then molten rock welled up repeatedly to surround, shatter, and metamorphose the older rock.

This newly upwelled magma cooled below the land's surface into hard igneous rock, mostly granite. The granite mass often cracked and new magma filled the gaps, creating dikes. Black basalt dikes contrast distinctively with their pink granite matrix. Hot rock ceased to flow here about 350 million years ago. During the long ages that followed, erosion stripped away thousands of feet of overlying rock to reveal the durable Mount Desert granite ridge, which was still part of the mainland.

Ice-Age Sculpture

About 3 to 4 million years ago, the ice ages began. The most recent of perhaps 20 to 30 continental glaciers began to form in north-central Canada 100,000 years ago. Spreading slowly southward, it finally reached the barrier of the Mount Desert granite ridge some 18,000 years ago.

First the sheet of ice spread around the ends of the barrier. Then ice piled higher and breached the lowest points on the ridge. Rough tongues of ice flowed down south-facing valleys on the other side, steepening the valleys' walls and widening their floors to create U-shaped profiles. The once-unbroken ridge became seventeen mountains separated by U-shaped valleys, such as the one that now contains Bubble Pond.

Ice found its way down the center of Mount Desert Island through a narrow gap between Acadia and Norumbega mountains; there, constriction forced the glacier to cut an especially deep valley. The valley eventually was flooded by the sea to become Somes Sound, the only fjord on the east coast of the United States. A former river valley, Somes Sound looks like a broad stretch of the Ohio or the Mississippi flowing quietly below river bluffs. But its salt water is as deep as 168 feet, providing a good home for lobsters.

Basins scoured in the floors of other glacial troughs became lakes, such as Bubble Pond, Eagle Lake, The Tarn, and Upper and Lower Hadlock ponds. Rubble from glacial excavations was transported within and on top of the ice mass and was abandoned as the ice melted, beginning about 13,000 years ago. Where glacial retreat halted for a few decades, debris piled up as glacial moraines, creating or enlarging lakes by damming their lower ends. Some boulders, such as the glacial erratics on the bald summit of Cadillac Mountain, were dropped at least 20 miles southwest of the ledges from which the ice had quarried them.

The Drowned Coast

The tremendous weight of ice perhaps as much as 3,000 feet thick actually depressed the surface of the land, forcing crustal rocks to sink at least 1,000 feet into the earth below their present level.

Simultaneously, the ice sheet locked up much of the earth's water, causing the sea level to drop to about 330 feet below its present level. As the ice melted and its weight was removed, the earth's surface rebounded until some 10,000 years ago. Although stabilized now, the land mass still is downwarped. Meanwhile, the sea level continues to rise worldwide by about 2 inches a century as polar ice continues to melt.

Depressed land and a rising sea create a "drowned coast," steep and ragged. Acadia, a classic example of this phenomenon, presents islands that once were mountains. Arms of the sea that incise Acadia's shores are former river valleys. Headlands and peninsulas were once ridges. Only a few dozen yards of drowned neck in the Mount Desert Narrows separate the island from the mainland.

Zones of weakness in the rock erode relatively quickly, allowing pounding waves to increase the coast's jagged appearance. Typical are the thoroughly cracked basalt dikes on Schoodic Point, which have eroded into steep-walled trenches tens of feet into the surrounding granite mass.

At Thunder Hole, on the southeastern edge of Mount Desert Island, frost and waves dislodge chunks and bits of granite along a large crack. Waves rolling into this steep-sided excavation trap and compress air in the end of the crack. From a small cavern worn in the back of the crack, water and air have nowhere to go but up. As the compressed air escapes amid splash and spray, it expands with a thundering sound when storms rage and waves crash into Thunder Hole.

Water erosion along the shoreline creates a great deal of rubble. Waves fracture the rock, transport the particles, and deposit them at the head of every cove. Wave action also piles up bars of stones that have been tumbled round and smooth. Such a bar, connecting the eastern side of Mount Desert Island with Bar Island, gave Bar Harbor its name.

Acadia's coast has few sandy shores. But currents near Thunder Hole have dumped tons of sand, mixed with bits of sea-urchin spines and pulverized clam and mussel shells, into Newport Cove. Here, Sand Beach may be diminished by the pounding waves of winter, only to be rebuilt by the gentler currents of summer. Rock promontories buttress each side of the cozy pocket of sand, framing it with dramatic cliffs that shield the beach from most assaults by waves.

Opposite: Both Jordan Pond and the two Bubbles were shaped by glacial erosion.

Climate

The sea moderates the climate of Acadia National Park, which is usually a few degrees warmer in winter and cooler in summer than inland Maine. The summer temperatures in the 80s are offset by damp, cool fog that forms along Acadia's coast on fifty to sixty days each summer. Swimmers at Sand Beach frolic in water that averages 55° to 60° F. Cooler weather in September and October contributes to the remarkable autumn colors in Acadia's deciduous forests, usually best during the first two weeks of October. Winter runs from November to April, usually providing plenty of snow to keep cross-country skiers happy, without imposing an endless bitter cold that would drive them indoors.

The Intertidal Zone

The area between high tide and low tide on a rocky coast is one of the sea's most complex ecological zones. The gravitational pull of the sun and the moon causes the sea at Acadia to rise and fall a tidal range of between 9 and 14 feet twice each day. The highest tides, called spring tides because they spring high on the shore, occur twice a month. The lowest tides, or neap tides, coincide with the first and third quarters of the moon. Between these extremes is an infinite variety of tide levels and times.

All these variables create extreme diversity in intertidal habitats and in the types of plants and animals that live there. Most species are adapted to particular ecological niches characterized by different levels of temperature, light, evaporation, and salinity. Most also possess specialized defenses against extreme battering by waves, ice, and storms.

Much of the variation within the intertidal area takes place in layers; this is especially obvious on such steep shores as Otter Point, where bands, or zones, of life are arranged one above the other.

Just above the high-tide mark—but within reach of ocean spray—is the Black, or Spray, Zone. It may be identified by a characteristic black stain on the rocks. The stain is actually a thin mass of blue-green algae known as *Calothrix*. (Blue-green indicates the phylum of algae, not necessarily the color, which is black for the Calothrix.) Under a microscope, each individual plant can be seen

Opposite: Stress lines in pink granite cliffs along Ocean Drive speed erosion.
Overleaf: Crowded northern rock barnacles may be forced to grow in height only.

The herring gull, most common in the northeast, lives along all U.S. seacoasts.

in its gelatinous covering, which prevents desiccation in sun and wind. When wet, the coverings constitute one of the slickest surfaces imaginable and are the cause of many slips and falls.

Periwinkles, marine snails from the next lower zone, venture into the Spray Zone to eat blue-green algae. A periwinkle (the largest is only about 1 inch long) scrapes algae from rocks with its radula, a tonguelike structure bearing about 3,500 teeth. New radula sections grow constantly and are pushed forward as the front sections wear away. Various periwinkle species graze throughout the tidal zones.

Perhaps the most exacting intertidal environment is the Barnacle Zone. This zone is exposed to the air for several hours twice a day and takes the heaviest wave pounding. It is marked by a whitish band made up of millions of acorn barnacles tightly cemented to the rocks.

The next intertidal zone is the Rockweed Zone. Rockweed is brown and rubbery, and it lies prostrate on the rocks at low tide. At high tide, it floats upright, supported by air bladders on its fronds. Although the wave pounding is less fierce in this zone than in the Barnacle Zone, rockweed must anchor itself to the rocks by hold-fasts, tentacles that sometimes are more difficult to dislodge than are the rocks they grasp.

At the normally lowest level of the intertidal environment,

The color and surface sculpture of the Atlantic dogwinkle species vary widely.

uncovered only twice a month, is the Irish Moss Zone. A rubbery red alga, like rockweed but not as long, Irish moss provides cover for sea stars, sea urchins, and crabs. Most of these creatures retreat to the Laminarian Zone during neap tides.

The Laminarian Zone is named for brown laminaria, or kelp. They live at depths from the very lowest tide mark (exposed only briefly semi-annually during equinox neap tides) to approximately 50 feet below the surface. Growing as single, leathery blades as much as 20 feet long, kelp take a fierce beating from winter storms but bend before the waves and cling tightly to rocks with their holdfasts. They are able to photosynthesize essential organic material in the dim light that penetrates fairly deep water.

Tidal pools make up a fragmentary tidal zone scattered among the bands of other zones; they are isolated bodies of sea water that give temporary shelter to forms of life incapable of withstanding prolonged exposure to the air at low tide. Tidal pools are not simply miniature versions of the sea, however. A shallow pool can heat up in the sun, causing the water to lose so much dissolved oxygen that many animals in the pool die. Evaporation of water can increase the pool's salinity so greatly that many animals die. Heavy rain can reduce the salinity so much that many animals die.

And yet, some animals have evolved tolerances that enable them to survive the tenuous balance of tidal-pool living. Sea stars, mussels, crabs, sponges, periwinkles, dog whelks, clusters of flowerlike sea anemones, and green sea urchins all contribute to the joy that can be had by gazing quietly for hours into tidal pools. Whether or not it really is a tranquil place, a tidal-pool garden appears peaceful in contrast to the foaming surf a few feet away.

Sea Animals

The waters around Acadia National Park swarm with life because of the abundance of tiny plants and animals collectively called plankton. An extensive food web based on plankton culminates in the marine mammals. Finback, humpback, right, and minke whales feed directly on the plankton. Harbor porpoises (visible from land), pilot whales, and harbor seals eat fish, squid, and other animals several levels of consumption distant from the plankton.

The most commonly seen sea bird of Acadia doubtless is the herring gull. Herring gulls, in their first and second years, already possess the 55-inch wingspread and pink webbed feet of mature birds, but their plumage is a mottled brown. In the adults, though, the gray back and black wing tips contrast attractively with the white head and body. The loud, clear bugling of herring gulls is a dominant sound on Acadia's coast.

Life on Land

Seaside spruces often are stunted and twisted by thin soil and wind, unlike typical trees of the same species that grow 70 feet tall with 2-foot-thick trunks beside streams and bogs in the park's interior. Needles of red spruce are about .5 inch long, stiff, and sharp. Cones reach lengths of up to 1.5 inches and have papery reddish brown scales. In good years, masses of cones cover the tops of red spruces. The cones are a primary food source for the red squirrel, the most evident of Acadia's forest dwellers. Other land mammals include white-tailed deer, chipmunk, raccoon, striped skunk, and red fox. Beaver and (rarely) river otter inhabit ponds and streams.

Although red spruces dominate the evergreen forests of Acadia, the forests also include black and white spruces; abundant balsam fir; and red, pitch, jack, and white pines. Unlike other needle-bearing trees, the tamarack, or larch, sheds its needles in winter. Before they fall, the needles turn a dusty gold, contributing to the autumn splendor of the park.

The most stunning of Acadia's trees in the autumn are the red

Opposite: Red and sugar maples in a display of New England's autumn splendor.

and sugar maples. In October, the leaves of sugar maples turn shades of vibrant yellow, orange, and red; simultaneously, those of red maples turn radiant crimson. Numerous maples at Upper Hadlock Pond create an unforgettable October vision.

Beginning with trailing arbutus, the spring wildflowers rival the autumn leaves in color. Later, the pink lady's-slipper brightens the woods. On Acadia's sunny mountain slopes, the rare wood lily holds erect its single orange cup. Spikes of the large purple-fringed orchid accent swampy edges of old beaver ponds, while fringed polygala, or gaywings, color damp meadows pink. Sunny meadows may be tinted with tiny bluets, or blue-eyed grass. Lupines are blue, pink, or white attention grabbers that were introduced to the cultivated gardens of Mount Desert Island from the Pacific Northwest and subsequently escaped to join the wildflower population.

With so many colorful blooms, it is easy to overlook the waxen, ghostly white Indian pipe; this small, slender plant, displaying not the slightest green hint of chlorophyll, obtains its food from decaying forest litter and the roots of living plants. Many nonflowering plants—ferns and club mosses—add a lush feeling to the woods. And lichens and mosses establish themselves on bare rocks and tree trunks.

Other colorful annual appearances at Acadia are made by its unusually diverse multitude of warblers—21 nesting species—which count among the more than 300 species of birds that have been spotted in the park. The 1947 fire encouraged the growth of much habitat needed by southern species, including the veery and the rose-breasted grosbeak. More typical of Acadia's northern latitude are species such as the gray jay and the evening grosbeak.

Sites, Trails, And Trips

Park Loop Road

The 20-mile Park Loop Road is the most heavily traveled stretch of Acadia National Park. At .5 mile along the Loop Road beyond the Visitor Center is an overlook of *Frenchman Bay* and the town of Bar Harbor. The bay, accented with islands, is one of the loveliest on the Maine coast and is as deep as 290 feet.

A stretch of one-way traffic starts with a left turn 3 miles south of the Visitor Center. In addition to the tile-roofed cover house over the *Sieur de Monts Spring*, the area boasts a wildflower garden; a Nature Center, which provides information for interpreting Acadia's natural and cultural history; and the Abbe Museum, which is devoted to Indians of the area.

From the flank of *Champlain Mountain*, 1.2 miles beyond the spring, the Loop Road passes a wide and especially dramatic vista. Below the overlook is Highseas, a mansion typical of the Bar Harbor "cottages."

At 1 mile beyond well-marked *Thunder Hole* is *Otter Point*, one of the best areas in the park to observe intertidal zones. Visitors should refer to tide timetable charts or inquire at the Visitor Center to learn when the tide will be at its lowest ebb. Brightly colored buoys bobbing in the water here and elsewhere along the shore mark the locations of lobster traps. Each lobsterman uses a different color pattern for his buoys and may pull up only his own traps. In order to conserve this resource, strict regulations prescribe what lobsters may be kept. Present regulations, however, are not stringent enough to maintain the lobster population, which is dwindling due to overharvesting.

At 6 miles from Otter Point is *Jordan Pond*, which occupies a steep-sided valley carved primarily by glacial ice. Near the north end of the pond stand two rounded hills called *The Bubbles*. In the area, a nature trail and a popular trail around the lake can be taken. Such walks often conclude with a light delicious repast of popovers on the lawn of Jordan Pond House, a restaurant established in the late nineteenth century. Farther along the road, *Bubble Pond* provides graphic evidence of how glaciers formed all these lakes. An overlook of *Eagle Lake* allows motorists to view this largest body of fresh water in the park—425 acres, with an average depth of 50 feet.

Cadillac Mountain Summit Road

The Cadillac Mountain Summit Road, a 3.5-mile spur of the Park Loop Road, winds past overlooks to the treeless granite summit of the highest point on the United States Atlantic coast. The *Summit Loop*, a foot trail at the summit, takes hikers in less than 1 mile past isolated glacial erratics and spectacular vistas of Frenchman, Blue Hill, and Penobscot bays; Schoodic Peninsula; and Mount Desert Island.

The Western District

Maine 102 and Maine 102A circle the west side of Mount Desert Island, passing through disjointed sections of the national park and through coastal villages to several points of interest. *Echo*

Overleaf: The Park Loop Road follows the eastern shore of Jordan Pond.
Following overleaf: A nearby carriage road brings visitors to Witch Hole Pond.

Lake is a charming glacial lake with a sandy artificial beach. *Seawall Pond* was dammed by the action of waves piling up rounded stones into a high beach. At *Wonderland* (a mixed coniferous and deciduous forest, .6 mile south of Seawall Campground) and *Ship Harbor* (.7 mile farther on), pleasant trails run through woods and along granite ledges above picturesque inlets. At *Bass Harbor Head*, the southernmost point on Mount Desert Island, rises one of the most photographed lighthouses on the Atlantic coast.

Isle au Haut

The "high island" was named in 1604 by Champlain. Its highest point is *Mount Champlain*, 543 feet. A 3,000-acre unit of Acadia National Park covers more than half of the 6- by 3-mile island and comprises some of the park's most wildernesslike terrain. Situated in Penobscot Bay about 15 miles southwest of Mount Desert Island, Isle au Haut is accessible by a ferry that runs three times a day in summer and once a day in winter. The boat departs from Stonington, at the end of Maine 15. No auto ferry is available. The only accommodations on the island are a few National Park Service campsites (which usually must be reserved far in advance) situated a 5-mile hike from the ferry wharf along the 12-mile road that circles the island.

Most of the road is not paved, and most auto traffic is limited to the vicinity of the village where the ferry lands. About 30 miles of trails open most of the island to hikers. Visitors should respect the privacy and property of island residents. Except around houses, most of the terrain is blanketed by thick spruce-fir forest. On the eastern side of Isle au Haut, the forest is broken by *Long Pond*.

Schoodic Peninsula

Schoodic Peninsula, the 2,000-acre mainland unit of Acadia National Park, is encircled by a one-way road that passes along some of Maine's loveliest coastline. Beginning at a turnoff about 2.3 miles inside the park boundary, a 1-mile unpaved road climbs to the left and goes most of the way up *Schoodic Head*. An easy .2-mile walk to the top ends at the highest point on the peninsula, 440 feet above the shore. Although commanding, the view is somewhat restricted by jack pines. A 1-mile hike down to the main, paved road reveals other vistas of Schoodic Harbor. This ramble is aided considerably if a generous volunteer drives a car down to meet hikers at the turnoff just beyond Blueberry Hill picnic ground. Hikers make a left turn at the junction of the trail and the road to reach the rendezvous point.

At *Schoodic Point* (a right turn 1.4 miles beyond the spur to Schoodic Head), pounding surf sculptures the sloping ledges of pink granite and black basalt dikes. Visitors should watch for lobstermen pulling their traps in Schoodic Harbor and for piles of traps and buoys outside the park boundary on the way to Birch Harbor.

Baker Island Cruise

During the summer, the Islesford Ferry Company provides tours from Northeast Harbor to Baker Island that are accompanied by a National Park Service naturalist or a ferry guide familiar with natural history. Seals and osprey may be seen along the way. A launch transports visitors onto the island from the ferry. In addition to its plant and animal life, 123-acre Baker Island features a white stone lighthouse, 43 feet tall, that was built in 1855.

Hiking Trails

Paths, nature trails, and carriage roads provide hikers in Acadia National Park with more than 200 miles of routes. These interconnect in webs that permit maximum flexibility in planning the length and difficulty of hikes. It is doubtful that more pleasant hiking exists anywhere.

Weather conditions may change swiftly on Acadia's trails, but hikers are far more likely to encounter discomfort than danger. Heavy fog can obscure routes above the tree line, where bare granite shows no path and navigation must proceed from one cairn to the next. Park rules permit hikers to enjoy canine companionship, if dogs are kept leashed. Horses also are allowed on most carriage roads. Wildwood Stables offers guided carriage rides on the carriage roads.

Witch Hole Pond Loop Carriage Road Trail. The easy, 3.5-mile Witch Hole Pond Loop Carriage Road can also be bicycled. It begins and ends at Duck Brook Bridge, a few yards off Duck Brook Road, which runs between Maine 233 and Bar Harbor. Completed in 1929, Duck Brook Bridge spans its namesake on three arches of hand-hewn granite.

The simplest way to follow the loop is to turn right after crossing Duck Brook and bear left at all carriage roads thereafter until the bridge is again reached. Most of the loop runs through deciduous woods: oak, maple, birch, and quaking aspen. Beaver love the aspen and have built several ponds along the way. Much larger than the beaver ponds is Witch Hole Pond.

TRAILS OF ACADIA NATIONAL PARK

There are about 120 miles of hiking trails in Acadia National Park, plus 44 miles of carriage roads, which are also used for hiking. Weather conditions may change quickly, so carry a light jacket or windbreaker on mountain hikes. Consult the "AMC Guide to Mount Desert Island and Acadia National Park" for additional trails.

ACADIA MOUNTAIN TRAIL: Starts and ends at Acadia Mountain parking area on east side of Maine 102, 3 miles south of Somesville; 2.5 miles round trip; 1.5 hours; strenuous route, with 681-foot climb to summit of Acadia Mountain; excellent view of Somes Sound.

BEECH MOUNTAIN TRAIL: Starts and ends at Beech Cliff parking area; 1.8 miles round trip; 1.25 hours; climbs to fire tower atop Beech Mountain; excellent view of Great Pond.

BEEHIVE TRAIL: Starts and ends just north of Sand Beach parking area on Park Loop Road; 1.2 miles round trip; .75 hour; this steep trail should be avoided by those who are bothered by heights; excellent views of Frenchman Bay, Sand Beach, and the Otter Cliff area.

GORGE PATH: Starts at gravel pullout on south side of Park Loop Road about 1.5 miles beyond third left-hand turnoff; ends at Cadillac Mountain summit; 1.8 miles one way; 1.5 hours; trail rises south up gorge between Cadillac and Dorr mountains for 1.3 miles, then swings southwest and west and climbs steeply for .5 mile to summit; this is highest point on Eastern seaboard, 1,530 feet; excellent views all around, including ocean and mountains 50 to 75 miles distant; on clearest days Mount Katahdin can be seen 120 miles away.

DORR MOUNTAIN TRAIL: Starts at Sieur de Monts Spring; ends at Dorr summit; 1.5 miles one way; 1.5 hours; first half has many stone steps and slabs; excellent views of Great Meadow and Frenchman Bay; several other trails join or branch off this trail.

GORHAM MOUNTAIN RIDGE TRAIL: Starts, ends at Gorham Mountain Parking area; 2.8 miles round trip; 3 hours; trail rises over open ledges to summit; return route drops down to Sand Beach by way of Bowl Trail and passes below Cadillac Cliffs. Follow Ocean Trail to parking lot.

NORUMBEGA MOUNTAIN TRAIL: Starts and ends at parking lot on west side of Maine 198 about .3 mile north of Upper Hadlock Pond; 2.5 miles round trip; 1.5 hours; trail ascends steeply through woods to granite ledges, then turns south to summit; summit is more wooded than most, but blueberries on north slope make it attractive; views of Somes Sound and mountains to the west are excellent; return route follows shore of Lower Hadlock Pond.

LONG POND TRAIL: Starts at pumping station at southern end of Long Pond; ends at junction with Western Trail; 2.9 miles one way; 1.7 hours; trail follows western shore of Long Pond before turning west and south; connection with Western Trail leads to Great Notch.

Opposite: Lifeguards watch over the cold waters of Newport Cove's Sand Beach in summer.

Winter sunrise over the Atlantic Ocean.

Hadlock Valley Loop Carriage Road. From a parking area near the impressive Brown Mountain Gate House, a short trail connects with the 4.2-mile Hadlock Valley Loop Carriage Road just inside the gate. At the first road junction, hikers should head right and then turn left at the next road junction, to make a gradual ascent of the flank of Cedar Swamp Mountain. Near the high point of the loop, two bridges curve over the forks of Hadlock Brook. Just upstream from the first bridge is the park's highest waterfall, particularly impressive after a rainstorm.

Two steep trails at the bridges offer shortcuts to lower sections of the road for hikers who lack time and must forgo traveling the entire loop. The loop eventually recrosses Hadlock Brook over a much smaller, yet very charming, bridge amid majestic white pines. The trees open for a brief view of Upper Hadlock Pond before the road ends back at the gate house.

Dorr Mountain and The Tarn Trails. A 5-mile loop, the beautifully constructed Dorr Mountain Trail is unremittingly steep along 1.6 miles of glacially sheered terrain between Sieur de Monts Spring and the summit of Dorr Mountain. On the steps and slabs above the spring, each switchback tempts hikers to rest, with the excuse of enjoying the progressively better views of Great

A bobcat sighting at Acadia is a rarity, occurring only about once a year.

Meadow and Frenchman Bay. Other trails join this one, but logic rightly indicates that the forks that lead up are the ones to take to reach the top. A trail junction just below Dorr's summit crosses over to Cadillac Mountain, another fine destination—especially for hikers who can arrange transportation both to Sieur de Monts Spring and from Cadillac's summit.

Hikers who continue climbing to the top of 1,270-foot Dorr Mountain are rewarded with views to the north, east, and south. The vast bulk of Cadillac blocks distant views to the west. To reach The Tarn, hikers must carefully follow the cairns down the south ridge of Dorr for 1.3 miles to a left turn on the Canon Brook Trail, and then descend for .3 mile to a left turn onto the Tarn Trail. This level 2-mile trail runs through mature deciduous woods, past beaver workings, and along the bouldery west shore of The Tarn.

Gorham Mountain Ridge Trail. The 4-mile loop of Gorham Mountain Ridge Trail offers a relatively easy mountain-summit hike that is also notable for its great variety and views. From the Gorham Mountain parking area along the Park Loop Road, the trail climbs through trees that took root after the 1947 fire, as well

Overleaf: Spring and autumn storm waves drench normally dry coastal ledges.

as some arboreal survivors of the conflagration. Vistas constantly broaden for .3 mile to a detour that leads below Cadillac Cliffs—cliffs and sea caves that were formed by waves before the land rebounded from the weight of glacial ice. The lower way, below the cliffs, is .2 mile longer than the upper route, which advances directly to the summit, about 1 mile from the road.

From the 525-foot top of Gorham Mountain, hikers may continue north down the ridge for .5 mile to an intersection. Left leads .2 mile to a small lake, The Bowl, and from there up Champlain Mountain to points north. Straight ahead leads .3 mile up to The Beehive, a steep round hill, from which hikers can descend on ledges and ladders over thrilling precipices to rejoin the loop without backtracking. After a sharp right turn at the intersection, the trail heads directly down to Sand Beach across the Loop Road. From Sand Beach, an ocean trail parallels the Loop Road past outstanding seascapes back to the point where the 1947 fire drowned in the ocean, across the road from the trail head.

Flying Mountain Trail. In the western district of the park, 284-foot Flying Mountain overlooks fine views of Somes Sound, Northeast and Southwest harbors, and the Cranberry Isles. Few trails contain so many pleasures at the cost of so little effort as does the 1-mile loop of Flying Mountain Trail. From a parking area where the Valley Cove Truck Road leaves Fernald Point Road, the trail climbs to the summit in .3 mile. After this 15-minute hike, visitors proceed to a view of Valley Cove, and then descend a steep trail through spruce woods. At Valley Cove, where the Acadia Mountain Trail begins, the end of the truck road lies about 75 yards up from the shore, providing an easy .5-mile loop back to the starting point.

Bicycle Routes

Bicycling is permitted on the Park Loop Road, on some other auto roads, and on park carriage roads that have been impressed with ground stone to provide traction and support for bicycle tires. The carriage-road routes feature rolling hills and other beautiful scenery. The park provides a bicycle guide that includes a map. Bikes may be rented in nearby towns. Some of the other carriage roads are open to horseback riding.

Opposite: Heavy fruit clusters of the showy mountain-ash mature in early autumn.

BISCAYNE
NATIONAL PARK

BISCAYNE NATIONAL PARK
P.O. BOX 1369, HOMESTEAD, FLORIDA 33090
TEL.: (305) 230-7275

HIGHLIGHTS: Coral Reefs • Marine Life • Elliott Key • Spite Highway Trail • Hammocks • Mangrove Forests • Convoy Point • Adams Key • Schooner Wreck Reef • Dome Reef

ACCESS: From Miami take Florida Turnpike or U.S. 1 to North Canal Drive and Convoy Point Information Center. Access to Elliott Key and offshore islands and reefs available through private concessionaire. Private boats may enter at several boat launch ramps or via Intercoastal Waterway.

HOURS: Park waters and Elliott Key open year-round, 24 hours daily. Convoy Point open 8 A.M. to 5:30 P.M. daily.

FEES: Fees charged by concessionaire for transportation offshore. Fee for boat launching out of Homestead Bayfront Park.

PARKING: 100 parking spaces available at Convoy Point. Slips at Elliott Key provide docking for 64 boats. Bulkhead docking at Boca Chita Key.

GAS, FOOD, LODGING: Available in Miami, Homestead, and the Florida Keys. Gas for boats only available at boat launching ramps.

VISITOR CENTER: Center at Convoy Point offers exhibits and sells publications; open year-round, seven days.

MUSEUM: None.

GIFT SHOP: Concessionaire-run gift shop at Convoy Point.

PICNICKING: At Convoy Point and at Elliott, Adams, and Boca Chita keys.

PETS: Pets on leashes of 6-foot maximum length allowed in parking and picnic areas, and at boat launching ramps.

HIKING: On Elliott and Adams keys.

BACKPACKING: At Elliott Key only. Free, required permit available at Convoy Point Visitor Center and Elliott Key Ranger Station.

CAMPGROUNDS: Elliott and Boca Chita keys.

TOURS: Access by boat only. Concessionaire-guided reef-snorkeling excursions, and ranger-narrated glass-bottom boat trips.

OTHER ACTIVITIES: Snorkeling, scuba diving, swimming, water skiing, and boating; fishing and lobstering per Florida state regulations.

FACILITIES FOR DISABLED: Biscayne vessels and restrooms at Elliott Key and Convoy Point accessible.

For additional information, see also Sites, Trails, and Trips on pages 66–72 and the map on pages 50–51.

The group of keys at the southern end of Biscayne; Elliott Key is at lower right.

SEEN FROM THE AIR, THE THIN CHAIN OF green islands divides the waters of Biscayne National Park into two palettes of color. To the east, coral reefs and grass beds dot the aquamarine Atlantic Ocean with splashes of sky blue, brown, turquoise, and deep cobalt. To the west, Biscayne Bay lies calm and quiet, the shallow water reflecting the vast blue expanse and puffy white clouds of the sky. This dramatic bird's-eye view reveals why Biscayne is sometimes called the "southern jewel" of the National Park System.

The jewel has many facets. Tropical fish with such fanciful names as rock beauty and queen angelfish glide through the multicolored coral formations. Trees and plants of both the West Indies and the north temperate zone, including red mangrove, mahogany, and the rare lignumvitae, lend their qualities to the islands' tropical appearance. Diving from above, terns and pelicans compete with humans for a dwindling harvest of seafood from Biscayne Bay and the Atlantic Ocean.

Although Biscayne is one of the newest national parks, the area reflects more than 500 years of southern Florida history. Indian mounds and pirate haunts coexist with millionaires' resorts. The park lies less than 30 miles from the heart of metropolitan Miami, but most people in the city are unaware of the hardwood hammocks, bonefish flats, coral boulders, and queen conch that have attracted others to the area for centuries. Biscayne is a jewel that has been admired by many people and yet has remained hidden from many more.

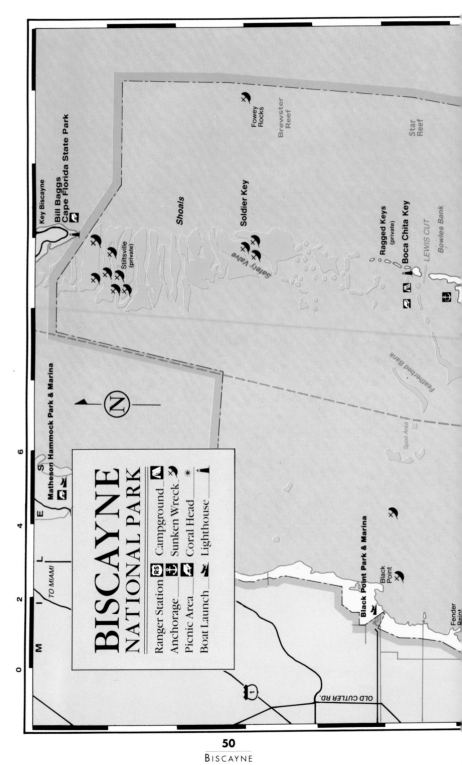

BISCAYNE
NATIONAL PARK

Ranger Station **RS**   Campground
Anchorage   Sunken Wreck
Picnic Area   * Coral Head
Boat Launch   Lighthouse

Key Biscayne
Bill Baggs
Cape Florida State Park

Matheson Hammock Park & Marina

Shoals

Stiltsville
(private)

Safety Valve

Soldier Key

Fowey
Rocks

Brewster
Reef

Star
Reef

Ragged Keys
(private)

Boca Chita Key

LEWIS CUT

Bowles Bank

Featherbed Bank

Spoil Area

Black Point Park & Marina

Black
Point

Fender
Point

TO MIAMI

OLD CUTLER RD.

1

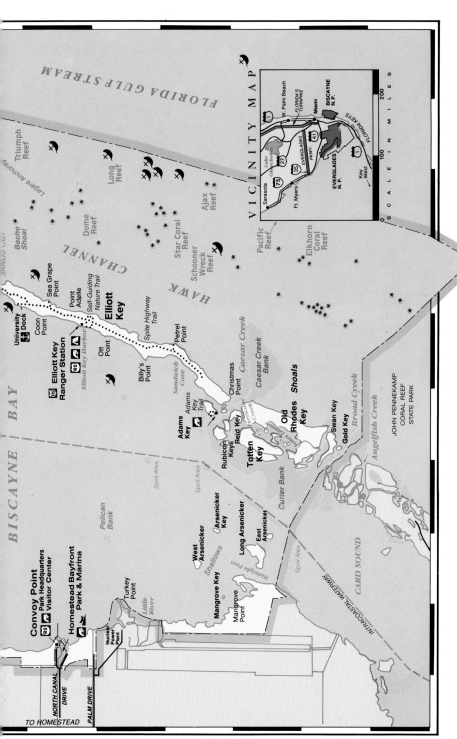

FLORIDA GULF STREAM

Triumph Reef

Legare Anchorage

Long Reef

SANDS CUT

Bache Shoal

Dome Reef

Ajax Reef

Star Coral Reef

Schooner Wreck Reef

HAWK CHANNEL

BISCAYNE BAY

University Dock

Sea Grape Point

Coon Point

Point Adelle

Self-Guiding Nature Trail

Elliott Key

Spite Highway Trail

Elliott Key Ranger Station

Ott Point

Elliott Key Harbor

Sandwich Cove

Billy's Point

Petrel Point

Christmas Point

Caesar Creek

Caesar Creek Bank

Adams Key

Adams Key Trail

Hurricane Creek

Reid Key

Rubicon Keys

Totten Key

Old Rhodes Key

Shoals

Swan Key

Gold Key

Broad Creek

Angelfish Creek

JOHN PENNEKAMP CORAL REEF STATE PARK

Cutter Bank

Convoy Point
Park Headquarters
Visitor Center

Homestead Bayfront
Park & Marina

Turkey Point

Little River

Pelican Bank

Spoil Area

Spoil Area

West Arsenicker

Arsenicker Key

Long Arsenicker

East Arsenicker

Shallows

Mangrove Key

Mangrove Point

Nuclear Power Plant

Midnight Pass

Spoil Area

CARD SOUND

INTRACOASTAL WATERWAY

TO HOMESTEAD

NORTH CANAL DRIVE

PALM DRIVE

VICINITY MAP

Sarasota

W. Palm Beach

Lake Okeechobee

FLORIDA'S TURNPIKE

Miami

BISCAYNE N.P.

Ft. Myers

EVERGLADES PKWY.

75

27

41

35

EVERGLADES N.P.

Key West

FLORIDA KEYS

1

Pacific Reef

Elkhorn Coral Reef

SCALE IN MILES

0   100   200

The Tequestas and the Spanish

What we know of the original human inhabitants of the Biscayne area is sketchy. The Spanish explorer Juan Ponce de León, who arrived in the area in 1513, found two groups of Native Americans in southern Florida: the Calusas, to the south and west of the Everglades, and the Tequestas, on the southeastern coast. The main Tequesta village was near the mouth of the Miami River, about 12 miles north of the future park, and the villagers undoubtedly visited the area on hunting and gathering expeditions. Scattered shell mounds and other archeological remains indicate the presence of seasonal camps on the islands. The heat and mosquitoes on the mainland—combined with the lure of manatee, conch (a large, tasty mollusk), spiny lobster, green turtle, and native fruits—would easily have justified an extended visit to the breezy shore during summer months.

Domingo Escalanter de Fontaneda, a thirteen-year-old boy shipwrecked off the Florida Keys in 1545, spent the next seventeen years with the Calusas and Tequestas, and it is from his accounts that we know of the life styles of these groups. The Tequestas relied on the bounties of the sea and the forest to sustain them. Daily activities of manatee hunting or berry collecting were punctuated with seasonal religious ceremonies or rites of passage. Women wore garments woven out of a type of Spanish moss and the men relied on simple leather breechclouts.

By the time the Spanish began to establish missions and forts along the Florida coast to strengthen their hold on the New World, the Tequestas were beginning to feel the embittering and decimating effects of slave raids and European diseases. A mission established at the main Tequesta village in 1567 lasted just a few years before the Spanish priests and soldiers were forced out by the hostility of the Tequestas. Nonetheless, during the brief existence of this outpost, the Tequestas helped rescue Spaniards from ships wrecked offshore, while killing non-Spanish survivors of other shipwrecks. In 1743, renewed interest in the security of the Miami River area sparked the establishment of a new Spanish settlement; but smallpox, yellow fever, and measles had left only a few scattered bands of Tequestas in the area.

Conchs and Pirates

The trade routes through the Straits of Florida and along the Florida Keys are among the world's most treacherous shipping lanes. Using inadequate charts to navigate the storm-plagued waters, captains sailing back to Europe with plunder from the New World frequently wrecked during unexpected hurricanes, scattering treasure and crew across the broad reef tract that parallels the arc of the Florida Keys. Two ships from the 1733 Spanish Plate Fleet, the *El-Aviso Consuelado* and the *Nao el Papulo*, wrecked off Elliott Key during one such storm, joining what would soon become more than forty shipwrecks within the future park's boundaries.

Spain lost Florida to Great Britain at the end of the Seven Years' War in 1763, and the American Revolution erupted thirteen years later. The Biscayne Bay area then began to take on another dimension. Settlers leaving unrest in the Bahamas, often Tories (British sympathizers) who had previously fled the rebellion in the North American colonies, began to settle the islands of the future park. Finding a land rich in seafood but harsh in climate, they eked out an existence by hunting sea turtles, salvaging shipwrecks, and harvesting mahogany for use in shipyards in the Bahamas. These island residents gradually became known as Conchs, after the large quantities of queen conch that they caught and their custom of using the empty shells as horns for long-distance communication.

When the United States acquired Florida in 1819, the area was well known as a haunt of pirates, who hid their sleek, lightweight sloops in the numerous small creeks and bays and emerged to ambush large cargo ships. The most famous of the pirates was Black Caesar, who used an iron ring on a small island to "careen" his vessel, concealing it as it lay in wait in a small creek. The process of careening involved tying down the mast so that the boat turned on its side while remaining afloat; it was more commonly used in those days to expose a boat's bottom for cleaning. Tales—perhaps exaggerated—of Black Caesar's buried treasure and cruel tortures provide a colorful episode of the park's history, and the present-day Caesar Creek and Caesar's Rock—the support for his iron ring—bear witness to his exploits.

Piracy in the area eventually was eliminated in the early 1820s by a naval squadron commanded by Commodore David Porter. But the salvaging of ships grounded on the reefs continued under the legal auspices of the territorial Wrecking Act, passed in 1823. Salvors of wrecked property were legally entitled to a portion of the salvaged goods or to a percentage of the profit on their sale, and the wrecking business soon became a major source of income for the Conchs. At the cry of "Wreck ashore!" all onshore work was dropped, and a mad rush toward the unlucky vessel ensued. The first person with a wrecker's license to reach a grounded ship

Sea turtle hunting on Key Biscayne, just north of the park near Miami, in 1928.

became the "master wrecker" and received the largest share of the spoils. Bradish W. "Hog" Johnson served as the master wrecker of the last ship in the Biscayne Bay area to be salvaged under these laws, the Havana-bound *Alicia*, which hit Ajax Reef in 1906 with a rich store of furnishings, wine, silks, and laces.

Wrecking revenue all but disappeared with the construction of lighthouses and other navigational aids to mark the treacherous reefs, leaving the Conchs to rely on turtling, sponging, and farming for income. Biscayne Bay provided an ample supply of green sea turtles and various species of commercially valuable sponges for sale in Key West. The soil of the islands, although present only in scattered pockets, yielded delicious "pines" (pineapples), key limes, and tomatoes for market in Miami and Key West.

Farming proved to be a risky venture, however. The hurricane of 1906 severely curtailed agriculture on the islands by salting the soil. Before Henry Flagler, a pioneer developer, extended his railroad to Key West in 1912, ferry service to the mainland breathed new life into the farming business, but higher freight costs and the importation of cheap Cuban pineapples and Mexican limes finally combined to put an end to agriculture on the islands. For the Conchs who were still willing to put up with the annoyance of insects, the threat of storms, the lack of fresh water, and the constant isolation, the only occupations that remained were smuggling rum or illegal aliens and guiding vacationers on fishing trips.

Establishment of the Park

Until the early 1960s, the Biscayne Bay area enjoyed a period of relative calm. It served chiefly as the site of a few weekend homes for city dwellers seeking respite from the hectic life style of a growing Miami. But the pressures of the outside world could not be held at bay for long. A proposal to develop a huge industrial seaport on the southwestern edge of Biscayne Bay was narrowly defeated when the Dade County commission became aware of the nature of the project. Sportspeople and conservationists also began to realize the degree of economic interest that developers had in this ecologically fragile area. Forming an organization called Safe Progress, these concerned individuals pushed for alternatives to protect the islands and their surrounding waters.

The push came none too soon. Some residents and property owners on the islands already had incorporated the area into Dade County's thirty-seventh municipality, Islandia, and were floating proposals to connect the islands to the mainland by a causeway and to begin development of a vacation paradise. Fearing the construction of another Miami Beach, Congress designated the area as Biscayne National Monument in 1968, citing the "rare combination of terrestrial, marine and amphibious life in a tropical setting of great natural beauty." When the vulnerability of the natural resources became fully known, Congress authorized new acquisitions in 1974 and changed the status of the area from national monument to national park in June 1980, thus completing the preservation of a slice of natural Florida ranging from mangrove estuary to offshore reef. The jewel was finally on public display.

Gathering for a portrait at an Elliott Key plantation, early twentieth century.

As recently as 25,000 years ago, during an interglacial respite in the Pleistocene epoch, the present-day Biscayne Bay area of southern Florida was covered by a warm tropical sea. Coral formations flourished on a narrow strip of the continental shelf, nurtured by abundant sunlight and clear ocean currents. No islands broke through the surface of the waters; shore birds seeking a sandy beach on which to land had to fly to what is now the Orlando area, 300 miles to the northwest.

The coral formations grew slowly. Individually crafted by its own minuscule coral animal, or polyp, each tiny limestone cup was cemented to the others, one by one, to form the branching horns or convoluted spheres that give each coral species its distinctive character. Each generation of polyps added its contribution to the growing fortress, using the wealth of calcium carbonate dissolved in tropical waters as the primary building material. Some species, such as the boulder-shaped star and the brain corals, added only 1 inch a year to their girth, while elkhorn and staghorn corals towered eagerly toward the sun with a comparatively rapid growth rate of 3 to 4 inches a year.

The final advance of the glaciers 12,000 years ago, during the Wisconsinan glaciation, spelled an end to this period of undisturbed reef growth. What had been 100 feet of sea water dwindled to 50 feet and then to none, as the glaciers sucked up the oceans to feed their advance. Deserted by their nurturer, the sea, the coral polyps died, and the vast system of patch reefs lay exposed to the mercies of wind, sun, and storm. During a period of rapid erosion, these elements cut deeply into the intricate architecture of the coral reef.

The story of this erosion can still be read in the rocky shoreline of the islands and in the form of the sinuous creeks that divide them from one another. Fossil corals of the formation called the Key Largo Limestone still sport the characteristic design of corals familiar to us today. The fall and subsequent rise in sea level also affected the area known today as Biscayne Bay. The calm, coastal lagoon of the Pleistocene gradually drained, only to be refilled by the same rain that fell on and helped erode the islands, becoming a small fresh-water lake. Finally, as the sea level rose again, Biscayne Bay took on its present form of a bay anchored at the edges by mangrove forests and influenced daily by tidal flow from the sea and by fresh-water runoff from the mainland.

Preceding overleaf: The Fowey Rocks Tower light guides Gulf Stream boaters.

Climate and Precipitation

A morning shower moves westward from the Atlantic. The thermometer has begun its daily climb toward 90° F, and the air is thick with moisture. Three-quarters of the park's yearly average of 55 inches of precipitation falls during the summer in these brief morning rain showers or in torrential afternoon thunderstorms that brew almost daily over the Everglades to the west. Summer is also hurricane season, when capricious storms form over the Atlantic and the Gulf of Mexico. Southern Florida's other season is its long winter, characterized by constant breezes, balmy days, and nighttime temperatures that drop into the upper 60s.

Hurricane Andrew, one of the century's most powerful storms, struck the park on August 24, 1992, with winds greater than 150 mph. All facilities were damaged or destroyed. About one-quarter of the coral reefs were damaged; some were almost scoured away.

A Cross Section of Natural Florida

Contained within Biscayne National Park is a remnant of the Florida that was, a natural system of interrelated habitats that mirrors the subtropical character of the area. On the western shoreline of the park, a fringe of mangrove forest filters fresh-water runoff

Tangled red mangroves along the park's shorelines buffer the fury of hurricanes. Overleaf: The mouth of a sea anemone is concealed by its waving tentacles.

from the mainland and stabilizes the mucky sediments. The result is a rich estuarine zone, in which miniature and larval marine creatures find food and protection. The shallow water of Biscayne Bay also shelters a variety of juvenile forms of marine life, many of which are commercially important species, such as the spiny lobster and pink shrimp. Thick mats of sea grasses and algae provide vital habitat for marine animals and help maintain the clarity of the water by binding sediments in a mesh of roots and rhizomes.

Biscayne's barrier system, which divides the park in two, comprises an extensive protective shoal area to the north—known as the Safety Valve—and a chain of more than forty small islands. The creeks between these shoals and islands connect Biscayne Bay with another natural zone in the park, the reef tract, where small backwater patch reefs lie behind fringing offshore reefs. These reefs constitute the northernmost extension of living coral reefs in the United States. The park boundary lies just east of the offshore reefs, where the water reaches a depth of 60 feet.

Marine Life

More than 95 percent of the park is covered with water. In the bay, rich undersea grass beds alternate with hard-bottom communities

Tiger grouper.

of sponges, algae, and soft corals to form a vital nursery ground for immature fishes and marine invertebrates of many species. Silver mullet and pinfish school near the submerged mangrove-root systems, attracting young gray snapper and barracuda. The bonefish, a game fish whose skeleton contains many small, fine bones, swims in the bonefish flats—the shallow-water areas above the grass beds. In areas that are not covered by turtle grass or algae, sponges and soft corals add a little relief to the flat underwater landscape. Stone crabs use small limestone crevices as impregnable fortresses, while such larger marine mammals as the bottlenosed dolphin and the West Indian manatee swim freely through the shallow water.

On the eastern side of the barrier system, the coral gardens dominate the scene and mesmerize even the most experienced snorkeler. Every color and design ever attempted by nature seemingly can be found on the reefs. Brown antlers of elkhorn coral branch toward the sun, providing a backdrop for the iridescent blues, yellows, and greens of the angelfish and parrotfish that swim between them. Every nook and cranny hides a new delight: a gold-flecked spotted moray eel, a diminutive but feisty damselfish, or a secretive Caribbean basket star, which has more arms than Medusa's head had snakes. Patrolling the tropical paradise are the

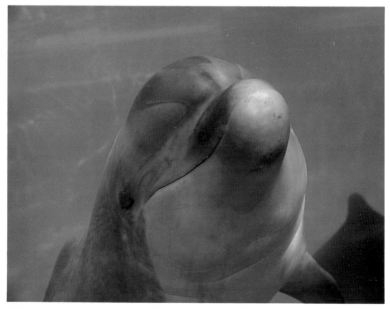

Bottle-nosed dolphins do not mind keeping company with snorkelers.

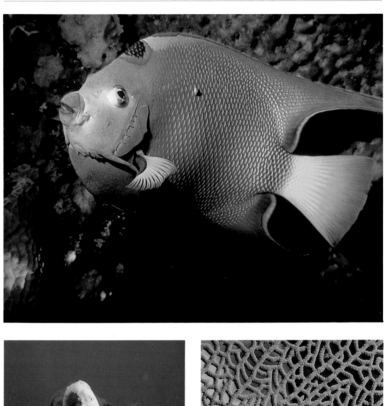

Top: Queen angelfish. Left: Feather duster. Right: A sea fan's branching network.

larger reef residents, such as various species of groupers and sharks.

The coral reefs provide one of the greatest natural laboratories for observing animal behavior. Cleaning shrimp wave their long white antennae to signal that they are open for business. The shrimp then proceed to pluck parasites from their temporarily docile but usually predatory clients, which include even the toothy barracuda. Brightly colored "supermales" of species such as the bluehead wrasse guide their retinues of females and juvenile males between foraging grounds. The supermale is one phase in a series of bizarre sex changes—still not fully understood—that are exhibited by many coral-reef fishes, including grouper and parrot fish. Look up, and a school of squid flees in unison from a pursuing gray snapper. Look down, and a yellow stingray disappears as it buries all but its eyes and spiracles (breathing holes) under sand. A lucky diver may even catch a glimpse of one of the five species of sea turtles that frequent the park's waters.

Terrestrial Life

The native vegetation of Biscayne can be classified into two distinct types: forests that are difficult to travel through, and forests that are impossible to travel through. The tangled jungle of a mangrove forest easily falls into the latter category, which is precisely why it is heavily used by brown pelicans, cormorants, and wading birds for roosting and nesting. Nonetheless, egg predators such as raccoons and yellow rat snakes will attempt to steal a meal in such locations.

The shoreline terrain and the interior hammocks on the larger islands are hospitable to many forms of life. West Indian trees and plants, whose seeds were originally transported in the waters of northward-flowing currents or in the winds of hurricanes, thrive in the ample rain and sun. Several specimens on Totten Key, such as a cinnamon bark and a tallow wood, have even been designated as the largest trees of their species in the United States. The colors are subtle in the hammocks—the thick subtropical forest that covers any high ground in southern Florida. Beige splotches on the milkbark, the gilded shimmering of a golden-silk spider's web, splashes of orange flowers on the Geiger tree, and the dark green of the quilted wild coffee leaf intermingle in the shade. These subtropical hammocks, fast disappearing because of development in the lower keys, shelter such endangered or threatened species as the Schaus swallowtail butterfly and eastern indigo snake and provide a breeding ground for some of the 175 species of birds found within the park, including the little blue heron and white-crowned pigeon.

Hurricane Andrew dealt heavy damage to the mangrove shoreline. In the hardwood hammocks, many trees were uprooted or stripped of their foliage by the high winds.

SITES, TRAILS, AND TRIPS

Many of the park's natural wonders and pleasures can be explored and enjoyed only in or on the water. Nothing can substitute for finding your first sea anemone or octopus while snorkeling near the Arsenicker Keys or for soaking up the sun and solitude on the deck of a catamaran off Pelican Bank. While most of the park is accessible only by boat, activities are available for landlubbers, too.

Convoy Point

The park headquarters on the mainland offers an orientation to the park. A ranger-staffed Visitor Center is the best place to get acquainted with the area. Activities such as guided snorkel trips and glass-bottom boat trips (year-round) provide an introduction to the unique vegetation and wildlife of Biscayne Bay and the mangrove shoreline. Convoy Point and the adjacent Homestead Bayfront County Park are also major boat-use areas; a dredged channel permits access to the shore through the shallow bay. Along the jetty bordering this channel, hikers can glimpse seasonal complements of shore birds and several species of salt-adapted shrubs and trees. A picnic area provides a view of the diving antics of brown pelicans and an opportunity to dangle a line for a seafood lunch or dinner. Development called for by the 1983 General Management Plan includes an enlarged Visitor Center, on which construction was scheduled to begin in 1995. Public tour-boat service to the islands and the coral reefs is provided by the park concession, Biscayne National Underwater Park, Inc., based at Convoy Point.

Elliott Key

From the harbor, a path leads across the island to a self-guided trail along the ocean side and back through a portion of the extensive hammock that covers most of Elliott Key. A boardwalk section of the trail along the shoreline facilitated travel across the craggy limestone outcrops; it was destroyed by Hurricane Andrew. Visitors should watch for hermit crabs, limpets, chitons, sanderlings, and other shoreline creatures along the way. As the

Opposite: Convoy Point overlooking Biscayne Bay.

trail cuts back through the hammock, it crosses a north–south path that traverses the entire length of the key. Appropriately named Spite Highway, the path is a remnant of a 120-foot-wide swath bulldozed by island residents eight months before the area was designated as Biscayne National Monument. Residents claimed the road was to become part of a transportation system connecting the islands with the mainland, and they named the proposed six-lane highway Elliott Key Boulevard. The bulldozed area has been reforested by second-growth vegetation and by nonnative vegetation, except for the 6-mile path, which is maintained by the park to facilitate movement up and down the island. Look for warblers flitting through the thick vegetation and for spurs of the trail that lead to old homesites on the ocean and bay sides of the key.

One of the few sandy beaches on Elliott Key is on the northwestern shore, and University Dock was rebuilt there with help from volunteers to allow continued use of the area. The waters to the south of the dock are a designated anchorage area; waterskiers are encouraged to use the area to the north of the dock or to the south of Billy's Point.

Adams Key

Once the site of a millionaire's retreat fashioned by Miami Beach developer Carl Fisher, Adams Key is a day-use area that overlooks Caesar Creek, a major access route to the waters of the open ocean. Construction on the Cocolobo Club began there in 1917, and the resort eventually included a two-story lodge, a caretaker's house, servants' quarters, a 70,000-gallon cistern, a power-generating plant, and a recreational building called the casino. Members of the club included such famous magnates as T. Coleman du Pont and Harvey Firestone. Four presidents—Warren Harding, Herbert Hoover, Lyndon Johnson, and Richard Nixon—vacationed on the island. The story is told that the infamous Teapot Dome Scandal may have been hatched at the club, as the guestbook records a visit on February 11, 1921, by Warren Harding, Albert Fall (his Secretary of the Interior), and petroleum magnate Edward L.Doheny (a friend) during a fishing vacation.

The buildings were constructed of resistant southern Florida slash pine. The lodge burned down in 1974 in an electrical fire. The "casino," which had been converted into a Visitor Center, was destroyed by Hurricane Andrew. A short trail leads through the hammock on the island; picnic facilities and rest rooms are available.

Marked Patch Reefs

Mooring buoys have been stationed at selected patch reefs on the

Manatees must surface for breath about once every four minutes.

TRAILS OF BISCAYNE NATIONAL PARK

ELLIOTT KEY SELF-GUIDING NATURE TRAIL: Starts and ends at Elliott Key Harbor; .5 mile; .75 hour; leads from Biscayne Bay through a tropical hardwood hammock; boardwalk section along shoreline; opportunity to see the endangered Schaus swallowtail butterfly on the trail, porpoises in both the bay and the ocean.

SPITE HIGHWAY TRAIL: Starts toward either north or south end of Elliott Key from two intersection points with Self-Guiding Nature Trail; total length of trail is 6.75 miles; rocky, uneven trail through dense hardwood hammock; spur foot trails lead to mangrove forests and shore.

ADAMS KEY TRAIL: Starts and ends near Adams Key dock; .5 mile; .5 hour; trail cuts through a hardwood hammock and loops back toward dock through a coastal transition forest.

CONVOY POINT JETTY TRAIL: Starts and ends behind Convoy Point Visitor Center; .25 mile one way; .5 hour; jetty on Biscayne Bay; glimpses of life in intertidal zones; birdwatching (especially good in winter); farther, older section of jetty may be underwater at high tide.

Overleaf: Wounds caused by contact with elkhorn coral tend to heal slowly.

ocean side of the barrier system. The shallow coral formations and associated reef fishes provide a representative sample of the marine life found throughout the reef tract. Two piles of ballast stones and a coral-encrusted gear box, the remains of a wreck believed to have been an eighteenth-century schooner, lie adjacent to *Schooner Wreck Reef*. The wooden hull rotted away long ago, but an observant snorkeler can pick out the original position of the keel between the two piles of ballast stones. The stones, typical of those found at other sites of wrecks, provide a playground for small wrasse and damselfish.

Elkhorn Reef and *Star Coral Reef* are excellent examples of these two forms of stony coral. Elkhorn Reef also demonstrates reef zonation, the different positions, or zones, that corals occupy on a reef as a result of the force of waves. Hardy fire corals (actually not corals, but look-alike hydroids) occupy the front rubble zone, where the wave energy is most intense. To the west, a snorkeler passes over the branching elkhorn and staghorn corals to find the quieter backwater species, such as small finger corals and lettuce corals.

At Star Coral Reef, the huge heads of mountainous star coral and various brain corals bear witness to the great age of the reef and are a drastic contrast to the delicate sea fans and sea whips that bend with every wave. The corals provide a meal for the colorful parrot fish, which can be heard munching away at the polyps with their hardened mouth plates.

Dome Reef is easily reached from the natural waterway known as Hawk Channel and is representative of many patch reefs along the channel's edge. Communities of sponges and calcareous algae, schools of grunts and blue tang, and solitary angelfish and spiny lobster all sport the decorative colors that brighten any coral reef.

The reefs are marked with blue and white buoys; using these for mooring eliminates damage to the fragile coral from carelessly thrown anchors. Bearings and specific directions to the marked reefs can be obtained at the Visitor Center.

After surfacing from an underwater survey of the magnificent array of colors and patterns on the reef, one feels drawn to gaze across the blue ocean waters to the green islands and the bay beyond. The treasures of the park are indeed hidden, but they do not lie buried in oaken chests guarded by the curses of long-dead pirates. Instead of gold and hand-cut gems, the subtropical hammocks and underwater habitats conceal a wealth of life that was unappreciated as recently as the 1960s. Properly cared for, the jewel that is Biscayne National Park can shine forever.

Opposite: Grunts from brown pelican young are often heard near nesting areas.

DRY
TORTUGAS
NATIONAL PARK

Remote Fort Jefferson was built on Garden Key, 70 miles from the Florida mainland.

Dry Tortugas National Park
P.O. Box 6208, Key West, Florida 33041
Tel.: (305) 242-7700

Highlights: Fort Jefferson • Beaches • Loggerhead Key • Coral Reef • Marine Life • Shipwrecks

Access: No regularly scheduled boat transportation. Access by private boat, commercial seaplane, and chartered boat. Limited docking facilities available. Contact Chambers of Commerce in Marathon, Key West, or Naples for information on boat and seaplane tours.

Hours: Fort is open from 8 A.M. to dusk year-round.

Fees: None.

Gas, Food, Lodging: No food, gas, or water is available in the park. All provisions must be brought in and all trash removed.

Visitor Center: Visitor Center, slide show, and museum are in Fort Jefferson.

Gift Shop: Small bookstore operated by Florida National Parks and Monuments Association sells titles on birds, fish, coral, and history.

Pets: Permitted if leashed at all times. Not permitted inside fort.

Picnicking: Tables and grills available on Garden Key. No food or beverages allowed inside fort.

Hiking: No trails. Seawall around fort offers a half-mile walk. Brochure guide available.

Backpacking: None.

Campground: Tent camping is permitted on Garden Key. Tables, grills, and salt-water toilets are provided. Special use permit, available from the park, is required for groups of 10 or more. No charge.

Tours: Self-guided tours of Fort Jefferson and the seawall. Ranger-led interpretive tours may be available.

Other Activities: Snorkeling, scuba diving, swimming, fishing, boating, birdwatching in season.

For additional information, see also Sites, Trails, and Trips on pages 88–89 and the map on pages 78–79.

O N A CALM DAY, WHEN THE WATER IS GLASS smooth, Fort Jefferson rises majestically, as if from an artist's canvas watercolored in blue and green. On stormy gray days, when the water tosses your boat like a carnival ride, the fort is a forbidding blip on the horizon. From the air, it looks like something out of a geometry textbook, a hexagon partly framed by a right-angled beach set in a mottled sea.

Closer inspection shows that the majestic fort is a half-finished pile of bricks so heavy that it is sinking into the sea, a military outpost obsolete before its cannons could be fired. The forbidding blip is what military prisoners saw as they approached: a distant, desolate outpost battered by the sea, but without fresh water. Stand in one of the cells, your brick-framed gaze scanning the horizon, knowing that civilization is almost 70 miles away, and you'll understand why one former resident borrowed a line from *Paradise Lost* and wrote, "Abandon all hope, ye who enter here."

Ah, but dive beneath the azure surface and you'll find tropical fish nibbling on brightly colored coral. Sea fans wave at the slightest motion and, on summer nights, endangered sea turtles come ashore to deposit eggs bearing the next generation. Overhead, magnificent frigate birds ride the thermals. On nearby islands, sooty and noddy terns nest, their only significant nesting ground in the contiguous United States.

Reachable only by charter boat, private yacht, or seaplane, the Dry Tortugas are a subtropical paradise close to the continental United States, yet worlds away.

Troops faced a big inconvenience : the islands are indeed "dry"—no fresh water.

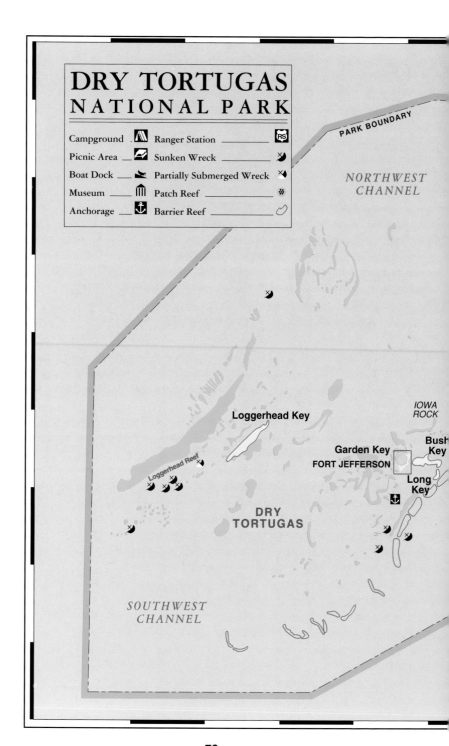

DRY TORTUGAS
NATIONAL PARK

Campground   Ranger Station   RS
Picnic Area   Sunken Wreck
Boat Dock   Partially Submerged Wreck
Museum   Patch Reef
Anchorage   Barrier Reef

PARK BOUNDARY

NORTHWEST CHANNEL

IOWA ROCK

Loggerhead Key

Garden Key
FORT JEFFERSON

Bush Key

Long Key

Loggerhead Reef

DRY TORTUGAS

SOUTHWEST CHANNEL

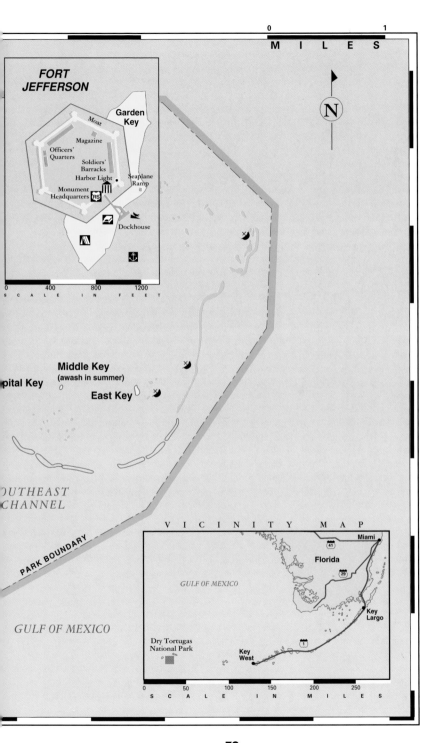

N

FORT JEFFERSON

Garden Key

Moat

Magazine

Officers' Quarters

Soldiers' Barracks

Harbor Light

Seaplane Ramp

Monument Headquarters RS

Dockhouse

0   400   800   1200
S C A L E   I N   F E E T

Middle Key
(awash in summer)

pital Key

East Key

OUTHEAST
CHANNEL

PARK BOUNDARY

GULF OF MEXICO

VICINITY MAP

Miami

Florida

GULF OF MEXICO

Key Largo

Dry Tortugas National Park

Key West

0   50   100   150   200   250
S C A L E   I N   M I L E S

Discovery

The seven tiny islands known as the Dry Tortugas have long been critical to mariners. Boaters sought safe anchorage in the natural harbor during storms, but were wary of the navigational hazards presented by the shoal. The islands were explored in 1513 by Juan Ponce de León, who left Puerto Rico in search of the Fountain of Youth. Seventy miles west of the Florida Keys, his crew captured 160 sea turtles in one day, prompting Ponce de León to name the small cluster of islands in the Florida Straits Las Tortugas, the turtles. Early navigational charts noted that the islands were "dry," meaning they lacked fresh water. Eventually they came to be called the Dry Tortugas.

Not everyone who sailed the Dry Tortugas was seeking safe harbor. Pirates used the islands as a base for attacking merchant vessels in the nearby shipping lanes throughout the seventeenth and eighteenth centuries. Boats not attacked by pirates ran the risk of running aground on sandbars and shallow reefs. And of course there were fierce tropical storms and hurricanes that seemed to blow up out of nowhere. Shipwrecks, many uncharted, are scattered throughout Dry Tortugas National Park. Some date to the 1600s.

The invention of rifled cannon made Fort Jefferson obsolete before it was completed.

Fort Jefferson

The flags of three countries have flown over Florida since its discovery: Spain (until 1763), Great Britain (until 1783), Spain again (until 1821), and the United States. The Tortugas were surveyed and named while under British control, but the Americans recognized the islands' navigational and military importance. For ships coming through the Straits of Florida, the Tortugas, with their natural harbor and navigable channels, offer a shortcut from the Atlantic Ocean to Florida's west coast.

In the 1820s, the United States Congress appropriated funds to build a lighthouse on the east side of Garden Key near the deepwater channel used by ships. The first lighthouse was a whitewashed brick structure with a fixed, rather than flashing, light. Despite its presence, ships still ran aground. The light was far from the shoals and its reflector was frequently dirty. Major repairs were made in 1838, and the situation improved dramatically. A second lighthouse was built on Loggerhead Key thirty years later.

Lighthouse keepers lived on the isolated islands, periodically sailing to Key West for supplies and provisions. Between trips, the sea turtles provided sustenance. Females laying eggs on the beach were turned on their backs and kept alive for several weeks. This kept the meat fresh until it was needed.

As travel and commerce through the Straits increased, so did the strategic importance of the islands. Tension between Great Britain and Spain led the U.S. War Department to draw plans for a fort with walls 8 feet thick, 50 feet high, and a half-mile in diameter. It was to be armed with 450 cannons. A moat would be built around the fort to prevent enemy boats from getting too close and beneath the cannons.

When construction began in 1846, Fort Jefferson was expected to become a superfort, one of many stretching down the east coast. Unfortunately, huge brick fortresses like Fort Jefferson were made obsolete when the rifled cannon was invented, fourteen years after construction began. Complicating matters was inconsistent War Department funding, especially during peacetime, and the difficulty of shipping workers and supplies, including 16 million bricks, to such a distant outpost. Thus construction was sporadic for thirty years, and Fort Jefferson was never completed.

Despite its unfinished state, troops were stationed at Fort Jefferson throughout and after the Civil War. During the war, President Lincoln ordered all coastal forts secured, but Fort Jefferson, the southernmost defense, was only half finished.

Because it couldn't be used for defense, the fort was turned into a military prison for convicts sentenced to hard labor. Many Union deserters were among the prisoners. Dr. Samuel Mudd, the physician who set the leg of John Wilkes Booth, Lincoln's assassin, was convicted of conspiracy and imprisoned at Fort Jefferson. Mudd later became a hero among the staff and prisoners when he emerged from his dank cell to wage a three-month battle against a deadly yellow-fever epidemic that swept through the islands (some of which were then populated) in 1867. He was later pardoned and released. Mudd's cell is still there for all to see.

Abandoned in 1874, Fort Jefferson was returned to service twenty-four years later. It spent two years as a quarantine station where personnel from ships and cargo were treated for disease and pests. In January 1898, while in the Dry Tortugas, the battleship *Maine* was ordered to proceed to Havana. Its destruction there, by an explosion, precipitated the Spanish-American War. In 1898, the U.S. Navy built a coaling station outside the fort, but a hurricane promptly destroyed much of the facility. Nonetheless, the fort served as a naval refueling station until 1908.

Establishment of the Park

In the spring of 1908, the sooty tern colony nesting on Bush Key prompted an executive order that created the Dry Tortugas Keys Reservation. Sooties are large blackish-brown birds who spend most of their time in the air over tropical seas. Though they also nest on islands off the Texas and Louisiana coasts, the birds had been decimated by commercial egg harvesters prior to establishment of the reservation.

In 1935, Fort Jefferson National Monument became the world's first marine area to be protected, by order of President Franklin D. Roosevelt. Unfortunately, the boundary was little more than an oval scrawled on a map. Boaters, surrounded by few landmarks and all that water, had no idea where the park boundary began. This made it difficult for Park Service managers to enforce the law and protect the resources. A new legal boundary, based on latitude and longitude and marked by buoys, was established in 1980. At the same time, the law gave greater emphasis to protecting and interpreting the natural resources. It specifically mentioned coral formations, fish, and nesting and migrating birds.

In 1990, the Florida Keys National Marine Sanctuary was established, offering federal protection to the water and undersea resources between Key Biscayne (near Miami) and the Dry Tortugas bank. In 1992, President George Bush signed legislation establishing Dry Tortugas National Park. Park status afforded additional protection to "the nationally significant natural, historic, scenic, marine and scientific values in South Florida." At the same time, the Loggerhead Key lighthouse was turned over to the National Park Service by the U.S. Coast Guard.

GEOLOGY

To understand Dry Tortugas geology, one must first become acquainted with a tiny animal called the polyp. Consisting of a soft tubelike body, a mouth, and tentacles for bringing in food (plankton), polyps are like hard-hat construction workers tenaciously putting up a building. As polyps grow and divide, they excrete calcium carbonate, which forms the coral reef skeleton. It's an extremely slow process; some reefs grow only half an inch a year, others gain 4 inches in the same period.

The coral reef is a living entity, a seascape community attracting plants and other animals to shallow waters in tropical and subtropical regions of the world. Its growth is aided by the presence of turtle grass, long thin flat-bladed plants with dense root systems. Turtle grass nabs sediments that eventually sink to the

A cannon from a sunken ship becomes a base for the growth of coral formations.

seafloor and are trapped. The grass helps keep the water clear, and clear water is necessary for coral to grow.

In some places, the coral rock foundations have become virtual skyscrapers. When the sea level dropped, during the glacial period, some reefs were exposed to air, rain, and surf. The corals died and fused together. Sea debris collected on the resulting coral rock, eventually creating soil which later attracted plant material that took root. This was the beginning of the Florida Keys, of which the islands of the Dry Tortugas are a part.

NATURAL HISTORY

Climate

On a clear day, the Dry Tortugas are the tropical islands of everyone's dream. Temperatures are comfortable, ranging from the mid-50s to the mid-80s. Humidity, ranging from 40 to 80 percent, is less noticeable than on the mainland thanks to balmy breezes. Cold fronts sometimes pass through during the winter, bringing storms with high winds and buffeting waves, but little rain.

More notable are summer's tropical storms and hurricanes. Fort Jefferson has weathered numerous hurricanes, some clocked at more than 100 miles per hour. Many are near misses, but the effects of wind and water are still felt. Hurricane-jarred waves, although a natural phenomenon, are damaging to the coral reefs. Repeated wind whippings and salt sprays have taken their toll on the old brick fort. Hurricane season extends from June through November.

Because the islands are "dry," rain water is collected and stored on Garden Key in 109 cisterns. If all were functional, they could hold 1.5 million gallons of water, but as little as 15,000 to 20,000 gallons of water may be available at any given time. Therefore, fresh water is precious on the islands and it is reserved for on-site park employees and day-to-day operations at the fort. Visitors must bring their own fresh water.

The Coral Reef

Because of its isolation and federal protection, the coral reef within Dry Tortugas National Park is widely recognized as one of the most pristine on the east coast. On the west side, it is known as a fringing barrier reef. These grow in shallow water around the fringes of islands. On the east side, the reef has developed spur

A Park Service scuba diver inspects the underwater world of the Dry Tortugas.

The smooth trunkfish, one of 442 speices of fish reported in the Dry Tortugas vicinity.

and groove formations. This happens when coral projections grow out from the reef, and the spurs become covered with dense coral growth. Grooves between the projections are swept by waves and currents, becoming deep sand channels.

Divers and snorkelers will find plenty to explore. Perhaps the most easily recognized formation is brain coral, whose round shape and tiny meandering ridges resemble the human brain. Sea fans are leaflike formations that sway with wave action, much like a leaf blows in the wind. Staghorn coral, looking somewhat like underwater tumbleweed, is delicate and easily broken.

Many beautiful and ordinary fish are found feeding around the coral or hiding in its crevices. There are yellow and silver porkfish swimming in schools for protection. Blue striped grunts stay close to coral during the day, but venture out at night to graze on seagrass. Green parrot fish, blue angelfish, and sea urchins are found close to shore. Scuba divers report seeing loggerhead turtles, jewfish, lobster, and snook.

The Islands

Though dominated by water, Dry Tortugas National Park is dot-

The male frigate bird inflates its bright red throat pouch during courtship.

ted with interesting little islands. The first stop for most visitors is Garden Key, largely occupied by Fort Jefferson. Though once thought to be solid coral rock, the 16-acre island is actually composed of shifting sand and coral boulders. A small beach provides opportunities for snorkeling and swimming. Fishing is allowed from the dock on Garden Key.

Loggerhead Key is the site of the Dry Tortugas Light Station, operated until recently by the U.S. Coast Guard. A small beach is near the lighthouse. Snorkeling is good just off the beach.

Bush, Long, East, and Hospital keys are important nesting sites for many birds. Sea turtles nest on East Key. The area just off Long Key is a breeding ground and nursery for nurse sharks. These islands may be closed during breeding and nesting times.

The Birds

The Dry Tortugas lie on a flyway between the United States and Cuba, resulting in a melodious procession of birds between April and September. Most birds pay only a brief visit to the Tortugas during migration, and their presence is heavily influenced by weather.

Still, more than 100,000 sooty and noddy terns nest on Bush Key, while roseate terns nest on Hospital, Bush, and Long keys. Frigate birds soar overhead during the summer. Noddy terns are one of the few species to make their home in the Tortugas. During the winter, gulls, terns, and migratory shore birds head for the islands.

SITES, TRAILS, AND TRIPS

Although Dry Tortugas National Park has some 80 acres of sand islands, 99 percent of the park is open ocean and submerged lands. Getting there requires planning, because the facility is 70 miles west of the nearest airport, road, and boat dock. Visitors must be self-sufficient, bringing in all their food, water, and recreational gear. They must haul out all their trash.

Fort Jefferson

Most of the brick fort is open during daylight hours. Begin with an introductory slide show and a visit to the museum. Follow with a self-guided walking tour through the parade grounds, where the Soldiers' Barracks and part of the Officers' Quarters remain, along with the powder magazines and cisterns. Climb the stairs and walk the corridors, peek into Dr. Mudd's cell, and gaze out to sea. On the roof you'll find cannons, a close-up view of the lighthouse, and a good vantage point for watching boaters, seaplanes, or frigate birds.

Outside the fort is a moat and seawall. Within the moat are turtle grass, jellyfish, sea squirts, yellow stingray, queen conch, mangrove snapper, bristle worms, and sea cucumber. The wall itself is designed to protect the fort from storms and enemy attacks. You can walk the half-mile circumference, but watch for loose bricks and the uneven surface.

Underwater Exploration

Several coral reefs are close to shore in shallow water, making them readily accessible to snorkelers. Just off Garden Key are snorkeling areas where staghorn coral, brain coral, and purple sea rods grow. They attract a good variety of fish, including parrot fish, angelfish, and sea urchins. Patch, or lagoon, reefs are found on the western side of Loggerhead Key. Corals are close to the surface here. Look for staghorn, brain, and gorgonian corals.

A number of wrecked ships lie beneath Tortugas waters, but

Visitors must bring all their food and water and carry out their trash.

the Park Service provides little information about them in an effort to protect these historical resources. The windjammer site is the best known, and interpretive handouts are available. One mile south of Loggerhead Key, only partially submerged, is the final resting place of the *Avanti*, which was lost in a 1907 storm. Maritime archeologists who examined the site found the portholes sealed, standard practice for ships in stormy seas. In addition, the port anchor is missing, although its chain was found secured to the ship and running out of its hatch. The crew probably lowered the anchor in an attempt to hold the ship, but the anchor broke from the chain and the ship drifted onto the reef and broke up. Many fish are found near the wreck, including grunts, snapper, porgies, and jewfish.

Prime fishing sites are marked on the official park map. Most are situated in open water or near barrier reefs, but several good spots are near Loggerhead Key. The south end of Long Key is closed to fishing, as is the moat and swimming area of Garden Key. Common catches include grouper, amberjack, cobia, tarpon, permit, and mackerel. There are closed seasons for snook and red snapper. Several species must be landed on the mainland unless they are for immediate consumption. Check with park rangers for current regulations.

EVERGLADES NATIONAL PARK

Birdwatching at Mrazek Pond is excellent, especially in the dry winter months.

EVERGLADES NATIONAL PARK
40001 STATE ROAD 9336, HOMESTEAD, FLORIDA 33034 TEL.: (305) 242-7700

HIGHLIGHTS: Saw-Grass Prairie • Bird Life • Alligators and Crocodiles • Subtropical Plant Life • Florida Bay • Manatees • Snake Bight • Chokoloskee Island Shell Mounds • Cape Sable • Wilderness Waterway • Shark Valley Tram Tour and Observation Tower

ACCESS: From Miami, take Florida Turnpike or U.S. 1. Free boat launching at Flamingo. Airboats not permitted in the park.

HOURS: Open year-round, 24 hours daily. Park is crowded at Christmastime.

FEES: At entrance and at campgrounds.

PARKING: Ample, throughout park; camper and RV parking at Long Pine Key and Flamingo Campgrounds.

GAS, FOOD, LODGING: Available in Homestead and Everglades City. Gas and limited groceries available at concessionaire-operated motel and restaurant at Flamingo, open from November 1 to May 31.

VISITOR CENTER: At Park Headquarters, Royal Palm, Everglades City, Shark Valley, and Flamingo; open year-round, seven days.

MUSEUM: Exhibits at Visitor Centers.

GIFT SHOP: At Visitor Centers.

PETS: Leashed pets allowed, but prohibited on trails.

PICNICKING: At various locations in park.

HIKING: Short, developed walking trails, reached via spur roads off main park road; longer trails include 15-mile Shark Valley Loop Road, network of fire roads in the pinelands, and Flamingo-area trail network.

BACKPACKING: Permit required for overnight backpacking. Most travel is by boat or canoe; campsites are raised wooden platforms.

CAMPGROUNDS: 108 sites for tents or RVs at Long Pine Key; 235 RV and tent sites and 60 tent sites (near shoreline) at Flamingo. Water available. 14-day stay limit from December 1 to March 31.

TOURS: Concessionaire-operated charter fishing and scenic boat cruises through park water systems. Shark Valley Loop Road tram tour. Ranger-led activities.

OTHER ACTIVITIES: Boating, swimming at Flamingo Inn pool, birdwatching, bicycling; fishing per Florida state and park regulations.

FACILITIES FOR DISABLED: All National Park Service facilities accessible. Audio tape trail guidance for vision-impaired.

For additional information, see also Sites, Trails, and Trips on pages 120–133 and the map on pages 94–95.

Black mangroves cope with a saline environment by excreting salt through their leaves.

MENTION THE EVERGLADES TO A FRIEND who is unacquainted with this unique national park, and he or she is likely to picture fathomless pits of quicksand, swamps seething with serpents, and alligators waiting to devour every passerby. Such are the myths that novelists and Hollywood film producers have conjured up about this vast wetland; yet nothing could be further from the truth. Everglades National Park is a gentle place where myriad tropical and temperate life forms interact in ways that are only beginning to be understood. True, harsher elements become involved when natural fires crackle across the saw-grass prairies or when hurricanes churn the shallow waters of Florida Bay far inland. But even these powerful forces of nature are merely agents of renewal to which the Everglades ecosystem has adapted over many millenniums.

Just a short drive from the concrete sidewalks of downtown Miami, the glades offer solace and spiritual renewal to vacationers and to residents who grow haggard from the hustle and bustle of

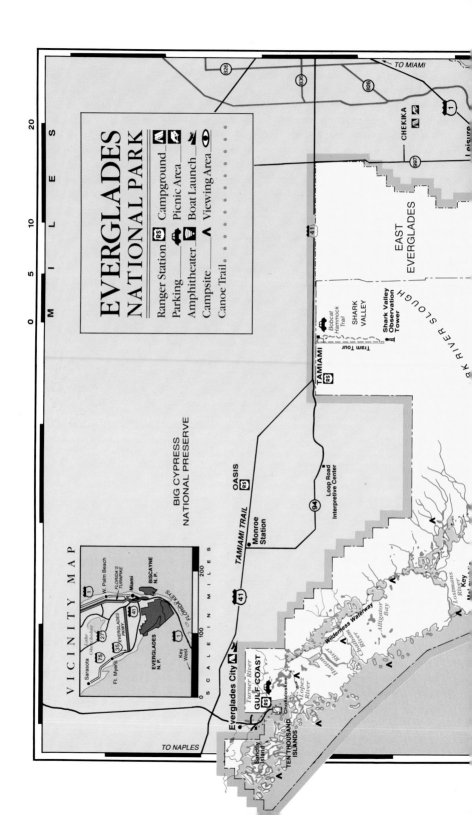

EVERGLADES NATIONAL PARK

Ranger Station RS	Campground		
Parking	Picnic Area		
Amphitheater	Boat Launch		
Campsite	Viewing Area		
Canoe Trail			

VICINITY MAP

W. Palm Beach
FLORIDA'S TURNPIKE
Miami
BISCAYNE N.P.
Sarasota
Ft. Myers
Lake Okeechobee
EVERGLADES PKWY
Key West
EVERGLADES N.P.
FLORIDA KEYS

SCALE IN MILES
100   200

BIG CYPRESS NATIONAL PRESERVE

OASIS RS

TAMIAMI TRAIL

Monroe Station

Loop Road Interpretive Center

TAMIAMI RS

SHARK VALLEY

Bobcat Hammock Trail

Shark Valley Observation Tower

Tram Tour

EAST EVERGLADES

SHARK RIVER SLOUGH

CHEKIKA

TO MIAMI

Leisure

Everglades City

GULF COAST RS

Turner River

Chokoloskee

Sandfly Island

TEN THOUSAND ISLANDS

Wilderness Waterway

Chatham River

Lopez River

Huston River

Lostmans River

Alligator Bay

MILES
0   5   10   20

TO NAPLES

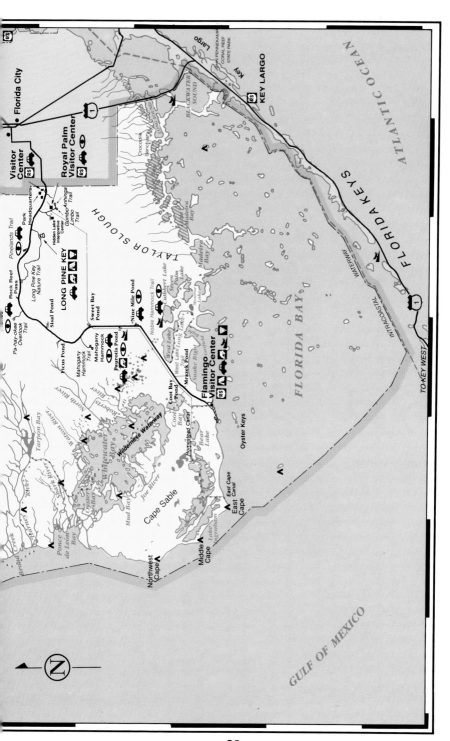

urban southern Florida. When gazing at the swaying saw grass that stretches from horizon to horizon—interrupted only occasionally by a low tree island—one gains release from the confines of the city. An incredible diversity of plant and animal life is sustained in the park's mangrove forests, coastal prairies, fresh-water sloughs, cypress strands, pinelands, and hardwood hammocks. Who does not gaze in wonder when a giant soft-shelled turtle; a dozen alligators; scores of herons, egrets, and ibis; and numerous 2-foot garfish are all visible from a single vantage point?

The park is best known for its varied and abundant bird life and its omnipresent alligators. It is home to fourteen species of threatened or endangered animals. Visitors may chance to see a southern bald eagle above Florida Bay, a snail kite at Shark Valley, an American crocodile in the salt-water estuaries, or perhaps an elusive Florida panther crossing the highway near a field or cypress swamp. Also resident in the park—and by no means endangered—are at least sixty-seven species of mosquitoes, which play an important role in channeling food through the ecosystem. A drop of human blood directly contributes to the web of life in the Everglades!

HISTORY

Shell Mounds and Middens

In this flat and watery land, the highest points of ground were not raised by geologic forces; instead, they were built over centuries by the indigenous Glades people. These mysterious shell mounds are found most often in the Gulf Coast section of the park. One mound along the Chatham River covers 40 acres. Sixty acres of ridges and mounds alter the topography of Dismal Key. Chokoloskee Island, reachable by road and surrounded by park lands, contains numerous shell mounds. One site, mostly destroyed by development on Chokoloskee Island, covered 135 acres and rose as high as 20 feet. A remarkable earthen mound 400 feet long and 30 feet wide lies a few miles north of Flamingo near Bear Lake.

Archeologists have determined that some mounds were used as burial sites and ceremonial sites. Most probably began as refuse piles, or middens, of discarded shells. When hurricanes inundated the land with storm tides, the mounds became places of refuge.

The Everglades region has been inhabited by human beings for at least 11,000 years. By 4,000 years ago, a substantial population of people lived in the maritime and wetland environment. Ample supplies of easily obtained food gave the Glades people the necessary free time to pursue their massive shellwork construction projects. Remains of turtles, deer, birds, small mammals, manatees, West Indian seals, crabs, lobsters, oysters, clams, and conchs have been found at ancient village sites. Coontie roots, palmetto berries, coco-plums, sea grapes, and prickly pears supplemented their diet.

During the time the Spanish occupied Florida, from the early 1500s through 1763, there were likely 5,000 to 20,000 Indians living in southern Florida. The Spanish recognized two groups of Native Americans living in the region. The west coast, where most of the large mounds are found, was inhabited by the Calusas. On the east coast, from what is now Pompano Beach south to Cape Sable and the Florida Keys, lived the 800 Tequestas. Portions of both tribes resided within the boundaries of present-day Everglades National Park. Hammering and digging tools made of conch shells, knives equipped with shark-tooth blades, and potsherds of gritty clay are frequently found in the park.

The Calusa and Tequesta people in southern Florida were reduced to a handful of survivors by 1800. Some may have departed with the Spaniards, but most probably succumbed to diseases brought by non-natives. These people, who lived among the mangrove waterways and coastal prairies, possessed no immunological defenses against European contagions. Tuberculosis, polio, influenza, and even the common cold probably struck the villages like waves of plague.

Taking in the scenery at "The Big Swamp of Florida, U.S.A.," circa 1906.

Escape and Survival in the Glades

After 1700, new groups of Native Americans emigrated to northern Florida. English settlements in the Carolinas and Georgia were pushing members of the loosely knit Creek Confederacy to the south. Among these people were the Miccosukee, who live today on the northern park boundary. After the Creek War of 1813 and 1814, the Creeks and other tribes abandoned extensive lands in Alabama and Georgia, and a large number of Muskogee Creeks emigrated to Florida. Together, the two groups of Creeks became collectively known by non-natives as Seminoles. The Seminoles, who numbered about 5,000 in Florida by 1821, provided refuge for runaway slaves, which, in part, served as a catalyst for white hostility. Sequestered on a reservation to the north of Lake Okeechobee, the Seminoles retaliated by raiding white villages. Congress decreed in 1830 that all Indians be moved "far beyond the possibility of any contact with white men." Many Native people were forced to travel west on the Trail of Tears to present-day Oklahoma, then known as Indian Territory. Numerous Seminoles, however, refused to be pushed west. During the Seminole Wars of 1835 to 1842 and of 1855 to 1859, they sought seclusion deep within the Everglades. The warfare inflicted heavy losses on the Seminoles as well as on the United States Army and government. Fifteen hundred soldiers lost their lives, and more than $20 million was spent. The wars finally ended on May 8, 1859, when Chief Billy Bowlegs and 164 others were sent west for relocation in Indian Territory. But the Seminoles had not been defeated, and the fighting had ended with a truce. Perhaps 150 Seminoles remained in the cypress strands and saw-grass prairies of southern Florida.

On hammocks within the Everglades, the Miccosukee built villages consisting of open-air, thatch-roofed structures called *chickees* and cultivated squash, corn, sugar cane, and citrus fruits. Poling dugout canoes was an ideal method of transportation through the watery glades. The opening of the Tamiami Trail between Tampa and Miami in 1923 induced the Miccosukee to build settlements along that thoroughfare. Lowering water levels, resulting from attempts to drain the Everglades, also may have encouraged Miccosukee people to move close to the highway. Today, many villages allow public visitation and offer vividly colored skirts and blouses for sale. Miccosukee children attend a school within the park. Classes are offered in traditional culture and language, along with courses designed to help the children succeed in the environs of Miami. Every spring, the Miccosukee retreat to secluded hammocks where they celebrate the traditional Green Corn Dance. Miccosukee culture has endured.

Spaniards and Outlaws

Although Juan Ponce de León discovered southern Florida in 1513, permanent white settlement of the region was delayed for almost three centuries. Spain established missions to the northeast of the Everglades to convert the Tequestas, but the missions, along with their protecting soldiers, departed in 1763 when Spain surrendered Florida to British control. Exploration of the Everglades began in earnest as the United States Army pursued Native Americans during the Seminole Wars. In 1838, Fort Poinsett was established on the East Cape of Cape Sable. Fort Cross was built nineteen years later on the Middle Cape. The first proposals to drain the Everglades were made by the military in 1848. John James Audubon's visit to Cape Sable in 1832 was the first of many made by prominent naturalists.

Settlement of the coastal portions of the future park began in the 1880s and 1890s. Calusa shell mounds became sites for agriculture and for the construction of homes. Farming, fishing, hunting, and taking birds for their plumes (which were used to decorate women's hats) provided a modest economic base for the region's few inhabitants. Tales abounded that the mangrove islands were hideouts for many hideous villains. In 1905, Guy Bradley, a warden hired by the National Audubon Society to protect heron and egret rookeries, was murdered, allegedly by plume hunters. In later years, the poaching of alligators and the illegal taking of pig frogs to supply restaurants replaced plume hunting as a source of revenue. Illicit drug running is a more recent manifestation of this outlaw tradition.

Establishment of the Park

Outrage at the numbers of great egrets, snowy egrets, roseate spoonbills, and other wading birds that were being slaughtered for their plumes led many conservationists to call for complete protection of the few remaining nesting colonies. Guy Bradley's murder, while he was investigating shots heard from the direction of the Oyster Keys rookery, made him a martyr to the cause of bird preservation.

As well as for its spectacular bird life, the Everglades already was renowned for its botanical treasures. In 1893, the magnificent stand of royal palms on Paradise Key—site of the future Royal Palm Visitor Center—had been investigated by Dr. H. P. Rolfs, dean of the University of Florida College of Agriculture, and Dr. N. L. Britton, director of the New York Botanical Garden. As a result of their efforts following that trip, Paradise Key almost became a national park. Rolfs and Britton persuaded James E. Ingraham, vice president of the Florida East Coast Railroad, to turn over part of Paradise Key to the federal government; but before negotiations could be completed, Theodore Roosevelt's presidential authority from Congress to accept such gifts lapsed. An arduous fifty-year struggle was to follow before the establishment of Everglades National Park.

The smaller area of Paradise Key, however, was granted protection in 1916, with the creation of Royal Palm State Park. The Florida Federation of Women's Clubs was instrumental in the cause of Paradise Key's preservation and subsequent development of tourist facilities. Meanwhile, the greater part of the Everglades experienced many threats to its environmental integrity. Pine, cypress, and mahogany were being cut for lumber. Plant collectors were carting away rare orchids and bromeliads (epiphytic plants, or air plants, of the family that includes the pineapple). Clam beds of the Ten Thousand Islands declined suddenly. Real-estate developers had plans to drain and subdivide the land. Oil wells were drilled on proposed park lands.

The Royal Palm State Park Board, a unit of the Florida Federation of Women's Clubs.

Ernest Coe, wearing bow tie, lobbied for federal protection of the Everglades.

Ernest F. Coe, who had moved to Miami in 1925, became the park's foremost supporter and established the Tropical Everglades National Park Association. Congress eventually passed a park bill in 1934 that opponents dubbed the "alligator and snake swamp bill," but acquisition of park lands did not proceed during the Great Depression and World War 11. The dedication of Everglades National Park finally took place on December 6, 1947. Everglades was the first national park in the United States established solely for its biological attributes. The park later gained additional recognition when it was declared a World Heritage Site and an International Biosphere Reserve. The program sponsors the study of unique cultural and natural sites in an effort to develop ways to balance the use and protection of the environment.

Ooids and Bryozoans

A visitor's first step into the saw-grass marsh usually causes a bit of bewilderment and surprise. One does not sink into oblivion, but usually lands squarely on firm footing. Underlying the entire Everglades is hard limestone.

Geologically speaking, the Everglades is young. The extraordinary flatness of the land indicates that it was once a sea bottom and only recently became exposed to erosive forces. The highest point in the park, aside from the Calusa shell mounds, stands a mere 10 feet above sea level. The highway to Flamingo climbs over Rock Reef Pass at a towering elevation of 3 feet.

Over the past million years or so, the land on which the Everglades rests has been repeatedly exposed above the ocean and then inundated by warm, shallow seas. Colossal geologic forces have not pulsed the Florida mainland up and down. The periodic fluctuation is instead due to changes in sea level caused by the expansion and contraction of the polar icecaps. During glacial times, when much water is stored as ice, the ocean level drops, leaving Florida high and exposed. In interglacial periods, glacial meltwater raises the ocean levels, and most of Florida is flooded.

The Miami Limestone that underlies most of the Everglades was formed 100,000 years ago when a shallow sea covered the present-day park to a depth of about 25 feet. The processes that deposited the Miami Limestone Formation are being reenacted today in a similar environment across the Straits of Florida on the Great Bahama Bank. Beneath the warm, shallow sea there, tremendous numbers of tiny grains called ooids are precipitated from water that is supersaturated with calcium carbonate. The strong currents of the Gulf Stream pile the ooids into a long bar. Except that it has not yet consolidated into hard limestone, the ridge resembles the Atlantic Coastal Ridge, which runs southwestward from Fort Lauderdale into the park. Colonies of bryozoans flourish in slightly deeper lagoons of the Great Bahama Bank. *Bryozoan* translates from Greek as "moss animal," and it identifies the Bryozoa, an entire phylum of tiny marine invertebrates that secrete calcareous shells. The Miami Limestone beneath the park on the western side of the Atlantic Coastal Ridge consists of the remains of a species of bryozoan identical to the one now living on the Great Bahama Bank.

Opposite: In places, tidewater has eroded the Everglades' limestone substratum.

Aquifers and Tomatoes

To the northwest of the Everglades, in Big Cypress National Preserve, the older limestone of the Tamiami Formation can be found. This 6-million-year-old rock contains more quartz sand and is harder and less permeable than the limestone of the Miami Formation. Southward, the Tamiami Limestone slopes beneath both the Miami Limestone and the Fort Thompson Formation (a limestone that surfaces to the north of the park), where it provides an impervious barrier to water. The highly porous Miami and Fort Thompson limestones, in contrast, hold great quantities of fresh water. Through the Biscayne Aquifer, water that falls in the Everglades ecosystem quenches the thirst of several million people living from West Palm Beach to the Florida Keys. The water irrigates rocky lands in Dade County that produce at least fifty-one different commercial crops, including 75 percent of the winter tomatoes grown in the United States.

Everglades is probably the most threatened of the national parks. Many parks are situated in mountainous regions where rivers have their sources. The Everglades' watershed begins approximately 240 miles north of the park border in agricultural areas near Orlando. Water once traveled through the meandering Kissimmee River before it accumulated in Lake Okeechobee, which overflowed its banks during the summer rainy season, initiating the Everglades. The Army Corps of Engineers, however,

replaced the Kissimmee River with a 150- to 300-foot-wide drainage ditch that channels water south to Lake Okeechobee. An additional 1,200-mile labyrinth of canals, dikes, and levees takes water from Lake Okeechobee to burgeoning population centers on Florida's east and west coasts, to agricultural areas, and to Everglades National Park.

The almost imperceptible slope toward the sea allows water to flow across the park in a broad shallow sheet. The Everglades ecosystem has been described as a vast river of grass—originally a river 40 to 70 miles wide and 100 miles long. When flowing naturally, water moves along it at a barely perceptible average speed of .5 mile a day. The gradient is about 2.5 inches to the mile in the Shark River Slough. Most of the surface water in the park flows southwestward toward the Gulf of Mexico. Unseen, water also flows eastward through porous limestone beneath the surface.

Drainage of wetlands to the north, east, and west of the park has considerably reduced the flow of water entering and leaving the Everglades. Drainage of wetlands has allowed heavier salt water to creep inland from the sea in a process known as saltwater intrusion. As well, phosphorus pollution from nearby farms drains into the glades, increasing nutrients to an abnormal level and promoting the growth of cattails, which crowd out established species and choke water flow. In 1988, the U.S. Justice Department sued the state of Florida for disregarding its own laws and allowing pollution of the park. The parties agreed to a cleanup

Low tide in Flamingo Bay exposes the mudflats that surround mangrove islands.

plan, which the sugar industry challenged. The state and federal governments then entered into protracted negotiations with the industry. Meanwhile, the Corps of Engineers agreed to attempt to restore to some degree the natural flow of water in South Florida. In 1989, Congress added 107,000 acres to the northeast side of the park to further protect the water flow. In 1994, the State Legislature agreed to spend hundreds of millions of dollars to build 40,000 acres of filtration marshes around Lake Okeechobee to filter out farm pollution before it reached the Everglades; the action brought an end to thirty-six farm-industry lawsuits.

Natural History

Climate and Precipitation

Unlike most of the rest of the United States, which experiences spring, summer, autumn, and winter, the Everglades has but two seasons: dry and wet. Driest conditions prevail from November to the end of April. In contrast, 80 percent of a normal year's rain falls between May and October. Thunderstorms materialize quickly with towering cumulonimbus clouds, plenty of lightning, and heavy downpours. Lightning strikes with greater frequency in southern Florida than in any other location in North America. The Everglades' mean annual rainfall, 53 inches, masks an extreme year-to-year variability. In some years, the total exceeds 100 inches; in others, serious drought occurs.

The Everglades ecosystem has a subtropical climate. The Gulf Stream pumps warm water past Florida, and prevailing easterly and southeasterly trade winds bring warm tropical air inland. Frost, a rarity in the Everglades, occurs only when a strong winter cold front pushes arctic air down the length of Florida. The glades sustain a mixture of tropical and temperate vegetation that is unique in the world. Temperate plants such as willows, poison ivy, and Virginia creeper migrated down the Florida peninsula from the north. Coco-plum, strangler fig, and gumbo-limbo are tropical species that arrived from islands of the West Indies.

From November through March, the daytime temperature usually reaches a pleasant 60° to 75° F. Mosquitoes may be nonexistent or a minor annoyance in winter. The peak season for mosquitoes is April through November. Deer flies often become a nuisance in April and May. During summer, many areas of the park may be too heavily infested with mosquitoes to allow comfortable hiking. The intense heat and high humidity of summer can produce other

Preceding overleaf: Elevation changes of only a few inches determine vegetation habitat.

uncomfortable conditions. A long-sleeved, loose-fitting shirt, baggy pants, a hat, and good insect repellent are essential in the glades during summer. Plenty of water should be carried on all outings.

Saw-Grass Prairies and Hammocks

In mountainous regions, changes in vegetation appear over thousands of feet of altitude. In the Everglades, a difference of mere inches in elevation can totally alter the ground cover. The dominant plant of the open glades is saw grass, which is actually a sedge. Its needle-sharp teeth discourage foraging animals and help catch water during the dry season. On foggy winter nights, dew condenses on the teeth and rolls down the V-shaped midrib to thirsty roots. Through the wet season, saw-grass roots are deep in water. During winter, the parched saw-grass prairies are occasionally consumed by crackling-hot fire. The flames release stored nutrients in dead plant matter that stimulate new plant growth. Fire, once widely thought to be harmful, is now recognized as a vital element in maintaining a healthy and diverse Everglades ecosystem.

The tree islands that dot the vast expanse of the Everglades may develop from either high or low spots of the limestone bedrock. Sloughs (depressions or channels with slow-moving water), especially ones that contain accumulations of sandy peat, provide excellent ground conditions for cypress trees. Big Cypress National Preserve, to the northwest of the Everglades, was

Mangrove roots bind the mud of flats off the park's coasts, and form islands.

named not for the size of its bald cypress but for the extensive area they once covered. Most of the Big Cypress was logged between 1930 and 1950; the preserve was created in 1974.

Willowheads, low islands of coastal plain willows, also occur in areas of deeper water. Willows frequently serve as pioneering plants; their decomposed leaves and stems produce the peaty soil that other woody plants require to gain a foothold. When peat accumulation in a willowhead approaches the wet-season water levels, a bayhead usually develops. Coco-plum, red bay, sweet bay, dahoon holly, myrsine, and poison ivy grow in bayheads because their roots can tolerate being inundated for part of the year.

Islands that rise 1 to 3 feet above the limestone base and support a junglelike growth of tropical hardwoods and palms are called hammocks. The roots of trees that grow on hammocks remain above water and receive plenty of air. Mahogany, gumbo-limbo, and strangler fig are but three of the numerous species of hardwoods that have arrived from the West Indies. The gnarled and majestic live oak is the only common hammock tree of temperate origin. Overhanging trunks and branches in hammocks are draped with epiphytic plants: orchids, bromeliads, and ferns. An epiphyte is a nonparasitic plant that grows on or in association with another, larger plant. On smooth-barked trees, ornately colored *Liguus* tree snails consume lichens during the rainy season. Hammocks possess a fascinating defense mechanism against fire. Weak organic acids from decomposing plant material concentrate around the edge of the island. The acids dissolve underlying limestone rock and create a moat that usually stops fires.

In places where fires repeatedly burn elevated limestone ridges, a plant community strikingly different from the dense jungles found on hammocks emerges. Slash pine, with its thick, corky bark, has a natural resistance to flames. Fire prunes back competing hardwood vegetation and exposes mineral soil that slash-pine seedlings find best for germination. The park's pinelands support thirty species of endemic plants found nowhere else.

On August 24, 1992, Hurricane Andrew, one of the century's worst hurricanes, dealt a fierce blow to the park's plant communities. The mangrove forests were damaged; many hardwood trees were downed. About 20 to 30 percent of the pines were destroyed.

Mangroves and Estuaries

Fresh water flowing through the Everglades eventually reaches the coast and mingles with salt water. In this transition zone

Opposite: In order to obtain air, red mangroves have adapted stiltlike roots.

grows a belt of mangroves that varies in width from a few yards in some spots to 20 miles along the southwestern coast. Buttonwood is the mangrove species least resistant to salinity; white, red, and black mangroves tolerate progressively higher salt concentrations. Buttonwood and white and black mangroves cope with saline conditions by excreting excess salt through their leaves. Red mangrove is able to prevent initial absorption of salt by maintaining high osmotic pressure in its roots. Mangrove forests cover 25 percent of the park's total acreage. Red mangroves are the most distinctive, with their arching, spiderlike roots. From their extensive underwater root systems, black mangroves sprout hundreds of vertical breathing tubes called pneumatophores. Mangroves help stabilize the shoreline and provide a buttress against hurricanes.

An acre of mature red-mangrove forest produces, on the average, 7,000 pounds of leaf and twig debris each year. This material falls into an estuarine environment where it decomposes into detritus and provides nutrients for a vast web of marine organisms. Bacteria and fungi initiate the decomposition, and they also add microbial protein to the leaf fragments in the process. Small crustaceans and fish feed on the enriched detritus and they, in turn, become food for larger fish and blue crabs. Snook, spotted sea trout, crocodiles, bald eagles, and people occupy the top of the mangrove food pyramid.

Sea Cows and Green Turtles

Florida Bay covers 800 square miles with salt water that averages only 4 to 5 feet in depth. The cloudiness of the water is caused by suspended particles of marl (clay and calcium carbonate) stirred from the bottom by wave action. More than fifty species of fish live in the warm, shallow bay. Mullet often can be seen jumping into the air a few feet above the surface.

Marine grasses growing in the bay provide cover, food, and nursery grounds for innumerable fish and crustaceans. Two large and endangered herbivores, the manatee and the Atlantic green turtle, feed on the underwater grasses. Manatees are gentle sea mammals that can grow 15 feet long and weigh 1,500 pounds. During six to eight hours of daily feeding, they may consume 10 to 15 percent of their body weight. All too often, these slow-swimming "sea cows" are struck by the propellers of fast-moving motorboats. The resultant wounds often cause manatees to bleed to death or die later from infections. A significant number of manatees are also crushed or drowned in the gates of flood-control structures. Moreover, manatees are slow to rebuild their numbers.

At intervals of two to five years, and after thirteen months of gestation, a cow gives birth to one calf.

Green turtles are the only sea turtles that are primarily plant eaters. The low nutritional value in their diet of sea grass and algae retards their growth. A green turtle may be twenty to thirty years old before reaching maturity.

About 100 keys (*key* originates from the Spanish word *cayos*, which means "little island") covered with mangroves dot Florida Bay. West of the bay, broad shell beaches line the coast of Cape Sable. Coral reefs are not found within Everglades National Park but grow in the warm Atlantic Ocean on the eastern side of the Florida Keys. Biscayne and Dry Tortugas national parks and John Pennekamp Coral Reef State Park preserve fine examples of reefs.

An Abundance of Birds

When winter's dryness parches the land, leaving the only fresh water in alligator holes and human excavations called borrow pits, the Everglades hosts an extravagant display of wading birds that is unequaled on the continent. Roseate spoonbills are perhaps the most outlandishly spectacular of the waders. An adult spoonbill sports brilliant red legs and eyes, a greenish face and bill, a white neck and back, and crimson-pink wings. Its oddly shaped bill, swung from side to side through shallow water and mud, "spoons" up small fish, shrimp, aquatic insects, and other organisms. The great egret, with its all-white body, yellow beak, and black legs, is the most frequently seen heron in the park. It may be confused with the great white heron, a white variety of the great blue heron. The great egret has black legs, while those of the great white heron are yellow. The snowy egret is smaller than the other all-white waders, and its black legs end with brilliant yellow feet, the source for an alternative local name, golden slippers. Smaller than the snowy egret is the cattle egret, a recent immigrant from the Old World often seen along Florida's roadways. The only other uniformly white herons are the juvenile little blue heron and reddish egret, although on land white ibis and immature spoonbills look virtually all-white in plumage, too. If wading-bird identification seems confusing, consult a field guide. Mastering the wading birds should take less than a day. For a greater challenge, try identifying shore birds! Each species of wading bird has developed specific strategies for securing prey. Great egrets and great blue herons remain in a freeze position until they stab fish or frogs with their bills. Little blue herons, tricolored herons, and reddish and snowy egrets often

Overleaf: The roseate spoonbill. Inset: Great white egret.

dance wildly as they dart after food. White ibis probe their pink curved bills deep into muck, where they grab food by touch.

The tremendous numbers of wading birds present during winter congregate at the few remaining water holes, which hold dense populations of aquatic life. Wood storks typify the dependence of wading birds on the age-old cycle in which the summer's rainfall flows across the land in a sheet, followed by the winter's drying down. Wood storks, often referred to in southern Florida as iron heads because of their gray, unfeathered heads, are considered a barometer of the Everglades' health. A wood stork secures food by touch, not by sight. It moves its massive, down-curved bill slowly through the water. When the bill contacts a fish, an incredibly fast grabbing reflex is triggered. To gather the roughly 440 pounds of food needed to raise a brood, wood storks require fish to be densely concentrated in drying pools during winter. To find such concentrations, adults may fly distances of up to 75 miles. In 1984, wood storks were added to the federal endangered-species list, in part because they had experienced few successful nesting seasons during the preceding decade in Everglades National Park. In wet winters, excess water in the park has enabled fish to remain widely dispersed. Conversely, droughts have been exaggerated by the diversion of water away from the Everglades. Inordinate numbers of fish die as even relatively deep water holes evaporate, and the wood storks must abandon their starving young.

It was hoped that adding 107,600 acres to the park in 1989 would lead to the restoration of some of the storks' habitat. By the mid-1990s, the storks were nesting again, at Paurotis Pond.

Another endangered bird that suffers from manipulated water levels is the snail kite, also known as the Everglades kite. This dark, medium-size hawk, with its large white tail patch and bright orange beak and legs, often may be seen at Shark Valley. Snail kites feed almost exclusively on apple snails, brownish green fresh-water snails that lay pinkish white egg clusters a few inches above the water's surface on blades of vegetation. Rapidly rising water levels that follow the opening of water-control gates drown the snail eggs; this, in turn, adversely affects snail kites' chances of survival. Drought, exaggerated by water diversions away from the Everglades, causes tens of thousands of snails to perish. Without a food source, the snail-kite population plummets.

At least 326 species of birds have been sighted in the park, 240 of which are considered residents or regular visitors. One bird that human observers often look for in vain is the flamingo. Wild flamingos may never have nested in Florida. Around 1900, and perhaps for centuries before, flocks of several thousand flamingos visited Florida Bay from nesting colonies in the Bahamas, but these colonies were later destroyed. The occasional flamingos now sighted in Florida Bay are probably escapees from captive flocks. Across the open water of Florida Bay, endangered southern bald eagles are sighted much more often than are flamingos.

The Last Refuge of the Panther

One of the most elusive park animals is the Florida panther, a subspecies of the mountain lion. Development in Florida has forced panthers to retreat to Everglades National Park and adjoining land in Big Cypress National Preserve and Fakahatchee State Preserve. Only thirty to fifty of the endangered big cats remain in southern Florida. Many panthers have been struck at night by automobiles traveling roads in the park and in the preserve. In an effort to reduce the carnage, some nighttime automobile speed limits were lowered in areas of prime panther habitat. Construction of underpasses were seen as a means of allowing the cats to cross highways safely. In other efforts to save the species, the Florida Panther National Wildlife Refuge was established in 1989, a captive breeding program was initiated, and cats outfitted with radio collars were tracked from the air so that their habits could be studied.

Panthers eat the Virginia white-tailed deer that are commonly observed in the Everglades. Other panther prey includes raccoons, opossums, and armadillos, an introduced animal that is just becoming established in the park.

Visitors are more likely to chance on bobcats than on panthers.

The American alligator is North America's largest reptile.

River otters and marsh rabbits are among the smaller mammals often seen in the everglades.

The Domain of Alligators and Crocodiles

Many people consider the Everglades to be synonymous with alligators. The American alligator is the park animal that most visitors thrill to see. Its crocodilian ancestors first appeared almost 200 million years ago, when dinosaurs ruled the earth. Superb adaptation has permitted alligators to survive so long in the swamps. Like all currently living reptiles, alligators are cold-blooded. Their dark skin absorbs the warmth of sunlight. Without internal furnaces to fuel, alligators have low energy requirements. They also conserve energy by spending so much time basking motionless. In the wild, alligators probably take a meal only once or twice a week. They have been known to survive for up to six months without feeding. Their seemingly sedate life style can be deceptive, however. Alligators move with blurring speed and over short distances can run faster than a human being.

Alligators use their strong jaws to crush the bony garfish and other prey that constitute their diet. Food is usually swallowed whole. Turtles, wading birds, waterfowl, apple snails, raccoons, and small dogs may fall prey to alligators' opportunistic tendencies to consume whatever they can catch. Larger animals, such as white-tailed deer and even other alligators, are taken on occasion. After drowning a deer, an alligator waits for the carcass to rot, consuming whatever flesh it can tear off. An alligator has never killed or seriously harmed a human being within Everglades National Park. The National Park Service's strict policy forbidding people to feed alligators helps keep gators from investigating human arms as a potential food source.

Courtship generally takes place during April and May. Around sunrise on spring mornings, deep, rumbling bellows emanate from adult alligators. Members of both sexes allow close approach to one another during this time of the year. A female may let the larger male rest his head or front foot on her back while both gators peacefully sun. After a courtship that may last for several days, the mating takes place while the gators are submerged in the water.

The female alligator builds a nest mound of vegetation in which she deposits twenty to fifty eggs. It is crucial to the eggs' survival that rising water not flood the nest during the sixty-five-day incubation period. Submersion for twelve hours suffices to kill the embryos. The sex of hatchling alligators is determined by egg temperature during the first two to three weeks of incubation. Eggs

The American crocodile has a pointed snout; the alligator's is U-shaped.

that develop below 86° F produce females, while those kept above 93° F hatch males. Temperatures between 86° F and 93° F result in broods of mixed gender. The female guards the nest during incubation, and then cares for the young until they are one to two years old. Picking up a grunting 9-inch baby gator will elicit a hissing, lunging charge from the baby's mother.

Alligators play a crucial role as hydraulic engineers in the Everglades. During the dry season, gators take refuge in water-filled holes in the bedrock, which they clear of muck and vegetation. Gator holes serve as an oasis for myriad forms of life. In return for creating the holes, alligators find an abundance of food at their doorstep. When summer rains appear, life moves from the gator holes to repopulate the open glades.

Salt-water areas of the park provide refuge for the much rarer American crocodile. About 300 crocs reside in Everglades National

Park, but fewer than 20 females nest each year. A crocodile's skin is olive gray-green, and its head is pointed to a V. An alligator has a U-shaped head and almost black skin. Both reptiles grow to similar sizes and generally have nonaggressive dispositions toward people.

Some twenty-seven species of snakes are protected within the park. Only four are venomous: the dusky pygmy rattlesnake, the eastern diamondback rattlesnake, the eastern cottonmouth (water moccasin), and the eastern coral snake.

Sites, Trails, and Trips

The Everglades ecosystem exhibits wide diversity, and visitors can enjoy the park in many ways. Outings range from roadside bird-watching at an assortment of ponds to a 99-mile wilderness waterway for canoe and motorboat travel. Visitors who slow down and patiently observe nature's workings are richly rewarded by the drama of everyday life in the Everglades.

The main Visitor Center is at park headquarters, 11 miles southwest of Homestead by car. Exhibits, publications, a brief movie, and the rangers help provide orientation. Visitor Centers are also situated at Royal Palm, Flamingo, Everglades City, and Shark Valley. Facilities smashed by Hurricane Andrew were replaced.

The main park road winds for 38 miles from the Visitor Center at headquarters to the concession complex of Flamingo on Florida Bay. The road passes through fresh-water marl prairies, pinelands, cypress domes, mangrove forests, and coastal prairies.

A great white heron shares the domain of a single, pioneering red mangrove.

During winter, great numbers of wading birds may gather at Mrazek Pond and at other roadside water holes that were dug to provide fill for the highway.

Walks and Hiking Trails

Two of the park's most popular walks, the Anhinga Trail and the Gumbo-Limbo Trail, leave from the Royal Palm Visitor Center.

Anhinga Trail. A .3-mile combination of elevated boardwalk and asphalt path leads into Taylor Slough. The Anhinga Trail offers excellent opportunities for observing alligators, water snakes, purple gallinules, and a variety of herons and egrets. The anhinga, also known as the water turkey or snakebird, may be observed as it swims submerged to its neck or as it perches in a tree, drying out its water-permeable feathers. It feeds by spearing fish with its skewer-like bill and then swallowing them headfirst. During the spring, anhinga nests can be seen near the covered boardwalk viewing area at the trail's end. The boardwalk, destroyed by Hurricane Andrew, was rebuilt using synthetic lumber from recycled materials.

Gumbo-Limbo Trail. The Gumbo-Limbo Trail, .3 mile long, winds through a dense tropical-hardwood hammock. Gumbo-limbos are tropical trees with papery bark of an orange-bronze color. The tree

Overleaf: Sunset overwhelms the park's gentle terrain.

Dewy spider web at twilight suggests the fragility of the Everglades environment.

is also known as the turpentine tree because of the odor it emits when cut. Southern Floridians often jokingly refer to gumbo-limbos as tourist trees because the bark is always red and peeling. In addition to the gumbo-limbo, many other tropical plants grow in the hammock. Among the most imposing are the tall and majestic royal palms. Overhead, arboreal orchids, bromeliads, and ferns flourish. Visitors should beware of a small species of tree called poison-wood, whose three to seven shiny green leaflets have yellow mid-ribs and black spots. A tropical relative of poison ivy, it can produce a severe rash in allergic individuals. The area of this trail was severely damaged by the 1992 hurricane, but was showing rapid recovery within two years.

At Long Pine Key, an interconnecting system of old fire roads allows hiking and bicycling in a variety of habitats.

Slash Pine Trail. The Slash Pine Trail travels 7 miles from the Long Pine Key Campground road to the main park road. Two hundred species of plants grow in the fire-maintained habitat of the pinelands. White-tailed deer, raccoons, opossums, and the extremely rare Florida panther live among the pines.

Pinelands Trail. The .5-mile Pinelands Trail circles from the main park road through open slash-pine forest. Many of the thirty species of plants endemic to the pinelands bloom along the walkway. The path courses over low outcrops of limestone pockmarked with solution holes. The 1992 hurricane left many trees snapped off at from 6 to 12 feet above the ground.

Pa-hay-okee Overlook Trail. In the language of the Miccosukee Indians, *pa-hay-okee* means "grassy waters." The short, handicapped-accessible (less than .5 mile) Pa-hay-okee Overlook Trail leads to an observation platform that offers a fine view of the vast "river of grass." To the north and west, the broad Shark River Slough is dotted with hammocks. The fresh water slowly flowing to the southwest originated at locations as far away as Orlando, 260 miles to the north.

Mahogany Hammock Trail. The Mahogany Hammock Trail, an elevated boardwalk, winds for .3 mile through a dense, moist, and dark tropical hammock. The largest mahogany tree in the United States grows among the junglelike vegetation. A hike through Mahogany Hammock on a moonlit night can be especially eerie when the barred owls converse with one another.

Mangrove Wilderness Trail (West Lake). The Mangrove Wilderness Trail, a boardwalk slightly less than .5 mile long, enters the heart of a mangrove forest. White, black, and red mangrove, as well as buttonwood, grow here where the fresh water of the glades mingles with salt water. West Lake, a large, brackish estuary, provides a habitat for many species of fish and crustaceans.

Six longer trails that begin in the Flamingo area provide hiking

The saw palmetto is the only native North American palm that branches.

routes through mangrove forests and coastal prairies north of Florida Bay. Although coastal prairies receive ample quantities of rain, many plants usually associated with deserts grow in them. Visitors should remember to carry plenty of drinking water. Salt-marsh mosquitoes may make hiking unbearable during late spring, summer, and early autumn. Do not rule out the possibility of mosquitoes even during winter.

Bayshore Loop and Coastal Prairie Trails. The .7-mile round trip Bayshore Loop Trail and 13-mile round trip Coastal Prairie Trail begin near site C-54 in the Flamingo Campground, The Bayshore Loop branches off the main trail .3 mile west of the campground. The loop trail provides insights into the human and natural history of the Flamingo area. "Windows" through the mangroves afford beautiful views of Florida Bay. The longer Coastal Prairie Trail meanders through coastal prairies and buttonwood hammocks to a backcountry campsite at Clubhouse Beach. The trail is excellent for observing plant communities on the relatively dry coastal ridge. Hurricanes have swept huge quantities of marl from the floor of Florida Bay to build the ridge.

Bear Lake Trail. The Bear Lake Trail, a 4-mile round trip, follows the path of an old road lined with tropical hardwoods. The trail begins 2 miles north of Flamingo at the end of the Bear Lake Road. The canal that parallels the road supports many wading birds during winter. Roseate spoonbills are often seen near Bear Lake at the trail's end. The path passes several Calusa mounds hidden by mangroves.

Christian Point Trail. The 4-mile round trip Christian Point Trail begins at the main park road to the northeast of the Buttonwood Canal and ends on the west side of Snake Bight on Florida Bay. The trail courses through dense mangroves and open coastal prairie. Prickly pear cactus, barbed wire cactus, and yuccas seen along the trail have adapted to the saline conditions and winter droughts.

Rowdy Bend Trail. The 5-mile round trip Rowdy Bend Trail follows an old roadbed that leaves the main park road about 1 mile south of Mrazek Pond. The trail passes through junglelike mangrove forests with a small section of coastal prairie. It connects with the Snake Bight Trail.

Snake Bight Trail. The 4-mile round trip Snake Bight Trail takes

Opposite: After this photograph was taken, the pinelands were battered by Hurricane Andrew.

hikers to Florida Bay along a dirt road currently used for tram tours operated by the Flamingo Concession. Snake Bight Canal runs parallel to the trail. A boardwalk at Snake Bight offers excellent opportunities to view reddish egrets and many shore birds. A bight is a body of water bounded by a curve or an indentation. The mud flats of Snake Bight can suck shoes right off the feet of hikers, so it is wise to stay on the established trail.

Shark Valley, at the northeastern end of Everglades National Park, is a popular destination for people traveling across the southern part of Florida on the Tamiami Trail (U.S. 41).

Tram Road. An asphalt tram road (a 15-mile loop) ends at the Shark Valley Observation Tower, which provides excellent views of the open expanse of the glades. During the winter, dozens of alligators and wading birds may be feeding in the pond at the base of the tower. Water conditions permitting, the tram road can be traveled on foot, by bicycle, or on a concession-operated tram; this open-air bus ride is a 2-hour ranger-guided tour. Tram rides are very popular during winter; reservations are suggested.

Bobcat Boardwalk and Otter Cave Nature Trail. Bobcat Boardwalk and Otter Cave Nature Trail are short walks originat-

The Bear Lake/Cape Sable Canoe Trail passes through hardwood hammock habitat.

The bulge in the middle of its trunk identifies the Florida Royal Palm on the horizon.

ing from the Shark Valley parking area. Both trails provide good opportunities for watching endangered snail kites as they hunt for apple snails during the winter and spring.

Water Routes

Everglades City, at the northwestern edge of the park, is the gateway for motorboat and canoe travel through the Ten Thousand Islands and the broad belt of mangrove forests lining Florida's southwestern coast. Concession-operated boat tours depart regularly, weather permitting, from Everglades City.

Turner River. Turner River is one of the many popular canoe routes. The trip begins at the Tamiami Trail and ends 13 miles away at Chokoloskee Island, 4 miles southeast of Everglades City. The river flows through two mangrove tunnels and passes an extensive area of Calusa shell mounds.

Wilderness Waterway. From Everglades City to Flamingo, the well-marked 99-mile waterway winds through creeks, rivers, and open bays, giving an unequaled opportunity to explore the mangrove wilderness. The trip generally takes 7 days by canoe. A free back-country permit from the National Park Service is required.

Overleaf: Moonrise over coastal prairie and hardwood hammocks.

Campsites along the route—some atop ancient shell mounds—have pit toilets. All the water is brackish, so plenty of fresh water must be carried. During the wet season, from May through October, mosquitoes along the wilderness waterway are unbearable.

Many shorter canoe trails leave the Flamingo area.

Nine Mile Pond Trail. The Nine Mile Pond Trail loops 5.2 miles through fresh-water prairies, saw grass, and mangroves.

Noble Hammock Loop. The 3-mile Noble Hammock Loop meanders through alligator ponds, buttonwood and red-mangrove forests, and open saw grass. The trail was once utilized by bootleggers to gain access to larger hammocks.

Hells Bay Trail. The Hells Bay Trail is 14 miles round trip. It passes beneath canopied mangroves for long sections of the route.

West Lake Trail. The West Lake Trail crosses West and Long lakes before ending 8 miles away at Alligator Creek on Florida Bay.

Bear Lake/Cape Sable Trail. The Bear Lake/Cape Sable Trail runs 12 miles one way and ends at the contoured shell beaches of Cape Sable. A 20-foot portage is required near the end of the trip. Thousands of ducks and wading birds may be observed in flooded coastal prairies during winter.

Trails of Everglades National Park

The main park road runs 38 miles from the main entrance near Homestead to the Flamingo Visitor Center. All of the developed hiking trails originate along this road. Mileages given on the main park road are measured from the Royal Palm Entrance Station.

ANHINGA TRAIL: Starts and ends at Royal Palm Visitor Center at termination of spur road, 2 miles on main road; .5-mile loop; 1 hour; paved portion, otherwise elevated boardwalk extending over Taylor Slough; offers one of the best opportunities in park to see wildlife close up: alligators, turtles, fish, marsh rabbits, and many birds, including anhingas, herons, egrets, and purple gallinules.

GUMBO-LIMBO TRAIL: Starts and ends at Royal Palm Visitor Center; .5-mile loop; .5 hour; narrow, paved trail winds through a moist, junglelike hardwood hammock, with statuesque royal palms, gumbo-limbo trees, wild coffee plants, and lush aerial gardens of ferns and orchids.

PINELANDS TRAIL: Starts and ends at 6.5 miles on main road; .5-mile loop; .5 hour; narrow, paved trail circles through pinelands; the shallow bed of limestone that

Most Florida Bay islands are closed to boat landings to protect nesting birds.

underlies the pinelands can be seen clearly along this trail.

PA-HAY-OKEE OVERLOOK TRAIL: Starts and ends at parking area at termination of spur road, 12.5 miles on main road; .5-mile loop; .5 hour; elevated boardwalk leads through a dwarf cypress strand to an elevated platform offering a panoramic view of the vast "river of grass"; opportunity to see bird life, pygmy rattlesnakes, indigo and king snakes, and an occasional alligator along the trail.

MAHOGANY HAMMOCK TRAIL: Starts and ends at parking area at termination of spur road, 19.5 miles on main road; .5-mile loop; .5 hour; elevated boardwalk through a moist, dark hardwood hammock with rare Paurotis palms and massive mahogany trees (including the largest living specimen in the United States); excellent examples of hurricane damage.

MANGROVE WILDERNESS TRAIL (WEST LAKE): Starts at 30.5 miles on main road; ends at West Lake; .5 mile one way; .5 hour; elevated boardwalk winds through mangrove forest along the edge of the large, brackish lake; four types of mangroves—red, black, and white mangrove, and buttonwood—grow in this region, where the southward-creeping water of the glades meets salt water.

In summer, because of wet conditions, the developed walking trails are the easiest way to see Everglades by foot. In winter or after checking with the park, more ambitious hikers may choose the 15-mile **SHARK VALLEY LOOP ROAD,** or the network of fire roads at Long Pine Key. Several longer, backcountry-type trails near Flamingo lead into the southwestern parts of Everglades. These trails include the **CHRISTIAN POINT TRAIL,** 4 miles; **SNAKE BIGHT TRAIL,** 4 miles; **ROWDY BEND TRAIL,** 5 miles; the **COASTAL PRAIRIE TRAIL,** 13 miles; and **ALLIGATOR CREEK TRAIL,** 14 miles. Many of these trails pass through coastal prairie; salt-tolerant plants usually associated with deserts—cactus, agave, yucca—grow here; hardwood hammocks have developed in some prairies.

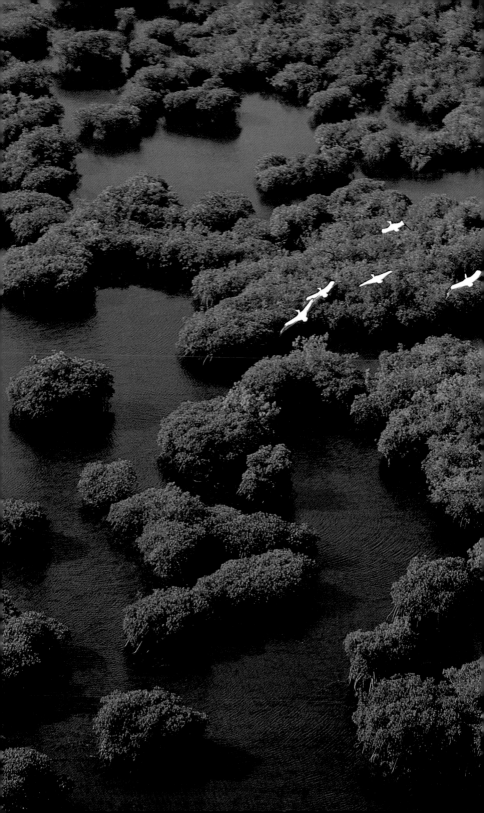

GREAT SMOKY MOUNTAINS NATIONAL PARK

A large population of black bears lives in the Great Smoky Mountains.

GREAT SMOKY MOUNTAINS NATIONAL PARK
107 PARK HEADQUARTERS ROAD
GATLINBURG, TENNESSEE 37738
TEL.: (615) 436-1200

HIGHLIGHTS: Newfound Gap • Clingmans Dome • Cades Cove • Oconaluftee • Rainbow Falls • Mount LeConte • Appalachian Trail • Cataloochee Valley • Charlies Bunion • The Chimney Tops

ACCESS: From Knoxville take I-40 to Tennessee 66, then U.S. 441 to Gatlinburg entrance. From Asheville, NC, take I-40 to Foothills Parkway.

HOURS: Open year-round, 24 hours daily. Clingmans Dome Road closed in winter; Newfound Gap Road may close in winter due to storms.

FEES: For camping.

PARKING: Ample parking throughout park.

GAS, FOOD, LODGING: Available in Tennessee and North Carolina communities near the park. Lodging in park at LeConte Lodge, open from April 15 to mid-November.

VISITOR CENTER: Major visitor center at Sugarlands; others at Cades Cove and Oconaluftee; Sugarlands and Oconaluftee Centers open seven days, year-round. Cades Cove open seven days, from April 15 through late November. Centers offer exhibits, trip-planning advice, and road-condition updates.

MUSEUM: Displays at visitor centers.

GIFT SHOP: Publications on sale at visitor centers.

PETS: Leashed pets permitted, but prohibited on trails.

PICNICKING: Numerous picnic sites available.

HIKING: More than 800 miles of hiking trails in park. Boil water.

BACKPACKING: Free permit and reservations required for overnight backcountry travel. "Backcountry" phone: (615) 436-1231.

CAMPGROUNDS: Developed campgrounds are at Smokemont, Elkmont, Cades Cove, Cosby, Deep Creek, Look Rock, Balsam Mountain, Cataloochee, Big Creek, and Abrams Creek. Reservations required from May 15 to October 31 for Cades Cove, Elkmont, and Smokemont. Water available. No utilities hookups. Showers available in nearby towns. 7-day stay limit from May 15 to November 1.

TOURS: Self-guiding nature trails and auto tours.

OTHER ACTIVITIES: Horseback riding, bicycling, fishing with Tennessee or North Carolina license, cross-country skiing, sledding.

FACILITIES FOR DISABLED: Extensive; brochure available from park.

For additional information, see also Sites, Trails, and Trips on pages 157–169 and the map on pages 140–141.

Fields in Cades Cove are still farmed to maintain their old agricultural appearance.

THE SOUTHERN APPALACHIANS CULMINATE IN the Great Smoky Mountains. Here, on mist-shrouded, rugged ridges are 520,000 acres of forest, rivers, wildlife, and history. Although the national park is the most popular one in the nation, with more than 9 million visits annually, its thick forest conveys a feeling of solitude. The sounds of wind and water dominate; the scents of fir and rhododendron stimulate the senses; cool air quickens the pace.

With sixteen peaks reaching above 6,000 feet in elevation, the Great Smokies are an ecological ark containing an amazing diversity of plants and animals. On ridges above 4,500 feet, the forest is filled with Fraser fir, and with red spruce much like those native to upper New England and Quebec. Farther down, at elevations between 4,500 and 3,000 feet, a deciduous forest typical of the Great Lakes region and central New England graces the mountains. Below that are the cove hardwood forests, where trees of great size and diversity thrive on just the right combination of rich soil and ideal climate. At the lowest elevations grow oaks and pines typical of the South.

Animals adapt themselves to these environments, each species

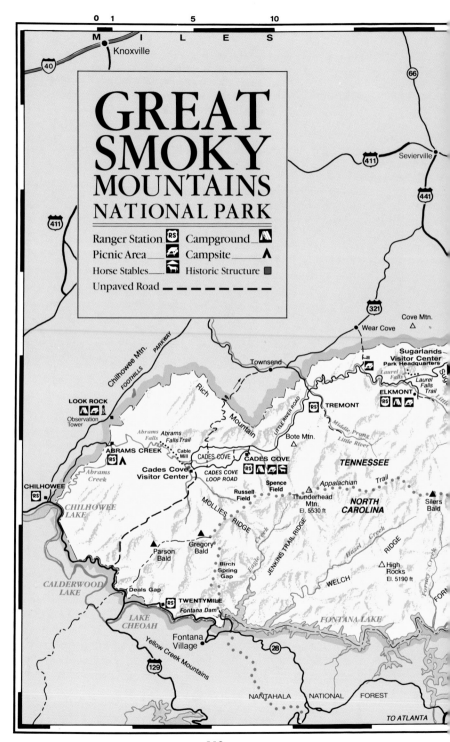

GREAT SMOKY MOUNTAINS
NATIONAL PARK

Ranger Station **RS**   Campground ⛺

Picnic Area 🐷   Campsite **A**

Horse Stables 🐴   Historic Structure ◼

Unpaved Road — — — —

Knoxville

Sevierville

Cove Mtn.

Wear Cove

Sugarlands
Visitor Center
Park Headquarters

Townsend

Laurel
Falls

Laurel
Falls
Trail

ELKMONT

TREMONT

LOOK ROCK
Observation
Tower

Rich Mountain

Bote Mtn.

Middle Prong
Little River

Abrams
Falls

Abrams
Falls Trail

ABRAMS CREEK

Cable
Mill

CADES COVE

CADES COVE

TENNESSEE

Cades Cove
Visitor Center

CADES COVE
LOOP ROAD

Spence
Field

Appalachian   Trail

CHILHOWEE

Abrams
Creek

Russell
Field

Thunderhead
Mtn.
El. 5530 ft

NORTH
CAROLINA

Silers
Bald

CHILHOWEE
LAKE

MOLLIES RIDGE

Parson
Bald

Gregory
Bald

Birch
Spring
Gap

JENKINS TRAIL RIDGE

High
Rocks
El. 5190 ft

RIDGE

WELCH

CALDERWOOD
LAKE

Deals Gap

TWENTYMILE

Fontana Dam

LAKE
CHEOAH

Fontana
Village

Yellow Creek Mountains

FONTANA LAKE

FON

NANTAHALA   NATIONAL   FOREST

TO ATLANTA

Chilhowee Mtn.

FOOTHILLS   PARKWAY

LITTLE RIVER ROAD

Eagle   Creek

Hazel   Creek

Forney   Creek

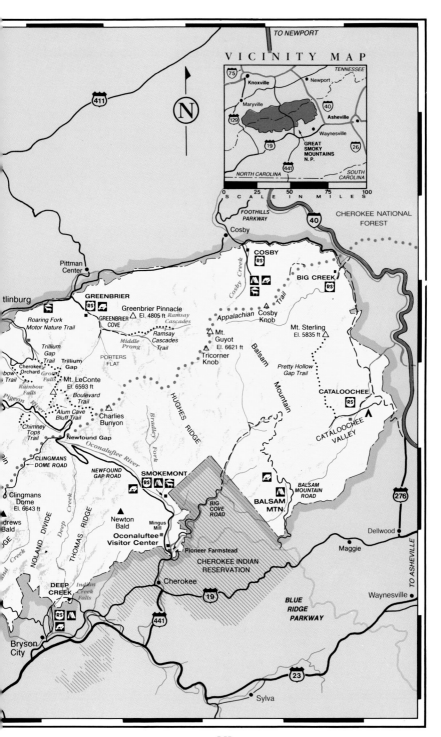

VICINITY MAP

TO NEWPORT

TENNESSEE

Knoxville   Newport

Maryville

Asheville

Waynesville

GREAT
SMOKY
MOUNTAINS
N. P.

NORTH CAROLINA

SOUTH
CAROLINA

SCALE IN MILES
0   25   50   75   100

FOOTHILLS
PARKWAY

CHEROKEE NATIONAL
FOREST

Cosby

COSBY
RS

BIG CREEK
RS

Pittman
Center

Cosby Creek

GREENBRIER
RS

Greenbrier Pinnacle
El. 4805 ft   Ramsay
Cascades

Appalachian   Cosby
Knob

Mt. Sterling
El. 5835 ft

tlinburg

GREENBRIER
COVE

Roaring Fork
Motor Nature Trail

Middle
Prong

Ramsay
Cascades
Trail

Mt.
Guyot
El. 6621 ft

Pretty Hollow
Gap Trail

Trillium
Gap
Trail

Trillium
Gap

PORTERS
FLAT

Tricorner
Knob

Balsam

CATALOOCHEE
RS

Cherokee
Orchard

Group

Rainbow
Falls

Mt. LeConte
El. 6593 ft

Mountain

Pigeon River

Alum Cave
Bluff Trail

Boulevard
Trail

CATALOOCHEE
VALLEY

Chimney
Tops
Trail

Charlies
Bunyon

HUGHES RIDGE

Newfound Gap

Bradley Fork

CLINGMANS
DOME ROAD

Oconaluftee River

NEWFOUND
GAP ROAD

SMOKEMONT
RS

BALSAM
MOUNTAIN
ROAD

276

Clingmans
Dome
El. 6643 ft

Deep Creek

THOMAS RIDGE

Newton
Bald

BIG
COVE ROAD

BALSAM
MTN.

ndrews
Bald

NOLAND DIVIDE

Mingus
Mill

Dellwood

Oconaluftee
Visitor Center

Maggie

Pioneer Farmstead

DEEP
CREEK
RS

Indian
Creek
Falls

CHEROKEE INDIAN
RESERVATION

Waynesville

TO ASHEVILLE

Cherokee

19

BLUE
RIDGE
PARKWAY

Bryson
City

441

23

Sylva

finding its own place. The wildlife includes more than 400 black bears, many hundreds of deer, uncounted small mammals, and some rarities: possible sightings indicate that the mountain lion may yet hunt the wilderness reaches of these mountains. Red wolves were reintroduced into the park in 1991.

But the life on the land could not survive without water. Great Smoky Mountains receives an abundant 55 to 80 inches of precipitation annually, depending on elevation. Sparkling streams and cascades are everywhere; indeed, the sound of moving water is almost always within range of hearing. From source to finish—from clouds to rivers—water provides the magic of the mountains.

HISTORY

The Cherokee Nation

Until the early 1800s, the Southern Appalachian Mountains and foothills were the land of the Cherokees. The Cherokee Nation maintained permanent towns and agricultural sites on level lowlands along rivers that flowed from such ranges as the Great Smokies and the Blue Ridge. The Cherokees hunted the elk, bison, and deer that grazed the high grasslands.

The Cherokee Nation reached from the Ohio River well into South Carolina and consisted of seven clans. Individually, Cherokees always described themselves in terms of clan, and they traced clan relationships matrilineally. Marriage between members of a clan was forbidden. Politically, each town governed itself and made decisions in town meetings, women and men sharing power equally. A typical town contained up to fifty log huts clustered around a town square and a town house, a dome-shaped building where decisions were made and rituals were conducted. The Cherokees were not nomads, as were the Plains Indians, but a settled people with a society based on agriculture.

Among the most famous Cherokees were Attakullakulla (Little Carpenter), a leader who traveled to London in the 1730s at royal invitation and later led his people against invading colonists, and Sequoyah, who in 1820 created a written syllabary for the Cherokee language and for whom the giant sequoia is named. They tried valiantly to adapt their people to the world of the Europeans, but their efforts could not save the Cherokee Nation. In February 1819, the Cherokees ceded to the United States the portion of their nation that contained the Great Smoky Mountains, and by 1839, they were forced westward into Indian Territory,

Opposite: Log skids were one means by which loggers stripped timber off the mountainsides.

present-day Oklahoma. Only a few remained in the East; their descendants are the Eastern Cherokees living near the park today.

European Explorers and Pioneers

Spanish explorer Hernando De Soto and his men traveled through the land of the Cherokees in 1540; they were followed soon thereafter by a Spanish missionary who reported the Cherokees' "prosperity and plenty." Much more was said about the Cherokees by botanist William Bartram, who visited the area in 1775. He later wrote about his visits to the Cherokee settlements and described mountains whose high ridges were much more open than those of today.

By the late 1700s, the first whites had begun to move into the mountains. Some of these settlements, established on Indian land, were illegal. More than a few settlers were slain by Cherokees, who did not readily tolerate trespassers. But the trickle of immigrants slowly grew to a flood. For these people, the dangers posed by the Cherokees and the wild land were little worse than those they had faced in Europe. Many came to escape religious persecution; others were ready to trade their Old World poverty for a chance to succeed on the frontier. Ethnic groups represented in the Smoky Mountains included Scots, English, and Germans.

Like the Cherokees, the pioneers settled the fertile lowland valleys, but as more of them arrived and available bottomland decreased, they began to establish homesteads in steep valleys. The population grew throughout the nineteenth century, and by 1926, about 6,000 small farms, large tracts, and other miscellaneous parcels existed in what is now the park. With skill and hard work, farming the lowlands could result in a reasonably good life, but eking out an existence in the steep valleys was not easy. Compare the homes in fertile valleys such as Cades Cove and Cataloochee with the cabins of hardscrabble farmers along the Roaring Fork Motor Nature Trail.

Loggers

For generations, the farmers lived in a society that was reasonably self-sufficient and stable. The outside world, with its cash economy, was secondary; surviving through folk remedies and home-grown food was more important. By the early 1900s, however, fundamental changes in this way of life had begun to occur. Large timber companies scouted the Great Smoky Mountains and saw here one of the last great forests surviving in the East.

Left: Horace Kephart, for whom the Great Smokies represented a healing force.
Below: 1927 photo of Harvey Broome, center at top, with friends on Mount LeConte.

Fortunes could be made off the trees; the land and its people were merely exploitable resources.

Up the valleys the loggers went, building roads and railroads, sawing and stripping, cutting and hauling. Sawmills gulped the huge logs and spat out boards: oak and maple, cherry and poplar. Fires consumed thousands of acres of debris. For the local people, all this activity meant money—the first cash-paying jobs most had ever had—but it also changed them. Along with 60 percent of the forest, the old ways were lost. By 1925, the only large tracts of uncut forest were in steep valleys and on the highest ridges.

Establishment of the Park

Away from the Great Smokies, events were occurring that would change the destiny of these mountains. National parks had been created throughout the American West, and the young National Park Service (established in 1916) was looking for park sites in the East in an effort to gain support for the park concept. A commission had suggested the Smokies, and a few farsighted people were about to add impetus to the suggestion with efforts of their own.

In the summer of 1904, Horace Kephart, a librarian from St. Louis, had come to the Smokies to restore his health. Within months, his vigor had returned; but as he remained to watch events in the Smokies, he saw the lumbermen draining the life out of the region's forests and people. By the 1920s, Kephart was actively promoting the idea of a national park in the Smokies. With the support of prominent residents of Knoxville, Tennessee, a citizens' organization was formed.

The United States government did not buy land for national parks in those years, but the National Park Service and various citizens' groups managed to convince thousands of people that a national park in the Great Smokies would be a source of pride and income for the area. Donations were made by millions of people, ranging from pennies given by children to a grant of $5 million from John D. Rockefeller, Jr. Old-time residents of the mountains and cash-conscious lumber companies were not easily persuaded to sell, but in 1934, Great Smoky Mountains National Park was established. Some residents retained lifelong rights of occupancy on park lands, and commercial in-holdings were permitted for many years; but like a jigsaw puzzle nearing completion, the park is now almost whole. The efforts of conservationists such as Harvey Broome of Knoxville and the many citizens who opposed building a second road through the park in the late 1960s continue to inspire those who today guard its wilderness from exploitation.

The Great Smoky Mountains are geologically ancient, and their rocks can be traced back almost 900 million years. Mountains existing at that time were slowly eroded into a sea, where they formed a thick layer of sediment. Between 500 and 400 million years ago, this primarily inorganic sediment was covered by a layer of organic sediment (limestone) from the sea. Pressures caused by movements in the earth's crust then changed the sediments into metamorphic rocks. At about the same time, the continent of Africa collided with North America, creating the original Appalachians, a huge mountain range. When the collision occurred, the more ancient underlying sediments, called the Ocoee Series, were tilted up and shoved over the younger organic sediments.

The Ocoee Series forms most of the Smokies—except in Cades Cove, where erosion has exposed the younger limestone beneath. In some places, the buckling of the crust tilted the rocks so steeply that cliffs and pinnacles were formed. Charlies Bunion and the Chimney Tops are examples of this phenomenon. The folding and buckling happened with imperceptible slowness. High mountains were gradually formed and worn away, not suddenly thrust up and torn down.

Rock surface near the Chimney Tops.

More recently, the climate of the earth cooled several times. During these ice ages, glaciers lay to the north of the Smokies, and cycles of freezing and thawing broke huge rocks from the mountains. These are the boulders seen in the park today. Running water also has shaped the land, carving the slopes into alternating V-shaped valleys and sharp ridges. The erosive forces continue, slowly washing the land toward the sea and sometimes sluicing off mountainsides. A gash on the side of Mount LeConte, created during a downpour in 1951, was a result of a landslide that occurred when the soil became so saturated with water that an entire area fell away from the mountainside. Occasional rock slides, such as the one that briefly closed the Newfound Gap Road in August 1984, provide further examples of water at work.

Tectonics determined the position of an Ocoee Series rock just below the Chimney Tops.

Natural History

During much of the year, weather in the Great Smoky Mountains is affected by storm systems that swirl down from the continental interior or sweep northward from the Gulf of Mexico. As they move across the Southeast, the Appalachian Mountains oppose them, forcing the winds to rise, cool, and drop their moisture. In summer, the continental storm systems rest, but hot, humid air rises along the slopes and then billows into thunderheads. Lightning flashes, and more rain falls. In the Great Smokies, the interaction of land and air is more pronounced than anywhere else in the East. Rain soaks the land, snow buries the heights, and precipitation totals as much as 80 inches a year on the high ridges.

The forest responds with growth, lush and green, and the sky bequeaths beauty: panoramas of peaks rising islandlike above fog-covered lowlands, and the silent motion of clouds forming on rising winds. During the warmer months, a smoky haze softens the contours of the mountains. Much of it is moisture rising off the vegetation, but hydrocarbons created by the forest and particulates from natural and human disturbance outside the park are also present.

An Assemblage of Forests

Above 4,500 feet, the Great Smoky Mountains take on the guise of a misplaced northern outpost. Red spruce and Fraser fir grip the rocks and fight the wind to shelter mosses and cloverlike oxalis. Clouds drift through the trees, and birds of the northern forest echo one another's calls in the stillness. With only the slightest bit of imagination, a visitor could take these highlands for Maine or Quebec.

This is the southernmost extension of northern coniferous forest in the East—a remnant of the much more extensive forest of spruce and fir that covered the East during the most recent ice age, only 12,000 years ago. (The Fraser fir, found only in the southern Appalachians, is a relict of the ice age.)

Mature Fraser firs may be eliminated from the park by a tiny European exotic the balsam woolly adelgid, which first appeared in the Smokies in 1963; by the mid-1990s, 95 percent of the mature firs were dead. The insect feeds only on the rough bark of mature trees and injects a toxin just as they are about to produce cones. The Park Service is able to spray enough trees with fatty acid soap, toxic to the adelgid, to prevent extinction of the firs. Meanwhile, red spruce trees are losing their needles; air pollution is suspected. The unique spruce–fir forest contains dozens of plants and animals found nowhere else; they could become extinct.

Moving down-slope is like coming south again—at approximately 250 miles per 1,000 feet. The far northern forest soon shades into a more familiar type of woods, the deciduous forest of central New England. Beeches, maples, birches (yellow, not white), buckeyes, and Allegheny serviceberries take over. This is a forest with beauty of its own; here, the autumn color is unsurpassed, and spring produces delicate and graceful blossoms and catkins.

Overleaf: Autumn view from Newfound Gap Road over the Deep Creek drainage basin.

Still farther down—perhaps below 3,000 feet—a more typically southern forest commands the slopes and extends into the coves. Called the cove hardwood forest by botanists, it nurtures huge trees; fifteen to twenty species reach near-record size in the park. In springtime, the dogwoods and silverbells seem to overwhelm the slopes with the beauty of their blossoms. Lumbermen sought this forest. Where it escaped them, the concentration of species—an astounding seventy varieties of trees in some valleys—and the largeness of individual trees make this the most lush temperate forest in the world outside the Pacific Northwest.

Nowhere in the Great Smoky Mountains is the climate dry, but on some ridges at low elevations the soil is so thin and the sun so strong that water quickly evaporates or runs off. In these places is another type of forest, in which oaks and pines are spaced away from one another so as to apportion the water and in which drought-tolerant mountain laurel forms the shrub layer.

Impenetrable Beauty

Trees are only a part of the Smoky Mountains botany, and they often are not the most conspicuous. In many places, evergreen shrubs form impenetrable thickets. Mostly rhododendron and laurel, these shrubs outdo themselves during June and July in producing clusters of pink or white flowers. Two species of rhododendron exist here: Catawba and rosebay. Both are members of a plant group known as heaths. Catawba rhododendron graces the highlands, in some places turning the ridge tops and meadow edges pink. Hardly to be outdone, rosebay produces its flower clusters deep in the forest, where they brighten the trail sides and stream edges. In winter, both serve as natural thermometers: the lower the temperature falls, the more the leaves shrivel and droop, until at 0° F, they look lifeless beyond recall. Whether waist-high on the ridges or 20 feet tall in the forest, rhododendron and laurel thickets are almost impassable. In deference to this density, local people refer to them as "hells"—a mild term to anyone who has encountered them while lost in the mountains.

On the forest floor, especially in early May, wildflowers of every color and description bloom in lush profusion. Trillium, spring beauties, trout lilies, bluets, and a multitude of others add lavish touches of beauty. Altogether, about 1,200 species of flowering plants, of which more than 300 are rare, are native to the park—an amazing profusion of life. As though in complement to all this, delicate ferns surround and mix with the flowers. Smaller in size,

Opposite: Passage through or out of a Catawba rhododendron "hell" is difficult.

The opposum is the only member of the marsupial order found in the United States.

but everywhere to be seen, are the mosses, lichens, and fungi that carpet boulders and fallen trees, rendering this green world even more captivating. Moisture and warmth encourage growth and variety, resulting in 2,000 species.

It has been said that the Great Smokies are changeless but that at the same time, the only constant is change. Over the centuries, the general patterns of vegetation in the park do remain the same, but there are always variations produced by storms, insects, and (rarely these days) fire. Each of these occasionally kills trees and opens the land to sunlight, stimulating a succession of growth that follows a pattern from tiny plants to massive trees. Death by disease and fire may seem unfortunate, but these natural occurrences create opportunities for a great variety of plants.

The Mysterious Balds

Trees cover the Smokies almost everywhere, but on some ridges at elevations above 5,000 feet open areas called balds appear. These grassy, meadowlike areas are edged with Catawba rhododendron and flame azalea, another member of the heath family. When spring warms into summer, the rhododendron and azalea respond with blooms in a wide spectrum of colors. Cool breezes swish through the grass, bees work the blossoms, and the balds seem perfect.

Despite intensive study, researchers do not concur about what caused the balds. Some say that they were areas the Cherokees

One of the Great Smokies' twenty-seven salamander species, the long-tailed salamander.

repeatedly burned in order to improve hunting; others suspect that the bison and elk that may have once grazed the high country maintained them; a few think that special conditions of soil, wind, and temperature may have been responsible. Early settlers girdled the trees to expand the balds, and in the spring they drove their cattle up to pasture in the balds. Whatever their origin, some balds in the Smokies are now being slowly overgrown by forest. Their disappearance will remove a bit of special Appalachian magic from the park. Two grassy balds, Gregory and Andrews, are being managed to remove invading trees.

Sharing a Trail with a Bear

Animals abound in the Great Smokies. Bears roam the forest, deer graze the open meadows of Cataloochee Valley and Cades Cove, opossums, raccoons, and skunks scavenge through the night, trout dart across clear pools, and salamanders (lizardlike amphibians) probe for insects and worms in the damp darkness. One species of salamander is unique here, and another, the hellbender, attains a length of 2 feet or more; with more than twenty different species, the Great Smoky Mountains are salamander heaven. Among birds, the raven is an example of one that is common far to the north, but that lives mainly on the high mountains this far south.

The mammals most commonly seen are roadside woodchucks and the many deer that emerge from shadowy forest edges at dusk, especially in Cades Cove. Rarely seen is one of the park's most destructive animals, the wild hog. These big, bristly pigs are descendants of animals that escaped from a game preserve early in this century and that entered the park about 1950. They have multiplied until they rank as a serious threat to the park's native flora and fauna.

Since 1991, the howl of the red wolf has echoed through the park's coves and valleys. A victim of predator-control programs and lost habitat, the red wolf had not been seen in the area for many decades. By the 1970s the species was nearly extinct, with fewer than one hundred red wolves surviving in Texas and Louisiana. Some of these were captured and bred in captivity, and a few were introduced elsewhere in the South. Their numbers grew to 250. As an experiment, two adults and two pups were released in Cades Cove in 1991. Full reintroduction began in 1992, with the release of two families. The goal is to sustain a population of fifty to seventy-five. The red wolf, which does not run or hunt in packs, has a slender body, long legs, and a gray-black coat with a cinnamon cast. It weighs 45 to 80 pounds.

Hikers along the park trails share one concern about the wildlife: the prospect of meeting a bear. With more than 400 bears roaming the Smokies, such an encounter is possible but not probable. Almost invariably, bears hear or smell approaching hikers and fade into the forest unseen. When a meeting does occur, the bear often simply turns and runs. If it does not, the hiker will probably never forget what happens instead. Bears are intelligent animals, accustomed to coping with people and with other bears—and they are good at it.

If two bears meet and feel antagonistic, they threaten each other by bluffing; they sometimes practice the same techniques on human passers-by. A large vocabulary of hisses, woofs, and growls is brought into use. If that fails to produce a satisfactory retreat, a mock charge or two may follow. People find this an unforgettable sight: bears are incredibly fast, and they do not slow down for trees, shrubs, rocks, or steep terrain. Genuine attacks on human beings are rare, and usually involve a mother protecting her cubs.

Most bears sighted in the park are just searching for food. Almost anything from berries to ants to small mammals to sides of bacon suits them—hikers' rations included. Sustaining 200 pounds or more is a full-time job, especially in the autumn, when winter sleep is imminent. From late November to March, bears in the Smokies sleep deeply, often high in hollow trees. Whenever the weather briefly warms, as it does frequently during the park's winter, the bears emerge and wander around. At this time of the year—January or February—the tiny, hairless cubs are born. The cubs, usually two in number, nurse and grow; by spring, they are

Heavy annual precipitation fills the Great Smoky Mountains' large number of streams.

ready to emerge from winter shelter along with their mother. It is then that hikers should be most wary.

SITES, TRAILS, AND TRIPS

The more than 800 miles of maintained trails in the Great Smokies range in length from short, self-guiding walks to the Appalachian Trail, which bisects the park into north and south sections for 71 miles along the main ridge. Well known and popular, the trail shows scars of overuse, yet it follows the heights and leads through the best high-elevation evergreen forest in the South. Backcountry campsites are assigned by the National Park Service; this arrangement ensures backpackers of camping space and protects the environment.

In general, trails in the Smokies are better categorized by the experiences they provide than by the places they go. Any trail leading into the spruce–fir forest presents hikers with the impression of being far northward. Hikers who follow streamside trails find another gift of the Smokies: the enchantment of water that is clear, cold, and swift. Some trails lead into virgin forest, where massive trees tower to form cathedrals of silence. Even the bird calls seem to echo, and the world beyond the park takes on an aura of unreality. From November through March or April, any trail to ridges above 5,000 feet becomes a journey into winter. The southern climate is replaced by snows and temperatures that may sink well below 0° F.

Overleaf: White-tailed deer are commonly seen grazing in Cades Cove at dusk.

Newfound Gap

Access to the interior of the park, including the highest elevations, is available at various places along the 35-mile Newfound Gap Road (U.S. 441) between Gatlinburg, Tennessee, and Cherokee, North Carolina. From north to south (Gatlinburg to Cherokee), the road ascends gently but steadily, first maintaining a straight course and then turning abruptly left as the grade increases. A boulder-strewn stream, the West Prong of the Little Pigeon River, tumbles beneath the road. Dramatic, rugged slopes, until now seen only at a distance, suddenly rise on every side. In spring and autumn, different stages of the seasons burst forth in progression along these slopes.

To increase the road's elevation, engineers designed it to pass through a short tunnel and then loop over itself. To the right near the loop are the Chimney Tops, at the summit of a steep, pinnacle-like peak. A trail leads to the summit. The road again follows the West Prong, still climbing and now reaching the elevation of the lowest stands of red spruce. Large and easy to identify, they become more numerous as elevation increases. Above, almost treeless areas called "laurel slicks" can be seen dominating the upper slopes. From the road, they look inviting—almost like swards of grass. In fact, they are impassable tangles of rhododendron, mountain laurel, and other plants in the heath family.

The air is noticeably cooler at this elevation, and clouds often drift through the spruce and fir. In winter, icicles hang from the road cuts, and rime (frozen cloud vapor) coats the evergreens. After a final switchback, the road reaches Newfound Gap, at 5,048 feet, and begins a gradual descent along less rugged terrain to the south. At the gap, an overlook with a large parking area, wayside exhibits, and rest rooms serves as a stopover for touring motorists and as a departure point for hikers.

Appalachian Trail. Along the Appalachian Trail and eastward 4 miles from Newfound Gap, at an elevation of 5,400 feet, is Charlies Bunion, a rocky prominence that was denuded by a forest fire in 1925. From the 1,000-foot cliff here, hikers can enjoy one of the best views of the park, extending north over Greenbrier Cove and northwest toward Mount LeConte. The Appalachian Trail passes through spruce–fir forest and occasional stands of stunted beech. It also provides access to Mount LeConte via the Boulevard Trail.

Clingmans Dome

From Newfound Gap, the 7-mile Clingmans Dome Road arcs along the crest of the Smokies to Clingmans Dome, whose crest at 6,643

View from the crest of Clingmans Dome.

feet is the highest elevation in the park. Thick stands of spruce and fir are often indistinct in the clouds that sweep low across the ridges.

On Clingmans Dome, an observation ramp spirals above the evergreens, offering a 360-degree view of the Smokies. The ramp is .5 mile from a large parking area at the end of the Clingmans Dome Road. Stands of dead Fraser firs are apparent.

Spruce–Fir Trail. The .75-mile (round trip) self-guiding Spruce–Fir Trail, which is 4 miles from Newfound Gap, explains the spruce–fir forest.

Andrews Bald and Silers Bald. Andrews Bald lies 2 miles south of the Clingmans Dome parking area and is the easiest of the Smoky Mountains balds to reach. Expansive views, soft grass, and flowering shrubs make this a rewarding destination. Five miles west of Clingmans Dome along the Appalachian Trail is Silers Bald. The distance from the parking area to that bald and the loss of elevation (1,200 feet) put the hike in the moderate category.

Mount LeConte

Reaching 5,000 feet above Gatlinburg, Tennessee—and 6,593 feet above sea level—Mount LeConte presents a vertical rise similar in elevation—although not in appearance—to that of the Grand

Tetons above Jackson Hole. Atop LeConte is a windblown fir forest interrupted by rocky cliff tops where waist-high shrubs struggle for life. In these places, known as Myrtle Point and the Cliff Top, the views and spiritual feeling of wilderness are unsurpassed. Hikers often visit these overlooks at dawn and sunset. Nearby, hidden in the forest, LeConte Lodge provides rooms and meals for hikers and horseback riders who have registered in advance.

Boulevard Trail. The 5-mile Boulevard Trail, through spruce–fir forest and atop narrow ridges, begins on the Appalachian Trail via Newfound Gap (3 more miles). It is the only LeConte approach entirely in the high country and the only one that does not require substantial climbing. At times, the trail ascends atop a narrow, steep ridge; it skirts the base of a cliff as it nears the peak of the mountain.

Alum Cave Bluff Trail. The Alum Cave Bluff Trail climbs 2,500 feet from the Newfound Gap Road through a variety of natural features. Clear streams, tall hemlocks, and a laurel slick are interspersed with unusual geology, such as Arch Rock (through which the trail tunnels), the 100-foot Alum Cave Bluff, and steep cliffs where hikers grip trail-side cables. Alum Cave Bluff, halfway up the 5.5-mile trail to Mt. LeConte, is a popular destination for day hikers, so the trail may be crowded to that point.

Rainbow Falls Trail. Two trails reach Mount LeConte from an area near Gatlinburg known as the Cherokee Orchard, and another ascends from Trillium Gap. All three require ascents of more than 3,000 feet. The 6.6-mile Rainbow Falls Trail is the most popular because it leads to an 80-foot cascade, 3.5 miles from the trail head. Beyond the falls, the trail climbs steeply to overlooks, laurel slicks, and the spruce–fir forest. The trail is also used by horses and may be muddy.

Cades Cove

Nestled at the base of the mountains near the western end of the park, Cades Cove is a broad, 6-mile-long valley maintained to preserve the nineteenth-century rural character once dominant there. Large pastures, cabins, churches, and a mill provide the foreground for panoramas of high ridges. In 1850, the population of the cove was about 685; then, drawn by opportunity elsewhere, people began to move out, and the population dropped to 275.

Opposite: Abundant high-elevation precipitation feeds Rainbow Falls.

The mountain laurel's flowers first appear as closed pouches, then open to reveal stamens.

Even in the pre-park days of the 1920s, the population had climbed back to only about 500.

Cades Cove Loop Road. The 11-mile one-way Cades Cove Loop Road is even better for bicycling than for driving. Along the roadside are nineteen tour stops—mostly cabins, churches, and the famous Cable Mill area. This area includes a Visitor Center, the John Cable Mill and adjacent Gregg-Cable house, barns, and other examples of nineteenth-century rural life.

Abrams Falls Trail. Level trails are unusual in the park, but the 2.5-mile Abrams Falls Trail involves very little climbing and leads to a 20-foot falls with a beautiful plunge pool. It begins along the Cades Cove Loop Road at tour stop 10.

Russell Field, Spence Field, and Gregory Bald Trails. Fairly strenuous hikes from Cades Cove are a prerequisite for reaching Russell Field, Spence Field, and Gregory Bald, on the crest of the Smokies. The trails climb 3,000 feet or more; however, the rich lowland forest, the hike through changing landscapes, and (in late June) the spectacular azalea on Gregory Bald make the effort worthwhile.

Cataloochee Valley

The Cataloochee Valley, along the eastern edge of the park, can be reached only from a poorly marked, winding road that enters the park at a point far from popular visitor areas; it is consequently less often seen than is Cades Cove. White farmhouses, barns, a schoolhouse, and a church identify the valley as another agricultural area, although one much smaller than Cades Cove.

Pretty Hollow Cap Trail. The route from the Pretty Hollow Gap trail head to the fire tower on 5,835-foot Mount Sterling is strenuous and climbs for more than 6 miles. Parts of three trails are covered, with much of the route along Pretty Hollow Creek. This trail and others in the area are often used by horseback riders.

Oconaluftee

At the southern end of the Newfound Gap Road is a Visitor Center and a living-history area; a nineteenth-century farm lies a short walk away. This is Oconaluftee, settled about 1800. Visitors can see cooking, sewing, and other farm-life chores being done at the John Davis house or can drive .5 mile to Mingus Mill, where corn is ground into meal.

A brown daddy-long-legs stakes out a grouping of robin's plantain blossoms.

TRAILS OF GREAT SMOKY MOUNTAINS NATIONAL PARK

HIGH COUNTRY TRAILS

APPALACHIAN TRAIL: Follows the crest of the Smokies for 71 miles, much of it through spruce–fir forest; often taken from Newfound Gap, from which it leads east 4 miles to Charlies Bunion, a popular overlook; from Clingmans Dome, the trail runs to the west through Silers Bald (5 miles), a high-elevation meadowlike area.

BOULEVARD TRAIL: Popular way to reach the summit of 6,593-foot Mount LeConte; 8 miles one way from Newfound Gap; 5–6 hours; follow Appalachian Trail from Newfound Gap to Boulevard Trail intersection; ascent of 1,545 feet.

TRAILS TO THE HIGH COUNTRY

ALUM CAVE BLUFF TRAIL: Starts at Newfound Gap; ends at Mount LeConte; 5.5 miles one way; 3–4 hours; ascent of 2,800 feet; Alum Cave Bluff about halfway along trail.

TRILLIUM GAP TRAIL: Starts at Grotto Falls parking area on Roaring Fork Motor Nature Trail; ends at Mount LeConte; 7 miles one way; 4 hours; steep climb, with ascent of 3,473 feet; Grotto Falls is 1.5 miles from trail head.

PRETTY HOLLOW GAP TRAIL: Starts in Cataloochee Valley; ends at fire tower on Mount Sterling; 6 miles one way; 3–4 hours; ascent of 2,400 feet; parts of three trails are covered; much of route parallels Pretty Hollow Creek.

CHIMNEY TOPS TRAIL: Starts at Newfound Gap Road at Chimney Tops parking area 8 miles south of Sugarlands Visitor Center; ends at twin pinnacles known as the Chimney Tops; 2 strenuous miles one way; 2 hours; 1,335-foot steep ascent; a final scramble up a rock face is necessary for view of Sugarlands Valley.

TRAILS TO WATERFALLS

RAINBOW FALLS TRAIL: Starts at Cherokee Orchard; ends at Rainbow Falls; 3.5 miles one way; 2–3 hours; 1,750-foot ascent; beautiful 80-foot waterfall deep in an old-growth forest.

RAMSAY CASCADES TRAIL: Starts at Greenbrier Cove; ends at Ramsay Cascades; 4 miles one way; 3–4 hours; 2,375-foot strenuous climb through forest of large deciduous trees.

ABRAMS FALLS TRAIL: Starts at Abrams Falls parking area at west end of Cades Cove Loop Road; ends at Abrams Falls; 2.5 miles one way; 2 hours; 340-foot elevation change round trip.

LAUREL FALLS TRAIL: Starts at Laurel Falls parking area on Little River Road; ends at Laurel Falls; 1.25 miles one way; .75 hour; 500-foot elevation change; paved trail leads through pine–oak forest; most popular waterfall trail in park.

Opposite: Depth and undertow of the pool below Abrams Falls make swimming dangerous.

Greenbrier Cove

From the Greenbrier Entrance, 6 miles east of Gatlinburg along U.S. 321, the entrance road parallels the fast, clear Middle Prong of the Little Pigeon River as it tumbles out of the Smokies. Along this stretch of river, the forest is young, and the remains of old stone walls can be glimpsed in the woods. Ahead, however, is the old-growth forest of Greenbrier Cove, with its shaded slopes of towering hemlocks and thick rhododendrons. The roadside beauty of the river would be enough to make the area popular, but two trails enhance its charm even more.

Ramsay Cascades Trail. The 2.5-mile (one way) Ramsay Cascades Trail leads through deep forest along Ramsay Prong, ascending almost 1,700 feet to the 60-foot Cascades, highest in the park.

Porters Flat Trail. A favorite for family hikes in the Smokies, the Porters Flat Trail starts on an old road that has been closed to public vehicles but that is open to hikers. It ascends slowly through beautiful old-growth forest. Porters Creek is delightful, the trees are huge, and the wildflowers are unexcelled in late April. After 2 miles, the trail crosses the creek; beyond that point, it continues to the Appalachian Trail. The trail is not maintained beyond campsite 31; it is steep, rugged, and dangerous, and should not be attempted.

Roaring Fork Motor Nature Trail

At the edge of Gatlinburg, the park boundary is marked by an abrupt transition from development to forest, but traces of human endeavor are hidden almost everywhere among the trees. The 5-mile Roaring Fork Motor Nature Trail winds through thick forest where once cornfields stood and cows grazed. With the aid of an interpretive booklet, visitors can identify forest areas that were farmed and can begin to learn about tree species, pioneer life, and the boulders that populate the slopes of the Smokies. Because the "trail" is narrow and crooked, it must be driven slowly—but the time is well spent. In order to reach the motor nature trail, visitors must take the Airport Road from downtown Gatlinburg and follow the signs.

Opposite: The disabled may visit Roaring Fork by taking the Motor Nature Trail.
Overleaf: Cades Cove with Methodist Church and graveyard from Rich Mountain

HOT SPRINGS
NATIONAL PARK

The Grand Promenade, begun as a public works project in 1934, was finished in 1958.

HOT SPRINGS NATIONAL PARK
P. O. BOX 1860, HOT SPRINGS,
ARKANSAS 71902
TEL.: (501) 624-3383

HIGHLIGHTS: Bathhouse Row • Hot Springs • Grand Promenade • Tufa Terrace • West Mountain Drive • Hot Springs Mountain • Dogwood Trail • Zigzag Mountains

ACCESS: From Little Rock take 1-30 and U.S. 70. From Glenwood take U.S. 70. From Mt. Ida take U.S. 270. From Texarkana take 1-30.

HOURS: Open year-round, 24 hours daily. Hot Springs Mountain Tower open daily: in summer, 9 A.M.–9 P.M.; in winter, 9 A.M.–7 P.M.

FEES: Charged at Entrance, for campsite, and for Hot Springs Mountain Tower.

PARKING: At city-metered spaces and commercial parking lots, and inside park at scenic pullouts.

GAS, FOOD, LODGING: Available in Hot Springs.

VISITOR CENTER: In former Fordyce Bathhouse, in the middle of Bathhouse Row; open 9 A.M.–5 P.M., extended summer hours, closed New Year's Day, Thanksgiving Day, Christmas Day. Offers information, orientation movie, tour of historically refurnished bathhouse.

GIFT SHOPS: At Fordyce Bathhouse Visitor Center and Hot Springs Mountain Tower.

PETS: Allowed on leash of 6-foot maximum length.

PICNICKING: At Gulpha Gorge Campground and on summits of Hot Springs and West mountains.

HIKING: 26 miles of hiking trails in park.

BACKPACKING: Overnight camping only at Gulpha Gorge Campground.

CAMPGROUNDS: 43 sites suitable for tents and RVs (no hookups) available at Gulpha Gorge Campground. Campfire programs in summer. Permit necessary; 14-day stay limit year-round.

TOURS: Self-guided tours of Fordyce Bathhouse. Guided tours of thermal features during summer months.

OTHER ACTIVITIES: Horseback riding, water skiing, swimming, boating. Baths, massage, and whirlpool available at bathhouses in downtown area; fees required.

FACILITIES FOR DISABLED: Fordyce Visitor Center, picnic sites, campsite, Bathhouse Row.

For additional information, see also Sites, Trails, and Trips on pages 190–192 and the map on pages 176–177.

HOT WATER FLOWING FROM THE GROUND must nourish the impulse to establish national parks. In 1832, forty years before the creation of Yellowstone National Park, Congress set aside another area containing hot springs—4 square miles of remote Arkansas wilderness. This was the first federal reservation to protect a natural resource.

Most of these "Hot Springs of the Washita" no longer freely discharge their vapors among remote wooded hills, and the national park is partly bounded by the city of Hot Springs. Yet this park still preserves the essence of relaxation that has drawn people to its springs for 10,000 years. Modern visitors relax not only in the hot waters, but also along tree-arched trails that provide natural seclusion and serenity.

Spring-fed fountain at Administration Building, and State Rehabilitation Center.

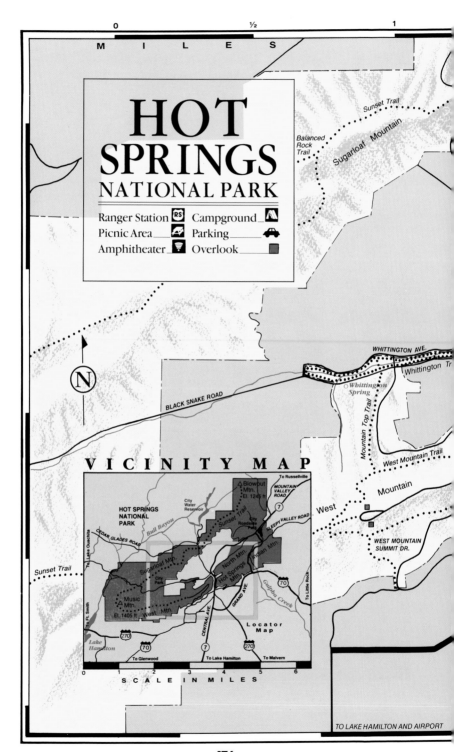

MILES

0 ½ 1

HOT SPRINGS
NATIONAL PARK

Ranger Station **RS**   Campground

Picnic Area   Parking

Amphitheater   Overlook

Sunset Trail

Balanced Rock Trail

Sugarloaf Mountain

WHITTINGTON AVE.

Whittington Tr

Whittington Spring

Mountain Top Trail

West Mountain Trail

BLACK SNAKE ROAD

Mountain

West

VICINITY MAP

HOT SPRINGS NATIONAL PARK

Blowout Mtn. El. 1246 ft

City Water Reservoir

To Russellville

MOUNTAIN VALLEY ROAD

7

Sunset Trail

Bull Bayou

City Roadside Park

SLEEPY VALLEY ROAD

CEDAR GLADES ROAD

To Lake Ouachita

Sugarloaf Mtn.

City Park

North Mtn.

Indian Mtn.

Hot Springs Mtn.

WEST MOUNTAIN SUMMIT DR.

To Ft. Smith

Music Mtn. El. 1405 ft

West Mtn.

CENTRAL AVE.

GRAND AVE.

Gulpha Creek

70

To Little Rock

Locator Map

270

Lake Hamilton

70

7 To Lake Hamilton

270

To Glenwood   To Lake Hamilton   To Malvern

0   1   2   3   4   5   6

SCALE IN MILES

TO LAKE HAMILTON AND AIRPORT

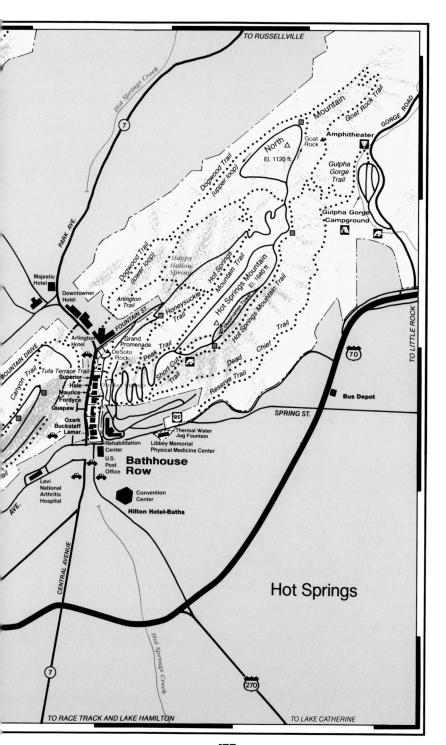

TO RUSSELLVILLE

Hot Springs Creek

7

Dogwood Trail (upper loop)

North Mountain

Goat Rock

El. 1120 ft

Goat Rock Trail

GORGE ROAD

Amphitheater

Gulpha Gorge Trail

Gulpha Gorge Campground

PARK AVE.

Dogwood Trail (lower loop)

Happy Hollow Spring

Hot Springs Mountain Trail

Arlington Trail

Majestic Hotel

Downtowner Hotel

FOUNTAIN ST.

Honeysuckle Trail

Hot Springs Mountain El. 1040 ft

Observation Tower

Hot Springs Mountain Trail

Arlington Hotel

Grand Promenade

Chief Trail

DeSoto Rock

Peak Trail

MOUNTAIN DRIVE

Canyon Trail

Tufa Terrace Trail

Superior

Hale

Short Cut Trail

Dead Trail

Reserve Trail

Maurice

Fordyce

Quapaw

Ozark

Buckstaff

Lamar

SPRING ST.

Bus Depot

70

TO LITTLE ROCK

Rehabilitation Center

RS

Thermal Water Jug Fountain

Libbey Memorial Physical Medicine Center

U.S. Post Office

Bathhouse Row

Levi National Arthritis Hospital

AVE.

Convention Center

Hilton Hotel-Baths

CENTRAL AVENUE

Hot Springs

Hot Springs Creek

7

270

TO RACE TRACK AND LAKE HAMILTON

TO LAKE CATHERINE

The First Bathers

Tradition holds that before Europeans arrived, the steamy vapors of the future park wafted above neutral ground, where hostilities between Indian tribes were put aside in favor of the tranquil ease of the hot water. There may have been spiritual significance to a ceremonial steam bath in an enclosed hut followed by a plunge into the cold water of Hot Springs Creek. Legends relate that the primal ancestors of the Native American people emerged from the mists of the springs and that their divine presence has remained evident in the place ever since. Like their white successors, Native Americans bathed in the springs for physical therapy.

Another attraction of the area for its earliest visitors was novaculite, or Arkansas stone, a very hard type of chert that is well suited to the manufacture of stone implements, such as knives and projectile points. The name of the rock comes from the Latin word *novacul*, which means "razor" or "sharp knife." Exposed on the park's ridge tops, novaculite was quarried extensively on Sugarloaf Mountain and Indian Mountain. Novaculite still is quarried outside the park and is used as natural whetstone for sharpening knives.

Arrival of the Europeans

Journals kept during Hernando De Soto's explorations on behalf of Spain indicate that the first European encounter with Hot Springs may have been in 1541. French fur traders visited the area a century later and bestowed French names on various landmarks.

President Thomas Jefferson sent various explorers into the Louisiana Territory. In the autumn of 1804, William Dunbar and George Hunter, leading an expedition up the Red, Black, and Ouachita (Washita) rivers to Hot Springs, found huts built by visitors the previous summer. Jefferson had included Dr. Hunter, a Philadelphia chemist, in the party to analyze the springs' waters. Hunter's competent reports encouraged visits by health seekers, for whom no journey was too intimidating if the reward might be renewed physical well-being.

Establishment of the Park

The first permanent non-native residents arrived in 1807. A hotel was up by 1828. Testimonials by recovered invalids inspired Congress to set aside the area as a federal reservation in 1832.

Bathhouses and lodgings proliferated and became less primitive as transportation to the reservation improved. Although Hot Springs imitated European health spas, federal ownership of the springs ensured that they would not be used only by the wealthy. Many homes and businesses were built on federal land; in 1877, Congress sought to bring more order to the area by establishing a planning commission. A federally planned city, also named Hot Springs, was separated from the federal reservation.

By the late nineteenth century, most springs had been covered, and their water was being piped to bathhouses along Hot Springs Creek. In 1884, the creek was protected by being buried in a pipe beneath what became Central Avenue in front of Bathhouse Row.

The newly created National Park Service was given administration of Hot Springs Reservation in 1916. In 1921, the reservation became Hot Springs National Park. Over the years additional land has been added to the park, and it now exceeds 5,000 acres in size.

Nineteenth-century visitors seek relief from foot ailments at Corn Hole Spring. Overleaf: Some early-twentieth century postcard views of the resort of Hot Springs.

Office of U. S. Government Reservation, Row Promenade, and E. C. Kropp Co., Pub., Milwaukee. 1210

Looking South on Central Avenue, Hot Springs, Ark.

Fountain Square, Hot Springs, Ark.

Central Avenue, looking North, Hot Springs, Ark.

Source of the Springs

The accumulation of silt in a shallow ocean basin for 180 million years and the collision of continents created the Ouachita Mountains of central Arkansas. These highlands, including the Zigzag Mountains, which contain the national park, are drenched by 53 inches of moisture annually. Much of this water percolates slowly (4,000 years are required) through cracks and pores in the rock to a depth of 4,000 to 8,000 feet, where it is heated by natural energy of uncertain origin.

At great depth, the heated water encounters a system of cracks, or faults, in the rock caused by the crumpling uplift of the Ouachita Mountains about 320 million years ago. These cracks provide a conduit through which hydrostatic pressure forces the water to rise quickly to the surface. Water that heated up during a 4,000-year descent rises to the surface within a year or two, little enough time for cooling. On an average day, the forty-seven springs disgorge some 850,000 gallons of water at 143° degrees F.

That's Tufa

As rain falls through the atmosphere and then trickles through upper layers of the soil, it picks up dissolved carbon dioxide and becomes mild carbonic acid. This acid dissolves bits of calcium carbonate, which are carried along through the soil as ions in solution. When the water again reaches the surface, it loses some of its carbon dioxide and thus its capacity to hold the calcium and carbonate ions in solution. Some of the calcium carbonate precipitates out of the water and collects in deposits as a limestone called tufa (TOO-fa).

Before the capping of the springs, Hot Springs Mountain was covered with frozen falls and terraces of tufa reminiscent of those at Mammoth Hot Springs in Yellowstone National Park. When the waters were diverted away from the mountain before they reached the surface, the continuing supply of tufa precipitate they carried also was cut off, as was the plant-killing heat of the natural flow. The Edenic climate of Arkansas soon covered the hillside with thickly growing plants.

The tufa is most easily seen today around the two uncapped display springs and at Tufa Terrace, a cliff behind Bathhouse Row. A large tufa boulder called De Soto Rock long ago tumbled from the

Opposite: Tufa deposits left by the 143° F water of an open spring near De Soto Rock.

cliff and rests across Fountain Street from the Arlington Hotel. At a site beside Tufa Terrace, water collected from upper springs on Hot Springs Mountain is liberated to flow in a somewhat natural manner amid masonry and iron railings. Here, tufa is forming again. Tufa also is forming unseen on the insides of pipes and covered reservoirs, where the flow from some of the forty-five capped springs is commingled before being pumped to fountains and bathhouses.

Were more springs to be uncapped, they probably would return to their natural flow and tufa deposition. But this would reduce to a degree the amount of hot water available for other uses and might cause some drainage problems in urbanized Hot Springs, where little spring water has flowed freely for a century. It also is possible that tufa deposition might plug a spring or that a new spring might emerge on the hillside.

Do Go Near the Water

Few visitors to Hot Springs National Park can resist the urge to taste water flowing from the several convenient fountains. Most agree that the spring water tastes pleasant, for it requires no added chemicals to be safe from organic contamination.

The natural sterility of Hot Springs water influenced the National Aeronautics and Space Administration to store moon rocks in this water while they were being examined for signs of life. (No such signs were found.) The capping of the springs to pipe their water to bathhouses has much reduced the possibility of contamination following the water's emergence from underground.

Although often called "mineral water," the water from Hot Springs contains relatively few minerals. Its traces of silica, calcium, magnesium, sodium, potassium, bicarbonate, sulfate, chloride, and fluoride, together with the spring water's warmth, give it whatever curative properties it may have.

The U.S. government asserts no health claims for the thermal water. Most people who bathe find that the experience makes them feel good. Many report that the water relieves pain and promotes relaxation.

The water also contains natural traces of radioactive radon gas, most of which escapes into the atmosphere of the closed reservoirs before it is pumped to bathhouses and drinking fountains. Whatever radioactivity is left presents about the same hazard as exposure to the sun. Regular drinking of the water probably does not pose radiation hazards any greater than the drinking of many other natural waters with similar levels of radioactivity.

The Visitor Center's courtyard drinking fountain issues hot spring water.

Hot Springs National Park luxuriates in a mild climate marked by relatively warm temperatures and much precipitation throughout the year. The growing season usually lasts from March to November. Snowfall averages 4.5 inches a year.

Humans have greatly influenced the park's natural environment. Gone are the big mammals—elk, bison, black bear, wolf. Ostracods—tiny crustaceans with hinged two-part shells—still survive in the hostile environment of hot-spring waters. Introduced Eurasian bird species, such as rock doves and house sparrows, are common. The warm microclimate near the springs that once kept herbs and ferns green throughout winter has been severely reduced.

But to the visitor who explores the park away from Bathhouse Row, the natural scene remains extremely fine. Squirrels—gray, fox, and flying—occupy their niches in the mature oak, hickory, and pine forests and also in the elm, hackberry, and yaupon woods that grew up after the capping of the springs. Other animals typical of eastern woodlands found in the park include opossum, red and gray foxes, cottontail rabbit, raccoon, and 150 bird species. Among the largest of the birds is the wild turkey.

Many nonnative plants have been introduced to the park. Only

Folds of skin behind the flying squirrel's forelegs, when extended, enable it to "fly." Opposite: Red fox kits begin to emerge from their den in mid March, five weeks after birth.

The wild turkey male uses its brilliant plumage to attract a harem of females.

an exceedingly hard-nosed purist would deny the beauty of such exotics as the southern magnolias that bloom along Bathhouse Row or the periwinkles that trail along the Grand Promenade.

The native plants are not shy about displaying their glory, either. Serviceberry, redbud, red buckeye, and dogwood are magnificent in spring, and the dogwood's bright red leaves and berries are lovely in autumn. Spring wildflowers include fire pink, dwarf iris, bluet, shooting star, bird's-foot violet, and wild phlox. They are followed in summer by cardinal flower, black-eyed Susan, and the leafless, white Indian pipe.

A rare blue-green alga reported in the hot springs by Dunbar still survives in the two display springs that remain uncapped and in spring water released beside Tufa Terrace. It is known to grow in only one other place on the continent.

Opposite: Bird's-foot violets bloom nearly year-round in upland sites.

189

The John W. Noble Fountain stands at the southern entrance to the Grand Promenade.

SITES, TRAILS, AND TRIPS

Hot Springs, one of the smallest national parks, is also the most urban. Nonetheless, it is certainly worthwhile to spend a little time reliving the era when leisure meant not doing much besides soaking and socializing. The park also boasts 26 miles of trails that loop through lush and fascinating eastern deciduous forest.

Getting into Hot Water

People with gallon jugs come to collect drinking water from several jug fountains, one of which is near the park's Spanish-style Visitor Center at the south end of *Bathhouse Row*. This line of eight large and ornate structures was built in the early twentieth century to surround spa enthusiasts with luxury. Most park visitors are fascinated by the architecture and by the elaborate carvings, paintings, fountains, patterned tile, and stained-glass windows that ornament the historic bathhouses, especially the *Fordyce Bathhouse*, built in 1914. Although the Fordyce bathhouse no longer is open for bathing, the building now serves as the park Visitor Center.

Therapy and recreational baths are still available to visitors in other bathhouses owned and operated by concessionaires regulated by the National Park Service. The full regimen of relaxation takes about one hour and forty minutes. The park also supplies hot water to facilities outside its boundaries.

Roads and Trails

Roads that climb the park's ridges were well planned. The gently curving road up *Hot Springs Mountain* was built for carriages in 1884, but autos travel it easily today. A 216-foot observation tower atop the mountain provides a good perspective of the park and the city. *West Mountain Summit Drive*, *West Mountain Drive*, and *Black Snake Road* are lovely boulevards through the park's lush woodlands.

Grand Promenade. Behind Bathhouse Row, winding along the base of Hot Springs Mountain, the Grand Promenade is a pleasant red and white brick walkway almost .5 mile long that took thirty years to build and landscape. A fine walk between Reserve Avenue and Fountain Street, the Grand Promenade provides access to the two open display springs immediately behind Bathhouse Row and to trails up the mountain.

The park's hiking trails undulate along crests and drop down slopes and gullies. Some overlooks reveal views of the city; others display natural scenes. Roads intersect the interconnecting trails at convenient points. Pets are permitted on park trails, if kept on a leash.

Sunset Trail. The longest park path, the Sunset Trail traverses the summit of Music Mountain, at 1,405 feet the highest point in the park. The Sugarloaf Mountain stretch of the Sunset Trail extends to Blowout Mountain, then winds down to Stonebridge Road. A spur to Balanced Rock, a novaculite formation, is also available.

Dogwood Trail. The loops of the Dogwood Trail are aptly named and especially lovely in spring and autumn. The entire route is less than 1 mile long.

TRAILS OF HOT SPRINGS NATIONAL PARK

GRAND PROMENADE: Starts at Reserve Avenue; ends at Fountain Street; .5 mile one way; .25 hour; a red and white brick, landscaped walkway designed as a transition between the highly developed bathhouse area and the mountain lands; provides access to the Stevens Balustrade and the open springs; designated a National Recreation Trail in 1982.

GULPHA GORGE TRAIL: Starts at Gulpha Gorge Campground; connects with the Goat Rock Trail and the Dead Chief Trail; ends at North Mountain Road near a historic trail shelter; .8 mile one way; 1.25 hours; crosses Gulpha Creek on stepping stones, then winds along the steep sides of the gorge.

DEAD CHIEF TRAIL: Starts near Gulpha Gorge Campground; ends at Grand Promenade; 1.4 miles one way; 1.5 hours; trail skirts south slope of Hot Springs Mountain.

GOAT ROCK TRAIL: Starts near North Mountain overlook; ends at Gulpha Gorge Trail; 1 mile one way; 1 hour; runs beneath Goat Rock, a fault-thrust rock pinnacle (short spur leads to its top); continues through meadowlike area with abundant wildflowers.

DOGWOOD TRAIL: Starts at northern terminus of Goat Rock Trail; 1 mile one way; 1 hour; follows crest of ridge through open forest of dogwood trees; passes large shortleaf pine tree; connects with parts of Hot Springs Mountain, Gulpha Gorge, and Goat Rock trails to return to start.

HOT SPRINGS MOUNTAIN TRAIL: Starts and ends at Hot Springs Mountain picnic area; 1.5 miles one way; 1.5 hours; gentle trail, with exceptional scenery, that connects with a number of other trails.

PEAK TRAIL: Starts at middle of Grand Promenade off Tufa Terrace Trail; ends at tower site on Hot Springs Mountain; .5 mile one way; .5 hour; moderately steep.

SUNSET TRAIL: Starts at West Mountain Summit Drive turnaround; ends at Stonebridge Road, with .5 mile spur to Blowout Mountain; 8.25 miles one way; 7 hours; skirts eastern slope of Music Mountain near summit (highest point in Zig Zag Mountains); section near trail head is the most heavily used in the park because of scenery.

BALANCED ROCK TRAIL: Starts along Sunset Trail on Sugarloaf Mountain; ends at Balanced Rock; .2 mile one way; .5 hour; offers exceptional view from Balanced Rock.

WHITTINGTON TRAIL: Starts and ends near the north end of West Mountain Drive; 1.1-mile loop; .3 hour; original bridle trail has been modified as a jogging and physical-fitness trail; trees along trail are of exceptional size.

WEST MOUNTAIN TRAIL: Starts and ends at roadside shelter on West Mountain Summit Drive; 1.2-mile loop; 1.25 hours; short connection with Mountain Top Trail leads to return route along upper portion of trail; West Mountain is rugged and has contrasting vegetation on various sides.

Top: One of the elegant but unused bathhouses along Bathhouse Row.
Above: The 216-foot-high Hot Springs Mountain Tower, and the city of Hot Springs.
Overleaf: Muscadine grapevines on Hot Springs Mountain produce a musky, edible fruit.

ISLE ROYALE
NATIONAL PARK

Fog at sunrise in secluded Chippewa Harbor, on the southeast side of Isle Royale.

ISLE ROYALE NATIONAL PARK
800 EAST LAKESHORE DRIVE
HOUGHTON, MICHIGAN 49931
TEL.: (906) 482-0984

HIGHLIGHTS: Rock Harbor • Windigo • Moose • Bird Life • Edisen Fishery • Lookout Louise • Rock Harbor Lighthouse • Monument Rock • McCargoe Cove • Greenstone Ridge Trail • Minong Ridge • Passage and Raspberry Islands • Shipwrecks • Minong Mine

ACCESS: U.S. 41 to park headquarters in Houghton, then shuttle boat from Houghton (or from Copper Harbor, MI, or Grand Portage, MN).

HOURS: Park open from April 16 to October 31. Houghton headquarters open five days, year-round.

FEES: Charged for shuttle boat to Isle Royale.

PARKING: At mainland departure points.

GAS, FOOD, LODGING: Boat fuel and groceries available on mainland and at marina stores in Rock Harbor and Windigo. Rock Harbor Lodge open from June to September.

VISITOR CENTER: Visitor Center dockside at Houghton headquarters offers boat reservations and sells publications. Visitor Centers at Rock Harbor and Windigo offer interpretive talks and walks.

MUSEUM: None.

GIFT SHOP: Concessionaire-run shop at Rock Harbor.

PETS: Not permitted on visitors' boats or in park.

PICNICKING: Permitted throughout park.

HIKING: 165-mile trail network covers 45-mile length of island. Boat dropoff arrangements available. Treat water.

BACKPACKING: Allowed with free permit, available at Rock Harbor, Windigo, and aboard shuttle boat from Houghton.

CAMPGROUNDS: Campers must register and file itinerary on arrival. 3-sided shelters and tent sites for up to 6 people/site available. Water and showers at Windigo and Rock Harbor.

TOURS: Concessionaire-operated boat tours along Isle Royale shore, with dropoffs at highlight areas. NPS-guided trail tours in summer.

OTHER ACTIVITIES: Boaters should check with park for information and regulations. Fishing in Lake Superior waters with Michigan state license.

FACILITIES FOR DISABLED: Shuttle boat from Houghton, Rock Harbor Lodge, Houghton headquarters, and restrooms on Isle Royale accessible.

For additional information, see also Sites, Trails, and Trips on pages 218–229 and the map on pages 200–201.

Islands stand where Siskiwit Bay basalt ridges break the surface of Lake Superior.

ISLE ROYALE IS A WILDERNESS ISLAND. REMOTE, isolated, and rugged, this "Royal Island" of the French explorers lies in the wildest and coldest of the Great Lakes, Lake Superior. It is 45 miles long and 9 miles across—the largest island in the broadest fresh-water lake in the world. Just 15 miles of water separate the island from Canada, while it is more than 50 miles from Michigan, of which it is part. Some 200 smaller islands are included in the park.

The park can be reached only by seaplane or by boat. No public roads exist on the island, which is 99 percent wilderness, and wheeled vehicles are prohibited. Visitors must explore on foot or by boat, or not at all. Even though Isle Royale is among the most inaccessible national parks, increasing numbers of people—fishermen, backpackers, boaters, guests at the comfortable lodge—are discovering its unique appeal. The park's 571,790 acres of ridges, valleys, and open waters fill a human need for nature, wildness, and separation from everyday cares.

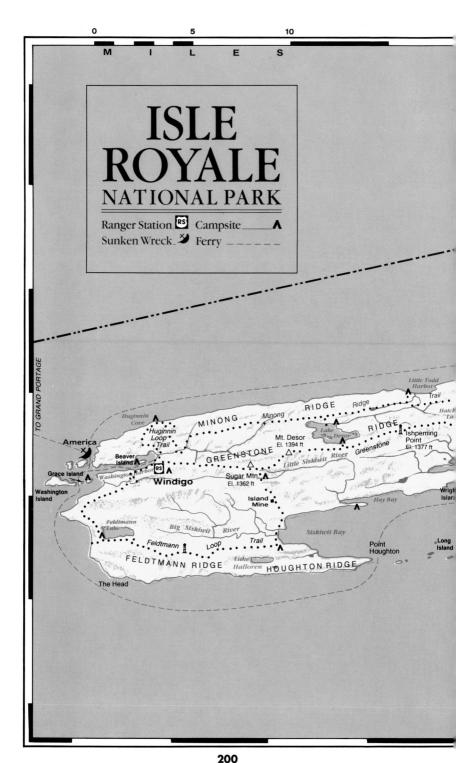

ISLE ROYALE
NATIONAL PARK

Ranger Station **RS**   Campsite _____ ∧
Sunken Wreck ⤹   Ferry ‒ ‒ ‒ ‒

0   5   10
M   I   L   E   S

TO GRAND PORTAGE

Little Todd Harbor
Trail
Hatch La

MINONG *Minong* RIDGE *Ridge*

RIDGE

Huginnin Cove
Huginnin Loop Trail

Lake Desor

Mt. Desor
El. 1394 ft

Ishpeming
Point
El. 1377 ft

America ✕
Beaver Island ∧
GREENSTONE
Little Siskiwit River
Greenstone

Grace Island ∧
Washington Harbor **RS** ∧
Windigo

Sugar Mtn.
El. 1362 ft

Washington Island

Island Mine

Hay Bay

Wrigh
Islar

Feldtmann Lake

Big Siskiwit River

Island Mine
∧

Siskiwit Bay

Long Island

Feldtmann Loop *Trail*

FELDTMANN RIDGE
Lake Halloren
HOUGHTON RIDGE

Point Houghton

The Head

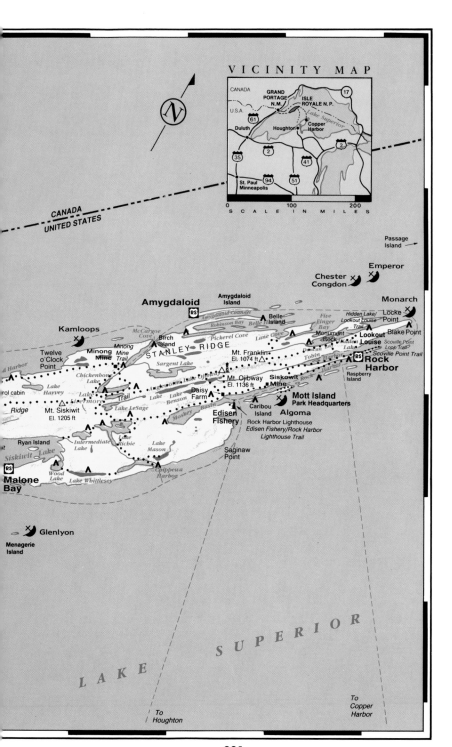

VICINITY MAP

CANADA

GRAND PORTAGE N.M.

ISLE ROYALE N.P.

U.S.A.

61

Duluth

Houghton

Copper Harbor

Lake Superior

17

35

2

41

2

St. Paul Minneapolis

94

51

SCALE IN MILES

0   100   200

CANADA
UNITED STATES

N

Passage Island →

Chester Congdon ✕

Emperor ✕

Monarch ✕

Amygdaloid

Amygdaloid Island

RS

Belle Island

Hidden Lake/ Lookout Louise Trail

Locke Point

Kamloops ✕

McCargoe Cove

Robinson Bay

Birch Island

Belle Harbor

Five Finger Bay

Monument Rock

Lookout Louise

Blake Point

Minong Mine

Minong Mine Trail

Pickerel Cove

Lane Cove

Duncan Bay

Scoville Point Loop Trail

Scoville Point Trail

Twelve o'Clock Point

STANLEY RIDGE

Mt. Franklin El. 1074 ft △

RS

Rock Harbor

d Harbor

Sargent Lake

Tobin Harbor

Raspberry Island

rol cabin

Chickenbone Lake

Mt. Ojibway El. 1136 ft △

Siskowit Mine

Lake Harvey

Trail

Daisy Farm

Ridge

Livermore

Lake Benson

Lake LeSage

Mott Island Park Headquarters

Mt. Siskiwit El. 1205 ft △

Moskey Basin

Edisen Fishery

Caribou Island

Algoma

Ryan Island

Intermediate Lake

Lake Richie

Lake Mason

Rock Harbor Lighthouse

Edisen Fishery/Rock Harbor Lighthouse Trail

wit

Siskiwit Lake

Wood Lake

Chippewa Harbor

Saginaw Point

RS

Malone Bay

Lake Whittlesey

✕ Glenlyon

Menagerie Island

LAKE   SUPERIOR

To Houghton

To Copper Harbor

A Thousand Mines in a Thousand Years

Human visitors probably reached Isle Royale in search of food and adventure as early as 7000 B.C., but the mining of copper that took place from about 2000 B.C. to 1000 B.C.—the earliest example of mining in North America—is especially noteworthy. Who were these ancient miners? No one knows, but archeologists calculate that they removed 280 to 375 tons of copper. Beads, blades, and pendants made from Isle Royale's copper were traded throughout the eastern United States. More than a thousand prehistoric mining pits from seven locations on the island have been excavated or recorded. These sites can be spotted by a trained eye scanning along the Minong Ridge and near Lookout Louise and Scoville Point.

The primary technique used in working the mines was probably battering at the rock face with hammerstones, which are large cobbles found on present and former shorelines. The miners are thought to have lived in small scattered camps, working copper only in conjunction with their quest for food. Isle Royale is one of a few places where the element occurs in its pure form, rather than as an ore combined with other elements; Native American prospectors traversing the island's barren rock ridges could easily spot the nuggets and veins of this unusual, shiny metal.

These early miners, breaking bedrock by repeatedly striking blows with hammerstones held in their bare hands, likely collected only several pounds of copper in the course of an entire summer. Yet they extracted tons of the metal over more than a thousand years. The mines of Isle Royale provide a unique archeological record of this significant achievement. It was once believed that an advanced civilization might have been responsible for moving such a great volume of material, but scientists now agree that the "mystery" of Isle Royale's prehistoric copper mines is really just the cumulative effect of a minor activity carried out over a millennium.

Historic Mining

The presence of copper on isolated Isle Royale was not general knowledge in 1843, when the Chippewa relinquished claim to the island and it officially became part of the United States. The glut of copper prospectors began in 1846—an overflow of the copper-mining boom that was creating millionaires on the Michigan mainland. This was America's first big metal rush, and it encouraged spirited individuals and a dozen eastern mining companies to explore Isle Royale aggressively for copper. The island's population stood at 120 in 1847. But because of changes in the mining law and general lack of profitability, this first period of mining came to an abrupt end by 1855, and the settlements at Daisy Farm, Siskowit Mine, Snug Harbor, and Todd Harbor were abandoned. The Smithwick Mine Pit, one often seen by Rock Harbor visitors, is a relic of this era.

The island's rock, however, still held plenty of copper, and two more boom-and-bust cycles ran their course in later years. After the Civil War, when copper prices were high, companies bought vast acreages on Isle Royale and sent trained mining engineers and geologists to explore for the metal. Diamond drilling—a new technique—supplemented the old haphazard search for exposed outcrops. Reliable transportation by lake steamer made life in the settlements more enjoyable. But by the 1880s, despite heavy investment, the Island Mine, Minong Mine, and Saginaw Mine had closed.

The final phase of mining involved a British syndicate called the Isle Royale Land Corporation. It purchased 84,000 acres of the island in 1889, set up a town of 135, and rigorously explored the Windigo area for copper. By 1892, when the accumulation of dia-

Hikers of the Feldtmann Ridge Trail may explore abandoned Island Mine equipment.

Early photograph of Isle Royale shows the foaming waters of a Siskiwit Lake outlet.

mond-drill cores revealed that the rock was too poor to mine profitably, the syndicate ceased exploration, closed down its settlement, sent home its workers, and began to sell its land. Hikers traveling the Huginnin and Minong Ridge trails may see traces of the exploration activity at Windigo. Other abandoned mining sites—with their piles of poor rock, tramways, ore cars, and old shafts—are spread around the island. A weekly tour goes to Minong Mine, the largest of these.

Commercial Fishing

Isle Royale is famous for commercial fishing, which began when the American Fur Company set up fish stations to harvest the abundant supply of lake trout, whitefish, and herring. By 1839, there were seven stations and a total crew of thirty-three fishermen. The three to five fishermen at each station were sometimes assisted by a barrel maker and by voyageurs who transported the fish to a central depot. Fishing was done in small boats propelled by oar or sail. For a while, the company salted 3,000 to 5,000 barrels of fish each year and shipped them in its own schooners to Sault Ste. Marie, from where they were transported to faraway markets. But the enterprise did not prosper, and by 1841, it had failed. The houses and docks eventually were taken over by independent fishermen, however, and through the years the enterprise expanded into almost every accessible cove and beach front on the island.

Hulk of the Algoma, wrecked off Mott Island in a November 1885 Lake Superior gale.

Links to this era still exist. Four of the more than forty gill-net fisheries once found around the periphery of the island continue to operate on a limited basis. The boom years are gone because of over-fishing and the predation of lampreys, but several individuals still manage operations that use small boats and long gill nets to catch fish. The historic fishery at Rock Harbor may be visited by tour boat throughout the summer. Here, visitors can see various tools of the fishing family—nets, floats, barrels, and boxes—and learn the story of the growth and decline of commercial fishing at Isle Royale.

Resort Development

Tourism began in earnest at the turn of the century. Resorts were developed on lands sold by the mining companies. Long famous for its subtle beauty, isolation, and unusually pure air and water, the island attracted a small but consistent tourist trade. By 1920, sizable resorts existed at Washington Harbor, Tobin Harbor, Belle Isle, and Rock Harbor. Adjacent to each, private cabins were built by many individuals. The opportunity to escape pollen and pollution attracted families (especially hay-fever sufferers) from throughout the Midwest; some of these families continue to visit the island every year.

Of the resorts of that era, only Rock Harbor Lodge remains in operation The rest fell victim to decay and archaic facilities.

Today's modern but rustic facilities at Rock Harbor include lodge and housekeeping cabins that attract old-timers and newcomers every summer to relive the early days of Isle Royale tourism.

Establishment of the Park

The fight for national-park status for Isle Royale began in the 1920s, as part of a national movement calling for more parks, especially in the East. The idea was promoted in the enthusiastic editorials of Albert Stoll, Jr., of the Detroit *News*, who argued that Isle Royale should be preserved for future generations because it possessed "practically the only bit of unspoiled nature east of the Mississippi River." He was the first to sound the wilderness-preservation theme for Isle Royale that has influenced management of the park to this day. Stoll challenged Congress to take action. He organized tours and won the endorsements of Stephen Mather, director of the National Park Service, and Francis Farquhar, future president of the Sierra Club. Many people, including most island landowners, agreed that Isle Royale was "eminently fitted" for the national-park system, but Congress was slow to act.

Ironically, when Stephen Mather died in 1930, the Isle Royale idea caught fire. Mather's death brought about much public mourning, and a general call even went out that Isle Royale be established as "Mather National Park" as a memorial to the great American conservationist. In February 1931, Representative Louis Cramton of Michigan introduced the Isle Royale bill into Congress; by March, legal conditions under which Michigan could offer its Isle Royale holdings to the federal government had been established. On March 3, 1931, President Herbert Hoover signed the bill into law.

The legislation provided that the national park be established whenever all remaining lands, including all surrounding islands, were donated to the federal government. It was not until 1940 that title to all such remaining lands had reached Washington. The park's formal dedication ceremony was also delayed because the government was preoccupied with fighting World War II. In August 1946, the park was finally dedicated—a quarter-century after Stoll began his call for a wilderness national park at Isle Royale.

Events of two subsequent years further distinguish Isle Royale National Park. In 1976, it was made a part of the National Wilderness Preservation System under the terms of the Wilderness Act of 1964. Then, in 1980, the island was selected by UNESCO as an International Biosphere Reserve, where research of global importance might be carried out.

The conspicuous linear ridges and valleys of Isle Royale are the result of fire and ice, two stages in a geologic story that began 1.2 billion years ago. Volcanism fired up this part of the earth before modern life forms even existed. Enormous volumes of basaltic lava flowed out intermittently from great cracks in the planet's surface. The island's tilted bedrock clearly displays these lava flows. Over time, layer after layer piled up to a thickness exceeding 10,000 feet and covered an area of hundreds of square miles. In fact, the greenstone flow that forms the high backbone ridge of the island may be the largest lava flow on earth.

Looking more closely, a visitor can see layers of sedimentary rock—sandstones, siltstones, and conglomerates—bedded between various layers of lava. This happened when sands and gravels from faraway mountains washed out onto the lava plains between periods of volcanic activity. After untold millennia, this great rock sandwich of lava and sedimentary rock fractured, sank, shifted, and tilted from its own weight, and the early Lake Superior basin was formed.

The glacial age of the past million years had a profound effect on the Lake Superior basin. Massive ice sheets—relentlessly powered by gravity—moved slowly across the rocks of what was to become Isle Royale. Sedimentary rocks were scraped and eroded more easily than was the harder lava rock. Today, these lava layers crop out in elongated northeast–southwest-trending ridges that extend the 45 miles from one end of the island to the other.

The mineral deposits on Isle Royale fascinate many visitors. Most such deposits were formed in vesicles, or bubbles, left by escaping gas as thick lavas cooled; others were concentrated along fissures in the bedrock and around pebbles in sedimentary deposits. Quantities of copper, the most important of the island's minerals, formed here in a pure metallic state, a freak of nature avidly sought during the nineteenth century.

Another mineral—found only at a few places in the world—is Isle Royale greenstone (chlorastrolite), which is Michigan's state gem. This green mineral, reminiscent of turtle shell, is much different from the hard greenish basalt that makes up the Greenstone Ridge. Other minerals—including little pink pebbles of prehnite, multicolored thomsonite, and hard, banded quartz agates—may also be found.

Overleaf: Thawing of ice in Todd Harbor in April; the park opens on April 16.

Climate and Precipitation

The cool waters of Lake Superior keep temperatures down in summer and moderate the coldness of winter by slightly "warming" arctic air masses that pass over the lake. Summer temperatures range from 40° F at night to 70° F during the day. Rain and fog are common throughout the visitor season, with snow and sleet sometimes falling in May and October.

Snow falls six months of the year, and ice coats the lakes and shorelines until mid-May. Lake Superior remains cold year-round because of its huge volume; surface water may warm up to 65° F in midsummer, but bottom temperatures hover around 36° F all year long. Some interior lakes warm up to 75° F, providing limited swimming opportunities for hikers.

The Wolf and the Moose

Isle Royale is famous for its wolf and moose populations and for the scientific studies of the relationship between them.

Howling by gray wolves seems to serve as a call for the assembly of the pack.

Isle Royale moose are most often sighted in summer near ponds and streams.

Researchers from Purdue University, in cooperation with the National Park Service, began to study the wolf and moose in 1958. According to Dr. Durward Allen of Purdue, "Isle Royale is probably the most ideal outdoor laboratory in the world." The isolation and largely natural state of the island have permitted observers to study the behavior of individual members of both species. Most research is done in winter by aerial tracking.

Moose came to the island early in the century, probably by swimming from Canada. Largest member of the deer family, the moose is a formidable creature. A bull moose can exceed 1,500 pounds and stand 7 feet at the shoulder. Despite its ungainly appearance, a healthy moose can move at speeds up to 35 miles per hour. The moose population on Isle Royale, initially free from predation, soared to as many as 3,000 individuals around 1930, and then crashed with the depletion of its browse. A fire in 1936 resulted in the growth of aspen and birch, and this renewed food supply led to a revived moose population.

A small pack of eastern timber wolves arrived on the island during the cold winter of 1948/1949, crossing on the ice from Canada. Since then, additional packs have been established, probably as offshoots of the first. Each pack—which may contain about ten members—is led by an alpha male and an alpha female, and other adults assume subordinate positions. The dominant wolves display erect tails and forward-thrust ears, while submissives may put their tails between their legs and flatten their ears against their heads. An alpha male may lead a pack for several years.

Most, perhaps all, mating within a pack is between the alpha male and alpha female. The litter of pups, born in the spring, is protected by all adults, with a foster mother often staying with the pups while the mother hunts. Such communal care strengthens the bonds among pack members and increases its chances for survival. The inevitable inbreeding does not affect the health of offspring. Nonetheless, the wolf population fluctuates; it fell from fifty in 1980 to fourteen in 1982. In 1994, there were fifteen known wolves on Isle Royale.

Some moose die of malnutrition or in drownings or other accidents. But most moose on Isle Royale are fated to be killed by wolves. Most of those killed are the very young, the old, and the ill or injured. By culling the weak and the old, wolves contribute to the health of the moose population. Culling ensures that the moose's limited food supply is available to the most vigorous individuals. In winter, moose are almost the only source of food for wolves, which can smell moose at a distance of 1.5 miles. Moose that stand their ground are not killed by wolves, but those that

Gray wolves form gender-based hierarchies of dominant and submissive pack members.

run are seen as vulnerable and are pursued by the pack. Only a small percentage of the pursuits are successful.

Barring an accident of nature or unwise human intervention, the wolves and moose are likely to remain in balance on Isle Royale. Some 1,700 moose roam the island today, and often are seen in summer at ponds and streams and near developed areas. Wolves, which have been killed off almost everywhere in the forty-eight contiguous states, are seldom seen on the island, but their piercing howls in the dark of night provide somewhat chilling reassurance that they do survive on Isle Royale.

Other Wildlife

Red squirrel, deer mouse, snowshoe hare, beaver, muskrat, red fox, and mink are among the mammals that visitors may see. Short-tailed weasel, otter, and the four species of bat are more rarely observed. The friendly red squirrel, a subspecies peculiar to Isle Royale, is especially conspicuous as it forages on the ground and chatters in the trees. The red fox, although commonly seen, is no friend of campers because it steals food and chews hikers' gear. Lynx, coyote, and caribou once lived on the island, but they have vanished as a result of trapping or competition from other wildlife.

The introduction of the white-tailed deer on the island in the 1920s was unsuccessful.

More species of birds frequent Isle Royale than do fish, mammal, reptile, and amphibian species combined; 120 bird species appear regularly, and 106 others visit occasionally or accidentally. Loons, mergansers, surface-feeding ducks, sandpipers, and gulls are regularly seen along the shore, and sparrows, woodpeckers, crows, and ravens are common in the interior. Predators such as ospreys and bald eagles are making a comeback at Isle Royale after decades of decline due to regionwide pesticide poisoning; the National Park Service is in the process of reestablishing the peregrine falcon.

Flora

Isle Royale has been a destination of botanical researchers since 1840, when explorer-surveyor Douglas Houghton described the vegetation in his journal. In 1847, William Ives gathered more field notes during his pioneering survey, and geologist George Dickenson wrote of encountering "hackmatack and thick undergrowth," cedar swamps, spruce, and fir. These early visitors had encountered the island's boreal (after Boreas, Greek god of the north wind) forest, a southern extension of the great belt of coniferous vegetation that girdles the North American land mass.

About 700 plant species grow on Isle Royale, and some are of special interest. A dozen—including the devil's club, Douglass hawthorn, and giant rattlesnake plantain—are characteristic of the western United States and on the mainland grow no closer to Isle Royale than in the Black Hills of South Dakota. Twenty-two species, mostly plants exposed to the constant cool temperatures and moisture of the island's eastern tip, are relics of glacial dispersal and are more commonly found in the Canadian and Alaskan tundra than elsewhere in this region. Thirty-nine plants on Michigan's threatened- and endangered-species lists grow on Isle Royale, and one, the round-leaved orchis (an orchid), is on the federal endangered-species list.

Isle Royale is a patchwork of many kinds of forest that may be generalized into two basic types. The boreal forest is characterized by balsam fir and white spruce, interspersed with paper birch and aspen. This forest occupies the cool and humid northeastern half of the island, where soils are shallow. The other principal forest type is the northern-hardwood forest of sugar maple and yellow birch,

Opposite: Red foxes prefer to live in open glades and fields adjacent to forest edges, and hunt in grassy areas alongside streams.

which grows in the warmer and more fertile southern half of the island.

Within the boreal and northern-hardwood forests are pockets of less common forest types that flourish where special environmental conditions exist. Red oak and white pine are found on dry ridge tops, black spruce and white cedar grow in swamps and bogs, and jack pine and aspen dominate fire-disturbed areas. Small islands also form their own ecological pockets. For example, Passage Island, 3 miles northeast of Isle Royale, has an unlikely abundance of mountain ash and Canada yew because of the historical absence of moose there.

Both fire and moose have affected the island's vegetation significantly. Copper miners burned vast stretches of forest to remove ground cover and expose bare rock that might contain deposits of the precious metal. In the early part of this century, natural and human-caused fires were not unusual, and travelers commonly remarked on the open expanses of charred and fallen trees. A catastrophic fire in 1936 burned during the entire summer and consumed 20 percent of the island's vegetation. The consequence of all this burning was loss of mature forest and of the humus that supported it. Today, a visitor can identify previously burned areas by the presence of almost pure stands of paper birch and quaking aspen.

Severe browsing by moose also changed the island's appearance. Moose relish Canada yew, and the vast thickets of this shrub described by early explorers are no more. Likewise, mountain ash and balsam fir make good "moose salad," as the chewed and gnarled branches of these trees attest.

Isle Royale is lush even in the understory. Common ground-cover plants include large-leaved aster, thimbleberry, alder, and beaked hazelnut. In some places, these can obliterate the view, snag backpacks, and host an abundance of biting insects; but amid the tangle are the understory's rewards, an assortment of delicious berries and colorful flowers.

Two dozen different ferns, 32 kinds of delicate orchids, and 525 species of fungi help provide splashes of color on the otherwise dark forest floor. One of the most colorful of all plants is the lichen, and nowhere else in America do lichens grow so luxuriantly. This is due to the purity of the island's moist air. More than 200 species have been collected, including such familiar ones as the gray, multi-branched reindeer "moss"; the brown, pendulous "hair" of old man's beard; and the vivid orange crustose rock lichen.

Opposite, above: Red berries of the rose twisted-stalk. Below: Calypso orchids.

The lush growth of white birch trees is seen along most Isle Royale shorelines.

SITES, TRAILS, AND TRIPS

Isle Royale is a waterlocked wilderness that can be experienced in different ways by backpacker, canoeist, boater, lodge guest, or day user. The park's 166 miles of trails, 36 campgrounds, moderate altitude, cool weather, and general absence of dangerous mammals and of poisonous snakes and plants make it a backpacker's paradise. Increasing numbers of canoeists are discovering the solitude of the interior lakes, which are knit together by a series of sixteen portages. Boaters can explore a dozen fjordlike harbors and can dock overnight at offshore islands as well as at the regular lakeside campgrounds. Lodge guests can rest in the comfort of modern rooms perched above the surging water of Rock Harbor or in housekeeping cabins nearby in a woodland setting. Day trips by ferry from Copper Harbor, Michigan, and Grand Portage, Minnesota (to Rock Harbor and Windigo, respectively), are available for people who lack the time to stay overnight.

The Rock Harbor Area

Most visitors enter the park at Rock Harbor because access is relatively easy and most development is there. Access is provided by daily concession ferry from Copper Harbor and by government ferry from the mainland park headquarters in Houghton, Michigan. Prices and schedule times are revised annually, so visitors should obtain the latest brochures beforehand from park headquarters.

Rock Harbor began to develop as a resort early in the twentieth century, after "Commodore" Kneut Kneutson built a small resort for hay-fever sufferers like himself. It prospered, and the resort (sold to the federal government in 1938, and now operated by National Park Concessions) has expanded ·to include sixty lodge rooms, twenty housekeeping units, a dining room, a snack bar, a gift shop, a camping-equipment store, and a full-service marina. The NPS visitor information station here sells natural-history publications and is the starting point for daily interpretive walks. Rangers give evening programs at the auditorium or in the amphitheater.

Various trails—long and short—originate at Rock Harbor Lodge. Several major long-distance hiking trails begin at the lodge and follow the Tobin Harbor or Rock Harbor shoreline to such overnight destinations as Daisy Farm, Moskey Basin, Lake Richie, and Chicken-bone Lake. (Long-distance trails are discussed in a separate section, below.)

Kneutson Trail. The self-guiding Kneutson Trail, less than .3 mile long, traces the history and development of the Rock Harbor resort. It terminates at the old America Dock, where steamers traditionally unloaded cargo and passengers.

Scoville Point Trail. The 4-mile signed self-guiding loop of the Scoville Point Trail leads to an exposed, wave-washed point of land where a bronze plaque commemorates Albert Stoll, who fought diligently to establish the national park.

From Rock Harbor, boat tours depart to half a dozen scenic and historical destinations that are impossible to visit without a boat.

Passage Island. Passage Island, 8 miles northeast of Rock Harbor Lodge, features a century-old lighthouse that is still active, plus a trail that leads through a gnarled and mossy forest containing devil's club, Canada yew, and other uncommon plants. The island lies beyond one of Lake Superior's principal shipping lanes, and it is not unusual to see 1,000-foot freighters approaching and leaving the major Canadian grain port of Thunder Bay, Ontario.

Raspberry Island. Raspberry Island is one of Isle Royale's scenic and rugged outer islands. Visitors here can explore a 1-mile self-guiding trail through a spruce bog.

Hidden Lake. Situated on Tobin Harbor, Hidden Lake has been a

Overleaf: Bog life may be encountered on the Raspberry Island Trail.

popular destination for boat tours since the 1920s. En route, visitors will pass a dozen colorful cabins perched along the wooded shore. These are held by life-lessees who built them before the park was established. A natural salt lick at Hidden Lake attracts moose, especially in the early summer when they urgently need salt in their diet. The 1-mile trail at the lake climbs up an ancient shoreline formed by an earlier stage of Lake Superior, past a 100-foot sea stack called Monument Rock (it once rose from the water when the level of the lake was higher), and over the ridge to scenic Lookout Louise. From here—320 feet above Lake Superior—visitors enjoy a grand view of the otherwise hidden bays and coves of Isle Royale's northern side, as well as of the cliffs of the Canadian shore 20 miles away.

Edisen Fishery. The boat tour to Edisen Fishery runs 7 miles from Rock Harbor Lodge to a historic commercial fishery; many kinds of nets, floats, boats, and other apparatus are on exhibit. A short path connects the fishery with the restored 1855 Rock Harbor Lighthouse, which houses exhibits that trace the maritime history of Isle Royale.

McCargoe Cove. McCargoe Cove, another popular tour destination, is accessible by boat after a 16-mile trip along Isle Royale's steep-cliffed northern side. It was used 4,000 years ago by the Native Americans who mined copper along nearby ridges. Named for a captain who hid in the cove with his ship for a year during the War of 1812, these deep waters were busiest during the 1870s, when the Minong Mine Company set up a town site, built a tram, and extracted copper ore that yielded 249 tons of refined copper. The historic mine and the prehistoric mine pits on the ridge are included on the National Register of Historic Places. The 1-mile walk to the mine from the cove is a moderate climb through a tall, shaded aspen forest.

The Windigo Area

Windigo is historically the park's western gateway. It appeals to visitors who want wilderness and a minimum of development. Access is provided by two concession ferries from Grand Portage; one ferry makes daily round trips, and the other circumnavigates Isle Royale three times a week. Situated at the upper end of Washington Harbor, Windigo originated as headquarters of a mining-exploration enterprise around 1890. The company closed

Opposite: Thimbleberry blankets the ground in Rock Harbor's spruce–fir forest.

because there was insufficient copper to mine commercially, and it sold its principal buildings to a group of Duluth sportsmen. Windigo Inn, a lodging venture built on that site by the National Park Service, was closed in 1976. At present, Windigo has a visitor information station, a self-guiding nature trail, an amphitheater, a store, and a modern rest-room building with washer-dryer and shower facilities. Rangers give daily interpretive walks, and evening programs are held in the auditorium or amphitheater. Washington Creek Campground is nearby.

Windigo is hiking country. From here, visitors can hike east to the Feldtmann Loop or west to the Huginnin Loop.

Feldtmann Loop. The Feldtmann Loop is 22 miles long and requires spending a minimum of three nights at campgrounds en route. The trail passes Feldtmann Lake, which is excellent for fishing, and climbs the rugged Feldtmann Ridge escarpment, which affords broad panoramic views reminiscent of those in western national parks. From there, it descends to Siskiwit Bay, and then climbs up to the abandoned Island Mine settlement, through maple and oak forest, before heading down again to Windigo.

Huginnin Loop. The Huginnin Loop is 9.5 miles long and passes through heavily forested, steep-sided valleys until it arrives at the small, picturesque bay called Huginnin Cove. Although the trail is short enough to be hiked in a day, hikers can enjoy the special beauty of this isolated little cove by camping there overnight.

The Long Trails

Backpackers who have at least a week to spend on Isle Royale generally trek the Greenstone Ridge or the Minong Ridge—the island's longest trails. Both trips, like any overnighter in the park, require a backcountry use permit, careful planning, maps, hiking experience, suitable equipment, and boots that have been broken in.

Greenstone Ridge Trail. The 40-mile, 5-day Greenstone Ridge Trail is rated as "moderate." It runs along the massive Greenstone Ridge, which tops out at Mount Desor, elevation 1,394 feet—792 feet above Lake Superior. The trail connects Windigo with Lookout Louise, although most hikers avoid the final 6 miles of the Greenstone in favor of a lakeshore route that enables them to terminate at Rock Harbor.

Minong Ridge Trail. The 26-mile Minong Ridge Trail is rated as "difficult"; it is Isle Royale's ultimate challenge for the experienced hiker. No fewer than 7 days are needed to tramp from Rock Harbor to Windigo on the Minong Ridge because the rugged trail is not maintained.

Canoe Portages

Canoeing and kayaking are gaining in popularity, but the National Park Service actively discourages these activities on the open waters of Lake Superior, where 6-foot waves and persistent swells make canoeing treacherous. The interior of the park, however, has many miles of waterways for the experienced canoeist. Sixteen portages—ranging in length from .2 to 2.1 miles—link backwoods bays and lakes. All are in the northeastern half of the island. Although most waters along the portage routes are fairly protected, sudden winds can whip up waves capable of swamping a canoe even in protected harbors and inland lakes. Therefore, every canoeist must wear a personal flotation device. A backcountry-use permit is required for overnight camping.

Shipwrecks

No description of Isle Royale would be complete without mention of the shipwrecks. This unusual collection, well preserved by the clear, cool water of Lake Superior, represents a cross section of Great Lakes shipping. A few ships broke up after running onto submerged sandstone and basaltic lava ridges; others rest on the bottom whole. The ten major wrecks, dating from 1877 to 1947, range in size from the 183-foot *America,* a passenger boat that sank near Windigo, to the 532-foot *Chester Congdon,* a package freighter that wrecked on the northern side of the island. The sinking of the *Algoma,* a passenger steamer, off Mott Island in 1885 resulted in about forty-five deaths, the greatest loss of life in the history of Lake Superior shipping.

Ten lesser wrecks also dot Isle Royale's coves and harbors. Despite the out-of-the-way location of most of these wrecks, they are being visited by an increasing number of experienced scuba divers. The National Park Service permits scuba diving and is managing these underwater cultural resources by protecting them, interpreting them, and making them accessible.

Overleaf: Canoeists favor Sargent Lake, although access to its waters requires a portage over an unmaintained trail.

Trails of Isle Royale National Park

Isle Royale National Park has 165 miles of trails and ideal weather for hiking and backpacking.

SHORT DAY TRAILS

WINDIGO NATURE TRAIL: Starts and ends at Windigo store; 1-mile loop; .75 hour; leads through old settlement area that is being reclaimed by wilderness; good introduction to the island's major plants and animals.

KNEUTSON TRAIL: Starts at Rock Harbor Lodge; ends at the old America dock; .25 mile one way; .25 hour.

SCOVILLE POINT LOOP TRAIL: Starts and ends at Rock Harbor Lodge; 4-mile loop; 2 hours; passes through spruce–fir forest to prehistoric mine pit and open waters of Lake Superior.

RASPBERRY ISLAND TRAIL: Starts and ends at Raspberry Island dock; 1-mile loop; 1 hour; leads through lichen-covered forest and passes wave-washed cliffs; boardwalk crosses black-spruce bog containing insectivorous plants; illustrated direction markers.

EDISEN FISHERY/ROCK HARBOR LIGHTHOUSE TRAIL: Starts and ends at Edisen dock; .5-mile loop; .5 hour; connects historic commercial fishery with restored 1855 lighthouse; passes grave from 1870s mining era.

PASSAGE ISLAND TRAIL: Starts at Passage Island dock; ends at boat cove; .5 mile one way; .5 hour; passes still-active 1881 lighthouse on major Lake Superior shipping lane; crosses over high cliffs, where uncommon plants grow; may be slippery due to fog and mist.

SISKIWIT LAKE TRAIL: Starts at Malone Bay dock; ends at Siskiwit Lake; .5 mile one way; .5 hour; follows creek to Siskiwit Lake and a panoramic view that includes Ryan Island, the largest island in the largest lake on the largest island in the largest freshwater lake in the world.

MINONG MINE TRAIL: Starts at McCargoe Cove dock; ends at Minong Mine; 1 mile one way; .5 hour; passes through forest of tall aspens along old route connecting settlement with 1870s copper mine; two horizontal tunnels, old equipment, and poor-rock piles may be explored; climb Minong Ridge to see prehistoric mine pits and to obtain an excellent view of Ontario, 20 miles away; use care when walking across sharp, loose rocks of the poor-rock piles.

HIDDEN LAKE/LOOKOUT LOUISE TRAIL: Starts at Hidden Lake dock; ends at Lookout Louise; 1 mile one way; 1 hour; skirts the shore of Hidden Lake and climbs up old beach ridges and passes a mammoth sea stack on the way to Lookout Louise, which offers a superb view of Isle Royale's north side and Ontario 20 miles beyond; steep in places; 320-foot change in elevation.

OVERNIGHT TRAILS

FELDTMANN LOOP TRAIL: Starts and ends at Windigo; 24 miles; 3 days; climbs Feldtmann Ridge, then descends to Siskiwit Bay Campground before passing

An Atlantis fritillary butterfly perches on a black-eyed Susan blossom.

abandoned Island Mine settlement; last leg of trail follows Greenstone Ridge; high point on Feldtmann Ridge is almost 600 feet above Lake Superior; excellent views.

Huginnin Loop Trail: Starts and ends at Windigo; 9.5 miles round trip; 9 hours; passes through heavily forested steep-sided valleys to small, picturesque Huginnin Cove Campground on Lake Superior.

Greenstone Ridge Trail: Starts at Windigo; ends at Rock Harbor; 40 miles one way; 4–5 days; follows the crest of the ridge of the Greenstone lava flow, the backbone of Isle Royale; high point on ridge is 792 feet above Lake Superior; no campgrounds on main trail.

Minong Ridge Trail: Starts at Windigo, ends at McCargoe Cove; 28.3 miles one way; 4 days; most difficult trail on Isle Royale—for experienced hikers only; rugged, unmaintained trail over open, rocky ridge; excellent views.

Overleaf: View from Feldtmann Ridge over Siskiwit Swamp, with distant Greenstone Ridge.

MAMMOTH CAVE
NATIONAL PARK

Crystal lake lies 60 feet below the route of the Frozen Niagara Tour.

MAMMOTH CAVE NATIONAL PARK
MAMMOTH CAVE, KENTUCKY 42259
TEL.: (502) 758-2251

HIGHLIGHTS: Mammoth Cave • Green River • Cedar Sink • Historic Cave Tour • Spelunking Tour • Frozen Niagara Cave Tour • Cave Life

ACCESS: From Louisville and points south take I-65. From points west take I-24 to Western Kentucky Parkway, then Kentucky 259 from Leitchfield.

HOURS: Open year-round, 24 hours daily. Cave tour schedules vary; no cave tours on Christmas Day.

FEES: For camping and cave tours.

PARKING: Ample parking at headquarters.

GAS, FOOD, LODGING: Available in nearby communities and at Mammoth Cave Hotel near park headquarters. Grocery store near headquarters campground open during peak season.

VISITOR CENTER: Next to park headquarters, open seven days, year-round; sells cave tour tickets and publications. Closed Christmas.

MUSEUM: None.

GIFT SHOP: Adjacent to Mammoth Cave Hotel lobby.

PETS: Must be leashed. Prohibited in Visitor Center, in food-service areas, and on cave tours. Kennel at Mammoth Cave Hotel.

PICNICKING: At headquarters, Sloane's Crossing Pond, Houchins and Dennison ferries, and at Maple Springs Group Campground.

HIKING: 7-mile network of trails in headquarters area; longer backcountry trails north of Green River. Seasonal ranger-led hikes. Treat water.

BACKPACKING: 60 miles of backcountry trails. Free, required permit for all overnight trips. Campers must camp at designated backcountry campsites on banks of Green and Nolin rivers.

CAMPGROUNDS: Free campground at Dennison Ferry (4 sites); Headquarters Campground has 110 sites. Water available at Headquarters Campground. 14-day stay limit year-round.

TOURS: NPS-guided cave tours and scenic boat tour on Green River.

OTHER ACTIVITIES: Recreational caving for experienced cavers; fishing in accordance with state and park regulations, no license required; boating; tennis and shuffleboard at Mammoth Cave Hotel.

FACILITIES FOR DISABLED: 2 campsites at Headquarters Campground and some restrooms accessible. Cave tours by special arrangement. Hotel accommodations.

For additional information, see also Sites, Trails, and Trips on pages 257–263 and the maps on pages 236–237 and 261.

WITH MORE THAN 340 MILES OF MAPPED passages, some extending beyond park boundaries, Mammoth Cave is the longest known cave system in the world. (The second longest is a 90-mile system in the Soviet Union. The United Nations has designated Mammoth Cave as a World Heritage Site and as a biosphere reserve.) The cave's collection of bizarre gypsum formations and water-deposited stalactites, stalagmites, draperies, and columns continues to develop. As the Green River cuts farther into the plateau containing the cave, more passageways are dissolved and then exposed as the water table drops. Because it is still growing, Mammoth Cave is said to be "living."

As interesting as the geologic "life" are the truly living and frequently unusual creatures that inhabit the passages of Mammoth Cave. More than 200 species of animals have been found in the cave. Some never leave, and the random course of natural selection has left many of them without eyes and without skin pigmentation in a lightless environment in which such features are extraneous.

Although less bizarre, the life on the surface of the park is more abundant and easier to enjoy than are the living creatures in the cave. The well-watered Kentucky forests atop Mammoth Cave provide ample opportunities for wildlife watching. The bright colors of wildflowers are surpassed only by the brilliant hues of autumn leaves on a wide variety of hardwoods.

Water erosion of the Mammoth Cave plateau's limestone layer results in sinkholes.

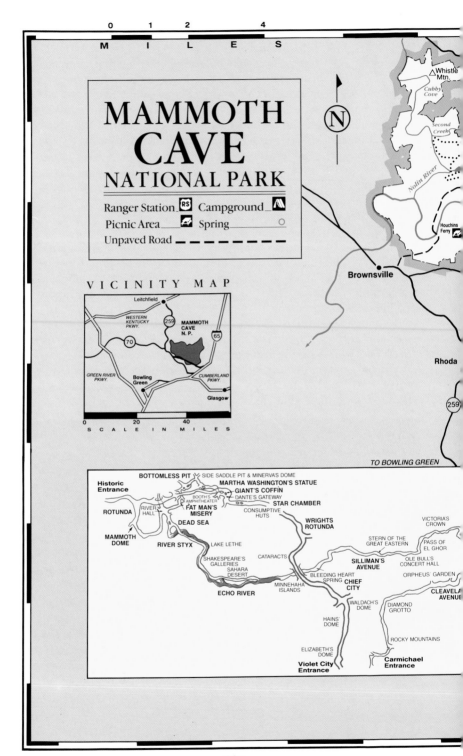

MILES
0 1 2 4

MAMMOTH CAVE
NATIONAL PARK

Ranger Station **RS** Campground **▲**
Picnic Area **🞉** Spring ○
Unpaved Road – – – – – – –

VICINITY MAP

Leitchfield
WESTERN KENTUCKY PKWY.
259
MAMMOTH CAVE N. P.
65
70
GREEN RIVER PKWY.
Bowling Green
CUMBERLAND PKWY.
Glasgow

0 20 40
SCALE IN MILES

Whistle Mtn.
Cubby Cove
Second Creek
Nolin River
Houchins Ferry

Brownsville

Rhoda
259

TO BOWLING GREEN

BOTTOMLESS PIT SIDE SADDLE PIT & MINERVA'S DOME
Historic Entrance MARTHA WASHINGTON'S STATUE
GIANT'S COFFIN
BOOTH'S AMPHITHEATER DANTE'S GATEWAY
FAT MAN'S MISERY STAR CHAMBER
RIVER HALL CONSUMPTIVE HUTS
ROTUNDA WRIGHTS ROTUNDA
DEAD SEA VICTORIA'S CROWN
MAMMOTH DOME STERN OF THE GREAT EASTERN PASS OF EL GHOR
RIVER STYX LAKE LETHE
SHAKESPEARE'S GALLERIES CATARACTS SILLIMAN'S AVENUE OLE BULL'S CONCERT HALL
SAHARA DESERT ORPHEUS' GARDEN
BLEEDING HEART SPRING CHIEF CITY
MINNEHAHA ISLANDS CLEAVELA AVENUE
ECHO RIVER WALDACH'S DOME DIAMOND GROTTO
HAINS' DOME ROCKY MOUNTAINS
ELIZABETH'S DOME CARMICHAEL Entrance
Violet City Entrance

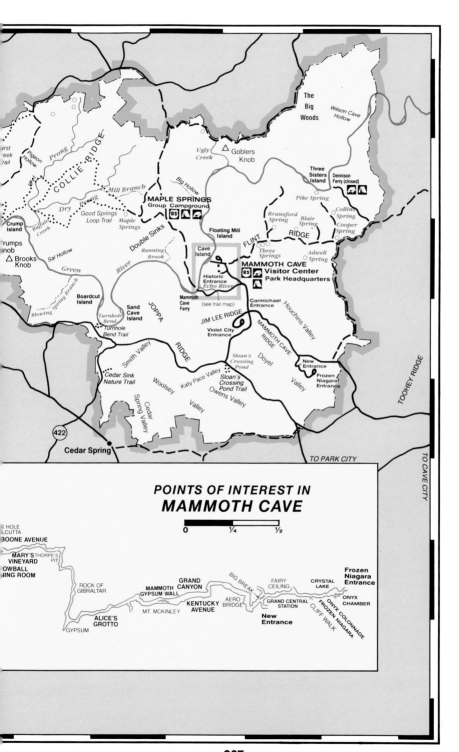

POINTS OF INTEREST IN
MAMMOTH CAVE

0   ¼   ½

Native American Miners

It is possible that Native Americans were exploring the cave extensively as many as 4,000 years ago. Using bundles of cane for torches, they sought mirabilite and epsomite, cave minerals that are effective laxatives. Native Americans also mined gypsum, probably to make a white paint. Some 2 miles from the Historic Entrance (still the main access to the cave), one of these early miners was killed in about 420 B.C. by the fall of a 5-ton boulder dislodged by his gypsum mining. His body, preserved by calcium nitrate, was discovered in 1935 and dubbed Lost John. He now lies in a secret place, still inside the cave.

Early Native Americans ventured far into depths that were not penetrated again by explorers until the twentieth century. The cave shows no traces of use by its first explorers, however, over the past 2,000 years.

Defending the Republic with Cave Dirt

The source of Mammoth Cave's calcium nitrate may have been water running through excrement deposited by the five species of bats that have used the cave for shelter for thousands of years. Alternatively, nitrogen-fixing bacteria within cave soils may have been the source. Whatever the source of this substance, also called false saltpeter, it was vital to the United States during the War of 1812. Saltpeter is an essential ingredient in gunpowder, and the British blockade had cut off foreign sources of both gunpowder and saltpeter.

Pipes made of hollowed-out yellow-poplar trunks carried water into Mammoth Cave, where slaves dumped tons of calcium-nitrate-bearing "peter dirt" into leaching vats. After leaching through the earthen material, the water was pumped back out through other wooden pipes. Nitrate crystals were precipitated by filtering the water through ashes (which contributed necessary potassium) and then boiling it off. Large quantities of potassium nitrate (true saltpeter) were shipped from Mammoth Cave to the Du Pont powder works in Wilmington, Delaware. This mining ceased after the war, when cheaper foreign supplies of saltpeter again became available. The remains of the saltpeter-leaching works still may be seen in Mammoth Cave.

Opposite: The Historic Entrance in the 1920s: at this time, local and state associations were seeeking to donate parcels of cave lands to the federal government.

In 1816, even before the mining of saltpeter ended, Mammoth Cave began to draw tourists. It has the reputation of being the second-oldest tourist attraction in the country; Niagara Falls is deemed the first. In 1838, Franklin Gorin bought Mammoth Cave and set his slave Stephen Bishop to learning about the cave and guiding visitors. Bishop's discoveries of 20 miles of passages, underground Echo River, and the river's blind fish soon gained him a measure of fame as a cave guide. Finally given his freedom in 1856, he died the next year at the age of thirty-seven. Bishop's grave is in the Old Guide's Cemetery on the park's Heritage Trail.

Mammoth Cave—and Bishop—had been purchased in 1839 by Dr. John Croghan, who soon increased the cave's success as a tourist attraction. He was determined to make part of the cave into a sanatorium for tuberculosis patients. Croghan theorized that the unvarying temperature and humidity would be good for them.

Eleven huts were constructed for fifteen consumptives in 1842, and food was brought to them by guides and slaves. All the patients got worse; two died within a year. In the face of these results, the experiment was terminated, but the remains of two stone huts still exist within the cave. Croghan himself died of tuberculosis in 1849.

Establishment of the Park

Inept management of Mammoth Cave by subsequent lessees caused a decline in tourist visits, accompanied by increasing local distress over lost revenue. Public support for the creation of a national park at Mammoth Cave began as early as 1905. In 1928, the Kentucky state legislature formed a commission to arrange the purchase of the cave and its donation to the federal government. After politically and legally complex land transfers, Mammoth Cave National Park was established in 1941.

Mammoth Cave, a tourist attraction since the early nineteenth century, did not gain national park status until 1941.

Modern Exploration

Exploitation for tourism of other caves near Mammoth Cave led to the serious exploration of many caves in the vicinity. Intrepid explorer Floyd Collins thought that the lovely gypsum passages he discovered in Crystal Cave in 1917 on his family's farm would make him wealthy. But Crystal Cave was too far from the flow of tourist traffic. In 1925, while Collins was trying to open passages in Sand Cave to divert tourists before they reached Mammoth, a rock fell on his ankle, trapping him in a low, narrow passage. He was facing out; no one could get past him to move the 27-pound rock.

For fifteen days, rescuers tried to extract Floyd, while journalists in a circuslike atmosphere outside the cave riveted America's attention on his plight. When a cave-in cut off Collins from food, water, and hope, a feverish effort to sink a shaft behind him at last began. Rescuers reached him ten days later, but he was dead.

After his family sold the property, Collins's body was entombed at Crystal Cave. In death, Collins drew the hordes of tourists that he could not attract while alive. In 1929 the corpse was stolen, perhaps by a competing cave owner, but was later recovered. The National Park Service acquired Crystal Cave in 1961 and halted tourist trips. Collins's body rested in the fine cave he discovered until 1989, when it was interred in a nearby Baptist Church cemetery.

The Flint Ridge Cave System and Mammoth Cave were believed to be connected, but the connecting passage was difficult to find beneath the Houchins Valley, which cuts between the two systems. Repeated exploration of extremely small, deep, and unpleasant passages beneath the valley failed to yield a connection between Mammoth and the Flint Ridge caves until 1972. In that year, Patricia Crowther, a member of a party of four explorers, wormed her tiny body through yet another muddy subterranean hole whose narrowness would have turned back a slightly overweight mole. Her contortions through the slimy, tight conduit paid off: in the next two trips the link was found, justifying the endeavors of the 628 other spelunkers who had participated in the effort to link the Flint Ridge and Mammoth cave systems.

In 1979, it was determined that Mammoth Cave extends to the southwest, after cave explorers followed an underground river from caves in Joppa Ridge. An additional 50 miles was added to the total in 1983, when a connection was made to a cave in Toohey Ridge. Mud-caked members of the Cave Research Foundation are still poking their carbide lamps into as yet unexplored byways, continually extending the cave system's record of mapped passages.

Water flowing down into the Historic Entrance will reappear at the Green River.

Water: The Underground Sculptor

Like most large caverns, Mammoth Cave has been dissolved out of beds of limestone. Limestone at this location was deposited some 300 million years ago in the shallow Mississippian sea. Changing conditions within the sea caused the accumulation on top of the limestone of deposits of sand and mud, which eventually were compressed into sandstone and shale. The deposition of sedimentary rocks stopped when the land began to rise and the sea retreated about 230 million years ago.

As soon as the rock appeared above the sea, erosion started to remove the sedimentary layers. The sandstone was much more resistant to erosion than was the underlying limestone, but 200 million years of weathering nonetheless removed a great deal of the sandstone cap. The cap atop the Mammoth Cave plateau is now 50 to 120 feet thick, and it has protected the limestone from dissolving. On limestone surfaces without protective caprock, the upper layers of limestone dissolved uniformly and rapidly. Whatever caves they contained were largely destroyed.

But the sandstone was not impervious enough to keep moisture out entirely. Water picked up carbon dioxide while falling as rain and trickling through decaying vegetation and became mild carbonic acid. It penetrated to the easily dissolved limestone layers, either through river valleys that had been cut through the sandstone or through holes in the sandstone.

By limiting its access to the limestone, the sandstone forced the water to concentrate its dissolving power in certain areas, which became cave passages. Water dissolved Mammoth Cave's passages as it percolated through a complex grid of cracks created in the limestone during the uplift of the land. The limestone also dissolved more rapidly along the edges of layers within the rock. The location, orientation, and gradient of the net of cracks and the composition of the limestone layers affected the direction, size, and shape of the passages. The passages range from huge subterranean rooms to tubes choked with silt that lie below the level of the Green River. (The river was elevated by debris washed from continental glaciers to the north.) Water from the surface also works its way straight down into the earth, forming vertical shafts. These intersect with abandoned passages at upper levels that had been drained as the Green River cut deeper into the plateau.

Opposite: The Frozen Niagara travertine formation was discovered in 1923.
Overleaf: The special environment of a forested sinkhole along the Turnhole Bend Trail.

The seemingly endless passages of Mammoth Cave began as conduits for water headed for the Green River. Subterranean water constantly sought the steepest, fastest route to the river, using gravity as its guide. Water abandoned upper passages as lower conduits were formed. Because the Green River did not cut its way into the plateau at a constant rate, some passages were filled with water longer than others. If water ran through a passage for a long time, a great deal of limestone dissolved from the surrounding walls and floors.

The stream-cut valleys in the Mammoth Cave plateau no longer have streams. The streams that carved the valleys now trickle quickly into the ground and flow through cave passages to the Green River. The surface of the plateau is pockmarked by perhaps 10,000 sinkholes—roughly basin-shaped depressions that either formed suddenly when subterranean caves collapsed or were gradually excavated by water flowing into caves. Sinkholes range in size from a few yards across and deep to .25 mile wide and 200 feet deep.

Flutes, Flowstone, and Gypsum Snowballs

Mammoth Cave's special features are its great length and vertical shafts. It is less richly endowed with spectacular formations than are many other caves. But in more than 340 miles, some passages contain notable decorations.

Scalloped indentations of various sizes were dissolved in cave walls as water flowed through the passages. Flutes are grooves dissolved by water flowing or dripping quickly down the walls. Bedding plane anastomoses are a third type of solution formation, a maze of interconnected, winding tubes on a passage wall or ceiling.

The most familiar cave features form from travertine, or calcium carbonate. As water charged with carbon dioxide trickles through limestone cracks, it dissolves the limestone into calcium and bicarbonate ions. As long as the ionic concentration of this dissolved material is less than that of the carbon dioxide, the water continues to dissolve the limestone. But when water enters a passage, it loses much of its carbon dioxide to the cave air. This increases the concentration of calcium and bicarbonate ions to a saturation point at which they precipitate out of the water as travertine.

Travertine assumes many shapes. Stalactites form when water drips slowly from a cave ceiling. When water drips too fast to deposit its excess calcium carbonate on the ceiling, it lands on the floor and builds up stalagmites. Eventually, a stalactite and a stalagmite may unite to form a column. A translucent drapery may grow along the edge of a stalactite. Flowstone forms where mineral-rich water runs across a limestone surface. Almost every heavily visited cave in North America has a flowstone formation that reminds people of a waterfall and is named for Niagara Falls. In Mammoth Cave, one of the largest travertine deposits is called Frozen Niagara.

While percolating through limestone, the water picks up small amounts of iron that color the travertine yellow, red, or brown. Traces of manganese add black.

White or golden brown crystals of shiny gypsum form only in dry passages protected by an intact cap of sandstone. Gypsum sometimes is a crust on a cave wall, or it may form in cracks and grow until it wedges off chunks of limestone. Appropriately named gypsum snowballs may burst open from the pressure of growing crystals behind the snowball and form gypsum flowers. Other deposits look like lilies, plant stems, or cotton; yet others are as straight and thin as needles. Some gypsum formations are among the most delicate objects in nature and could have developed only in the very still environment of a cave.

Gypsum formations.
Overleaf: Columns formed of calcium carbonate ions give the Lion's Cage its name.

There are, of course, two climates at Mammoth Cave. Temperature under the ground fluctuates somewhat, usually staying close to 54° F, the annual average of the surface temperature. Temperature inside the cave does not change significantly because the mass of cave air is insulated from changes in outside temperatures. Annual humidity averages a high 87 percent in those passages most often visited. The 52,830 acres on the park's surface receive abundant rain. The surface climate is uncomfortably hot and humid in summer, mild in winter, and competition for heaven during the long spring and autumn.

Cave Critters

Mammoth Cave's lightless environment imposes severe tribulations on cave animals, molding them in strange forms that engross biologists and the public at large. Cave animals are grouped as troglodytes (cave dwellers), troglophiles (cave frequenters), and trogloxenes (cave visitors).

Troglodytes, about thirty species that include two species of blind cavefishes, blind crayfish, blind spiders and daddy-longlegs, cave snails, cave shrimp, and blind millipedes, have so fully adapted to underground life that their loss of eyes and color or of tolerance to temperature or moisture change makes living on the surface impossible.

Eight species of blind cave beetles live in Mammoth Cave. About .25 inch long, sand beetles are the blind cave dwellers that are seen most often. They scurry about, digging cave-cricket eggs out of the silt and searching for other tiny cave animals, including their own species, to eat.

In the late 1960s, biologists thought that Kentucky cave shrimp were extinct. But sightings in the late 1970s and a comprehensive inventory in the 1980s indicate that their population is well established in several cave systems. Previously, the search for the shrimp had been conducted in the wrong parts of the cave. Cave shrimp are translucent, eyeless, humpbacked, and about 1.25 inches long. They are relatively long-lived, with a lifespan of some ten to fifteen years, and reproduce throughout the year.

Less rare are blind Mammoth Cave crayfish. Although their eyes have degenerated, these delicately pale creatures still have a light sensor in their tails. Their sensory antennae are longer and more efficient than are those of their surface relatives. This does

Opposite: The little brown bat is one of nearly a dozen bat species found in the park.

Top: Blind cave shrimp. Above: Blind cavefish.

not seem to be an adaptation to the darkness of the cave because surface crayfish are nocturnal. Surface crayfish use their eyes only for identifying predators, which cave crayfish do not have. The improved antennae of cave crayfish seem to be a result of the scarcity of food, which requires efficiency to locate. Cave crayfish interpret water movement as coming from potential prey. Wiggling fingers at the edge of pools is one way to attract the pincered creatures.

Troglophiles, such as spiders, can live all their lives inside caves but also can survive in cool, dim, and dank places outside. Perhaps the most attractive troglophile is the cave salamander, which is orange with black spots. It is not blind and seldom travels far from the cave entrance. It eats almost anything that moves through the dim light near the entrance and even snaps up bits of rock and plant litter that get in the way as it lunges at animal food. Typical of all troglophiles, it is not strictly limited to caves.

Bats and cave crickets are trogloxenes that feed outside caves at night or live just within the dimly lit cave entrances. Bats and crickets are important to the cave ecosystem because they transport the sun's energy into the system in the form of dung, which they deposit on the cave floor. This guano is an important food source for the cave community. Water washes other food into the cave, and careless human beings drop pieces of nourishing wood, paper, and other detritus.

Life on the Surface

Legend maintains that Mammoth Cave's modern discovery occurred in 1797 when a hunter named Robert Houchins pursued a wounded bear into the Historic Entrance. Some folks claim, to the contrary, that the bear was chasing Houchins, but no one seems to know what finally became of the bear. It is certain that bears do not inhabit Mammoth Cave National Park today.

Many other species of wildlife typical of eastern forests do thrive on the surface in the national park, however. For almost 150 years, farmers cultivated the river bottoms, valleys, ridges, and even sinkholes around Mammoth Cave. Natural plant succession in the humid Kentucky climate has caused farms purchased for the park to return to woods, creating ideal living conditions for a number of wildlife species.

White-tailed deer thrive in second-growth forests and have reverted to their natural fearlessness toward people because deer hunting is not permitted within the national park. With natural predators extirpated and human predation forbidden, the deer population in the park was controlled at one time by live-trapping and relocating. Walking the woodland trails atop Mammoth Cave, visitors may observe wild turkeys, woodchucks, cottontail rabbits, chipmunks, and gray and fox squirrels. Beaver, muskrats, and raccoons—or at least signs of their activities—can be seen along the Green River. The river contains 107 species of fishes and the world's most varied population of fresh-water mussels. More than 200 bird species may be spotted at Mammoth Cave during the course of a year.

Gypsum flowers within Mammoth Cave possess a rare beauty. But the wildflowers on the surface are even more lovely, although less startling because they are so common. Hepatica, columbine, trout lily, and trillium decorate the forest floor. Serviceberry, redbud, flowering dogwood, and mountain laurel bloom above.

The upland woods at Mammoth Cave are dominated by various oak species, together with shagbark hickory, persimmon, sassafras, and yellow poplar—also called the tulip tree because of its striking blossoms. Mixed in with the deciduous trees are Virginia and loblolly pine and eastern redcedar. Along the Green River, sugar and red maples, sycamore, black gum, beech, birch, and willow are very striking in the autumn.

American elm in foggy twilight.

Underground

Few of the sinuous passages that meander through Mammoth Cave are developed for cave tours. Some of the mineral wonders deposited in the cave are too delicate to permit public access because no way exists to protect the fragile stone from curious fingers. Some of the unique cave creatures, blind or sighted, cannot survive repeated contact with hordes of visitors.

Exploration is limited to researchers with National Park Service permits. Permits are granted for recreational spelunking unaccompanied by National Park Service rangers. This activity is limited to well-mapped Ganter Cave within Mammoth Cave National Park, to which access is limited by a locked door at the entrance.

National Park Service tours are the only way to see most of the accessible parts of Mammoth Cave. Tours may be attended by as many as 100 people. All the tours involve at least moderate walking and step climbing. Rest rooms are available on some tours. Pets are not permitted underground, but a concessionaire provides shaded kennels for a fee near the hotel.

Frozen Niagara Tour. The Frozen Niagara Tour takes in many of the cave's most interesting travertine formations. Tripods are not allowed in the cave, so those wishing to photograph the travertine by available light should load their cameras with a high-speed film for incandescent light. Flash pictures likely will be disappointing because of the direction of the light and the large size of the formations.

Historic Tour. The Historic Tour leads past remnants of the War of 1812 mining operations and Indian artifacts. Until recent years it included a torch-throwing demonstration that continued a tradition established by early guides, but the torch-throwing was seen as incompatible with the natural surroundings. The saltpeter works are best shot with fast daylight film, although nothing but flash works very well with the fluorescent tubes that light the saltpeter pit.

Wild Cave Tour. The Wild Cave Tour, limited to fourteen people, entails 5 miles of hiking and crawling through unimproved passages. Photographers must depend on flash to light pictures of fellow spelunkers.

TRAILS OF MAMMOTH CAVE NATIONAL PARK

CAVE ISLAND NATURE TRAIL: Starts and ends at Historic Entrance to Mammoth Cave; 1-mile loop; 1 hour; woodland trail that offers clues to the existence of the cave below; stay on trail and watch for poisonous snakes, poison ivy, and ticks.

HERITAGE TRAIL: Starts and ends west of hotel at end of parking lot near motor lodge; 0.5 mile; .75 hour; a leisurely stroll, designed to accommodate visitors with disabilities, and handicapped parking is available; illuminated at night; cassette describing walk may be borrowed at Visitor Center; points of interest include a lovely overlook, large trees, and the Old Guide's Cemetery, where Stephen Bishop and some of the patients from the Mammoth Cave tuberculosis-treatment experiment are buried.

GREEN RIVER BLUFFS TRAIL: Starts at picnic area north of Historic Entrance; ends at Visitor Center; 1 mile one way; 1 hour; trail bends around a bluff above the Green River.

CEDAR SINK NATURE TRAIL: Starts at parking area off Kentucky 422 inside park; ends at Cedar Sink; .75 mile; .5 hour; leads to large sinkhole with disappearing stream.

SLOAN'S CROSSING POND TRAIL: Starts and ends at Sloan's Crossing parking area on U.S. 70; .5-mile loop around a small pond; .5 hour.

TURNHOLE BEND TRAIL: Starts and ends at Turnhole parking area on U.S. 70; .5-mile loop; .5 hour; trail leads along wooded bluffs overlooking Green River; additional .25-mile walk leads to banks of river.

BACKCOUNTRY TRAILS

All of the backcountry trails at Mammoth Cave lie north of the Green River; check with park headquarters for information and additional trails.

GOOD SPRINGS LOOP TRAIL: Starts and ends at Good Springs Church; 10-mile loop; 5–6 hours; trail passes through lowland areas of the Buffalo Creek drainage basin; diverse wildlife, exceptional autumn foliage and wildflower display.

FIRST CREEK TRAIL: Starts at Temple Hill Cemetery; ends at Jaggers Cemetery; 8 miles; 4–5 hours; good fishing for bass, panfish, and catfish in Nolin River; trail provides access to First Creek Lake; vistas from higher elevations on trail.

McCoy HOLLOW TRAIL: Starts at Temple Hill Cemetery; ends at junction with Good Springs Loop Trail; 8 miles; 6–7 hours; trail passes along bluffs above Green River, overlooks McCoy Hollow; exceptional viewing of autumn foliage from river bluffs.

Preceding overleaf: Chief City is the largest room in Mammoth Cave.

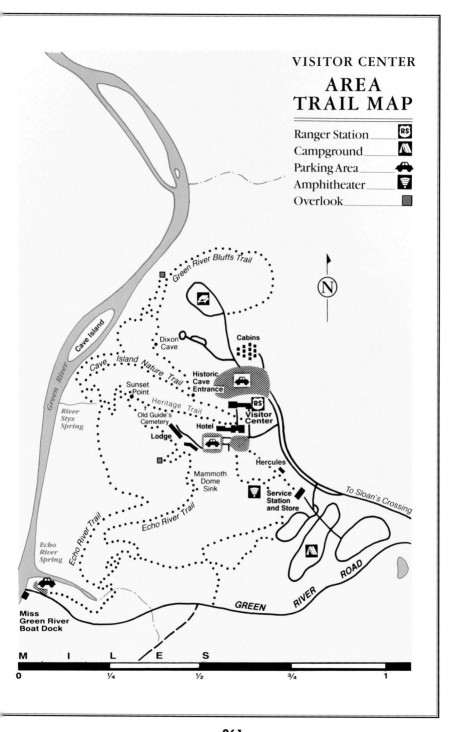

VISITOR CENTER
AREA TRAIL MAP

Ranger Station_____ RS
Campground_____
Parking Area_____
Amphitheater_____
Overlook_____

N

Green River Bluffs Trail

Cave Island

Dixon Cave

Cabins

Cave Island Nature Trail

Sunset Point

Historic Cave Entrance

Heritage Trail

RS
Visitor Center

Green River

River Styx Spring

Old Guide's Cemetery

Hotel

Lodge

Hercules

Mammoth Dome Sink

Service Station and Store

To Sloan's Crossing

Echo River Trail

Echo River Trail

Echo River Spring

GREEN RIVER ROAD

Miss Green River Boat Dock

M   I   L   E   S

0   ¼   ½   ¾   1

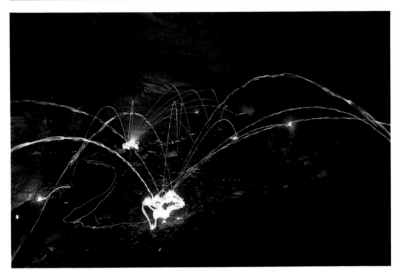

Torch-throwing demonstrations were conducted until about 1990.

Aboveground

Some 70 miles of hiking and horseback trails wind through woods to overlooks and springs on the park's surface. Dogs are permitted to travel all surface trails if they are kept leashed. Ticks and poison ivy abound off the trails, where poisonous rattlesnakes and copperheads also find suitable habitat.

Cave Island Nature Trail. The 1-mile Cave Island Nature Trail loops past hints of the cave lying beneath the surface. Dixon Cave, along this trail, was another site of saltpeter mining as early as 1800.

Echo River Trail. The 2-mile Echo River Trail, which loops to the Green River, leads past Echo River Spring, where Echo River emerges from the depths of Mammoth Cave. More interesting than spectacular, the spring is a quiet, green pool among the sycamores, with a flooded cave entrance visible when the water is clear.

Cedar Sink Trail. The sometimes steep and slippery .75-mile nature trail into Cedar Sink descends to the bottom of a collapsed cavern. At the bottom, an underground stream emerges into the open, flows for some distance in the sunlight, and then sinks back into blackness at the base of a cliff.

Turnhole Bend Trail. The Turnhole Bend Trail loops past three impressive sinks and offers overlooks of the Green River, with a .25-mile detour down to the river itself. Large loblolly pines in this area were planted by the Civilian Conservation Corps during the administration of President Franklin Roosevelt.

North of the Green River. The tilt of the plateau reduces the opportunities for ground water to form caves north of the Green River because underground water flows away from the surface outlet opened by the down-cutting of the river. The absence of caves makes this the lesser used section of the park. *Ugly Creek* got its name from flash flooding rather than from its normal waterless condition. *Goblin Knob* may have been named for the gobbling of wild turkeys. The *Big Woods* are dense and wild because limited timber cutting before the park was established left many old trees standing. A short, steep path from Temple Hill Cemetery drops to small *First Creek Lake.* This path is especially bright and colorful with wildflowers in early spring.

Paved roads through the park, mostly lined with dense forest, have a boulevardlike quality. Occasional turnoffs mark points of interest, such as an overlook of *Doyel Valley* or of *Sloan's Crossing Pond,* a likely place to spot wildlife attracted to the park's only significant body of water south of the Green River. This unique pond is the result of an effort by CCC dam builders, whose work was enlarged on by beavers reintroduced into the park.

An 8-mile cruise on the Green River aboard *Miss Green River II,* which seats 122 passengers, provides a different perspective of the park. Canoeists on the Green and Nolin rivers enjoy deep gorges bounded by precipitous sandstone and limestone cliffs visible through the dense woods that crowd the banks. Long stretches of these rivers are pooled to still water by a downstream dam. Upstream from the mouth of Echo River, the Green offers some 12 miles of flowing water to the eastern boundary of the park.

Overleaf: Mammoth Cave's fall foliage competes with the wonders of the cave itself.

SHENANDOAH NATIONAL PARK

View from the Big Run overlook on Skyline Drive.

SHENANDOAH NATIONAL PARK
ROUTE 4, BOX 348
LURAY, VIRGINIA 22835
TEL.: (703) 999-3500

HIGHLIGHTS: The Blue Ridge • Skyline Drive • Appalachian Trail • Big Meadows • The Limberlost • Dark Hollow Falls • Stony Man and Hawksbill Mountains • Camp Hoover • Overall Run and Lewis Run Falls • Old Rag Mountain • Big Run

ACCESS: From Washington, DC, take I-66. From points south take I-81.

HOURS: Open year-round, 24 hours daily. Skyline Drive may close temporarily in winter due to storms.

FEES: At entrance, for vehicles and persons on bicycles; for campgrounds.

PARKING: Ample parking at developed areas within park.

GAS, FOOD, LODGING: At Skyland and Big Meadows lodges; cottages at Lewis Mountain. Groceries, gas, and meals available at various locations along Skyline Drive.

VISITOR CENTER: Dickey Ridge Visitor Center and Byrd Visitor Center, open daily from spring through late fall. Centers offer exhibits, films, and sell publications.

MUSEUM: Displays at Visitor Centers.

GIFT SHOP: Concessionaire-operated shops along Skyline Drive.

PETS: Leashed pets permitted, but prohibited on designated trails.

PICNICKING: At Lewis and Loft mountains, Dickey Ridge, Elkwallow, the Pinnacles, Big Meadows, and South River.

HIKING: More than 500 miles of trails in park. Treat water.

BACKPACKING: Free, required permit available at park headquarters, Visitor Centers, and ranger stations. Trail shelters for day use only. 7 huts on Appalachian Trail available for long-distance hikers.

CAMPGROUNDS: At Big Meadows, Lewis Mountain, and Loft Mountain; check with park for dates open and reservations information. Camper and RV sites at all campgrounds. Water available; no trailer hookups. 14-day stay limit year-round. Group campsite available.

TOURS: Naturalist-guided hikes offered in summer. Self-guiding nature trails. Concessionaire-led horseback tours.

OTHER ACTIVITIES: Bicycling, horseback riding, cross-country skiing, fishing with Virginia state or park license.

FACILITIES FOR DISABLED: Park is widely accessible.

For additional information, see also Sites, Trails, and Trips on pages 291–309 and the maps on pages 270–271 and 295.

SHENANDOAH NATIONAL PARK IS DRAPED LIKE a long, narrow blanket over some 75 miles of the Blue Ridge mountains in northern Virginia. The blanket simile has become increasingly appropriate since the park was established in the 1930s, because the hardwood forest that constitutes the natural vegetation of the area has been allowed to reassert its dominance. Because the trees and shrubs are so dense, visibility is often limited to sights close at hand. But frequent openings at roadside overlooks and along trails provide opportunities to look eastward over the farmlands of Piedmont Virginia and westward into the valley of the Shenandoah River. The contrast between intimate short-range views into the forest and grand vistas of other mountains receding into the distance is one of the special pleasures of Shenandoah.

As years pass and land development increases, Shenandoah assumes more and more significance as a surviving remnant of the hardwood shield that once covered almost the entire northeastern United States. In the seventeenth century, a squirrel could have crossed eastern North America from the Mississippi River to the Atlantic Ocean without touching the ground. No longer is that possible, but a squirrel still can traverse the length of Shenandoah from tree to tree.

Skyline Drive extends the length of the park, always near the crest of the Blue Ridge, and affords the motorist a fine sampling of the area's scenic beauty. But the traveler on foot—strolling through a hemlock grove, climbing to a high peak, descending to a waterfall, or hiking along the 95 miles of the Appalachian Trail within the park—has a better chance to appreciate the essence of Shenandoah. The complex ecosystem of the hardwood forest can best be observed from within.

The Blue Ridge is deceptive. Even though it is old enough to have been flattened considerably by erosion, its peaks and ridges are often steep and rocky. Nonetheless, the Blue Ridge is for walkers rather than for rock climbers. Most of the park's 300 square miles have been walked over—by Native Americans, by settlers, and by park visitors. But that fact, too, is deceptive. Most walkers have followed trails. Anyone who steps off a trail may be standing on previously untrodden ground or on ground last crossed by a Native American stalking a deer or a pioneer woman gathering chestnuts. Such possibilities represent part of the mystique of the Blue Ridge forest.

Pages 272–273: Summer wildflowers in a mountain meadow above Shenandoah Valley.

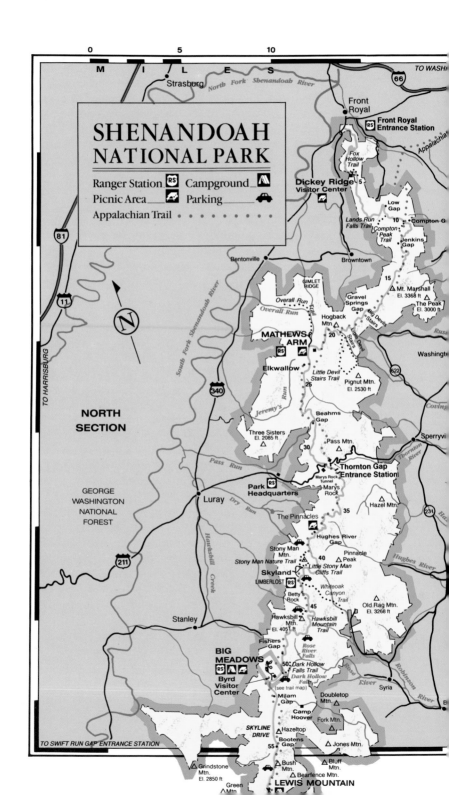

SHENANDOAH NATIONAL PARK

Ranger Station [RS] Campground [▲]
Picnic Area [🐷] Parking [🚗]
Appalachian Trail • • • • • •

MILES
0   5   10

Strasburg
North Fork Shenandoah River
TO WASH

Front Royal
TO WASH 66

[RS] Front Royal Entrance Station

Fox Hollow Trail

Dickey Ridge Visitor Center 5

Low Gap

Lands Run Falls Trail 10 Compton G
Compton Peak Trail
Jenkins Gap

Bentonville
Browntown

GIMLET RIDGE 15

Gravel Springs Gap △ Mt. Marshall El. 3368 ft
△ The Peak El. 3000 ft

Overall Run
Overall Run Trail
Hogback Mtn. 20

MATHEWS ARM [RS][🐷]

Elkwallow

Little Devil Stairs Trail 25 △ Pignut Mtn. El. 2530 ft

Big Devils Stairs
Little Devils Stairs

Washingto

622
Russ

Jeremy's Run

Three Sisters El. 2085 ft △

Beahms Gap

△ Pass Mtn. 30

Coving

Sperryvi

Thornton River

NORTH SECTION

Pass Run

Thornton Gap Entrance Station

GEORGE WASHINGTON NATIONAL FOREST

Luray

Dry Run

Park Headquarters [RS]

Marys Rock Tunnel
△ Marys Rock 35 △ Hazel Mtn.
231
Ru

The Pinnacles

Hughes River Gap

Hughes River

Stony Man Mtn. △
Stony Man Nature Trail

Pinnacle △ Peak 40

Little Stony Man Cliffs Trail

Skyland
LIMBERLOST [RS][🚗]

Betty's Rock

Whiteoak Canyon Trail

△ Old Rag Mtn. El. 3268 ft 45

Stanley

Hawksbill Mtn. △ El. 4051 ft
Hawksbill Mountain Trail

Fishers Gap

Rose River Falls

BIG MEADOWS [RS][▲][🚗]

Byrd Visitor Center

50 Dark Hollow Falls Trail
Dark Hollow Falls
(see trail map)

Milam Gap

Doubletop Mtn. △ Syria

Camp Hoover Fork Mtn. △

Robinson River

SKYLINE DRIVE
△ Hazeltop

Bootens Gap 55 △ Jones Mtn.

TO SWIFT RUN GAP ENTRANCE STATION

△ Grindstone Mtn. El. 2850 ft

△ Bush Mtn. △ Bluff Mtn.
△ Bearfence Mtn.

Green Mtn

LEWIS MOUNTAIN

81

11

TO HARRISBURG

340

211

Hawksbill Creek

N

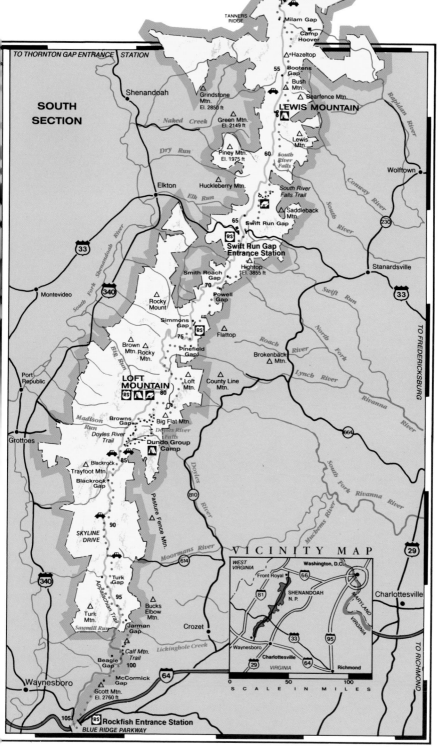

SOUTH
SECTION

TO THORNTON GAP ENTRANCE STATION

Shenandoah

TANNERS
RIDGE

Milam Gap

Camp
Hoover

Hazeltop

55 Bootens
Gap

Bush
Mtn.

Bearfence Mtn.

LEWIS MOUNTAIN

Grindstone
Mtn.
El. 2850 ft

Green Mtn.
El. 2149 ft

Lewis
Mtn.

60

Rapidan River

Wolftown

Conway River

Piney Mtn.
El. 1975 ft

South
River
Falls

Dry Run

Naked Creek

Elk Run

Huckleberry Mtn.

South River
Falls Trail

Saddleback
Mtn.

Elkton

65 Swift Run Gap

South River

230

RS Swift Run Gap
Entrance Station

Hightop
El. 3855 ft

Stanardsville

33

33

Smith Roach
Gap

70

Powell
Gap

TO FREDERICKSBURG

Montevideo

340

Rocky
Mount

Simmons
Gap

75

RS Flattop

Swift Run

North Fork

Roach River

Pinefield
Gap

Brokenback
Mtn.

Lynch River

Port
Republic

South Fork Shenandoah River

Big Run

LOFT
MOUNTAIN

RS

80

Loft
Mtn.

County Line
Mtn.

Rivanna River

664

Brown
Mtn.

Rocky
Mtn.

Madison Run

Browns
Gap

Big Flat Mtn.

Doyles River
Falls

Doyles River
Trail

Dundo Group
Camp

Grottoes

Blackrock

Trayfoot Mtn.

85

810

Blackrock
Gap

Pasture Fence Mtn.

Doyles River

South Fork Rivanna River

90

SKYLINE
DRIVE

614

Moormans River

Muckems River

29

VICINITY MAP

340

Turk
Gap

95

Bucks
Elbow
Mtn.

Appalachian Trail

Turk
Mtn.

Sawmill Run

Jarman
Gap

Crozet

Lickinghole Creek

WEST
VIRGINIA

81

Front Royal

Washington, D.C.

66

SHENANDOAH
N.P.

MARYLAND

Charlottesville

Calf Mtn.
Trail

Beagle
Gap

100

McCormick
Gap

64

33

95

VIRGINIA

Waynesboro

Scott Mtn.
El. 2760 ft

64

Waynesboro

Charlottesville

29

VIRGINIA

64

Richmond

TO RICHMOND

105 RS Rockfish Entrance Station
BLUE RIDGE PARKWAY

0   50   100
S C A L E   I N   M I L E S

Daughter of the Stars

The recorded history of the Blue Ridge began in 1669. Known from afar for more than half a century, it took its name from the almost perpetual blue haze of humid air that hangs over the forest. But early settlers were too occupied with homesteading and farming the river bottoms of Tidewater Virginia to be more than curious about the western mountains and whatever might lie beyond them.

Then, sixty-two years after Jamestown was founded in 1607, John Lederer, a visitor to the New World, hired three Native American guides and set out to explore the land lying to the west. According to his journal, Lederer crested the ridge nine days later and climbed a high peak (perhaps Hightop, perhaps Hawksbill—his description fits either one). He had half-expected to see the Pacific Ocean on the other side. Instead, he saw only a broad valley and row after row of mountains. Lederer made three more trips into the easternmost Appalachian Mountains before returning to his native Germany, but nothing in his accounts stimulated the colonists to move westward. Virginians had no use for mountains that could not be farmed or for remote valleys from which movement of goods to European markets would be difficult.

In 1716, Governor Alexander Spotswood of Virginia led a group of gentlemen, supported by servants and pack animals laden with amenities, westward into the mountains. They reached the top of the ridge either at Milam Gap, near Big Meadows, or at Swift Run Gap. The present highway through Swift Run Gap, U.S. 33, is known as the Spotswood Trail, and a monument to the expedition stands beside the highway at the crest of the Blue Ridge. The gentlemen are said to have marveled at the "Great Valley" of the "Euphrates River." Neither name remained in use for long; they soon were replaced by the Shenandoah Valley and the Shenandoah River. (*Shenandoah*, a Native American name, reputedly means "Daughter of the Stars.") Because of the gentlemen's favorable impression of the area and because of the growing population pressure that had caused Spotswood to organize the trip, several small settlements were established in the Shenandoah Valley between 1725 and 1730.

Archeological evidence indicates that two small tribes of Siouan stock, the Monacans and the Manahoacs, had had agrarian communities along the rivers east of the Blue Ridge. By the early eighteenth century, however, both groups had been absorbed or annihilated by the larger tribes that surrounded them.

The first Native Americans were food gatherers who lived seasonally on the Blue Ridge. Early European explorers found numerous clearings, indicating that hunting parties of a later period had used circle fires to confine and kill game. The burning also produced ashes that reduced the acidity of the forest soil and made it suitable for berry bushes. The early peoples are thought to have gathered chestnuts, hickory nuts, and other foods and medicinal plants on the mountains. The Stone Age implements of these visitors often were fashioned from the relatively hard rock of the Blue Ridge.

The Mountain People

The overall effect of the indigenous Americans on the land was negligible. But the European settlers had superior tools, which continued to improve. After a century of slow growth, both the European population and the amount of land under cultivation increased rapidly. The forest would never again be the same.

The landowners of the Piedmont and Blue Ridge were very different from the plantation owners of the Tidewater. They carved small farms out of the wild forest. Some, who preferred to harvest the natural bounty of the land, built homes near the mountains, clearing only enough land for gardens and small pastures. Others stayed near the rivers on either side of the ridge.

Clearings on the ridge sometimes were enlarged to provide summer pastures for cattle. Trees were killed by removing a strip of bark all around the trunk close to the ground. The dead trees were leafless the following year, and sunlight could reach the ground and promote the growth of grass. The wood of the dead trees cured as it stood, without taking up much space, and could be removed as needed. Much of the wood for homes, barns, wagons, furniture, and fences was obtained from such tree "deadenings" and from other logging of the gentler mountain slopes.

During the Civil War, the Shenandoah Valley became known as the breadbasket of the Confederacy. Several roads were built across the Blue Ridge to transport the goods of the valley to Piedmont and Tidewater markets. Some of them still exist as park fire roads. The two that cross Browns Gap and Fishers Gap were used by Stonewall Jackson during his successful Valley Campaign and during the maneuvering of reinforcements prior to the Battle of Fredericksburg. The only other military action within present-day park boundaries occurred at Browns Gap, where General Jubal Early skirmished with General Philip Sheridan.

By the time the Shenandoah Valley and the Blue Ridge had recovered from the impoverishment of the Civil War and

Reconstruction, a great deal of agricultural land had been opened farther west, and an expanded railroad system provided efficient means of transporting western goods to eastern markets. Most available timber in western Virginia had been harvested. Blue Ridge mines (copper, iron, and manganese), never very promising, could not compete with less expensive and more abundant ore supplies from western mines. The entire Shenandoah area—Piedmont, Blue Ridge, and Shenandoah Valley—became for a while a stable island bypassed in the westward surge.

By the last decades of the nineteenth century, however, several additional factors had begun to work against the economic health of the region. The mountain soil was thin, and years of clearing and logging had allowed much of it to wash away. The custom had long been to abandon gardens as their soil wore out and to clear new garden plots farther up the mountain. Similarly, successive generations usually homesteaded land bordering that of their parents. Eventually, they could find no more room down the mountain, so they had to move up—deeper into the hollows and higher on the fragile slopes. In ecological terms, the settlers exceeded the carrying capacity of the Blue Ridge.

Then, early in the twentieth century, a blight caused by a fungus killed the American chestnut. At one time, perhaps every fourth tree on the Blue Ridge was a chestnut, yet within three decades they all were gone. They were replaced in the forest by other trees, none of which could fill the economic niche occupied by the chestnut. It had provided a straight-grained hardwood that could be worked easily, was not too heavy, and contained enough tannic acid to resist rotting. Its bark had been sold as a source of the common tanning agent of the area. Its nuts had been marketed in the lowlands, too. After the chestnut disappeared, the economic situation of the mountain people worsened.

Establishment of the Park

Although the economic potential of the Blue Ridge diminished, its wild seclusion and alluring mystery attracted people who appreciated the land's natural beauty, even through the scars of exploitation. Resorts were constructed to provide vacationers a relaxing change from city life. The resorts opened some economic opportunities for the local residents and alerted Virginians to the econom-

Opening of the central section of Skyline Drive, from Thornton Gap to Swift Run Gap, in 1934.

ic potential of tourism. As a result, once the idea of establishing national parks in the East began to receive serious consideration, Virginians and former visitors to western Virginia promoted the Blue Ridge as an appropriate site.

Ultimately, two parks were to be established, one in the Great Smokies and one in Virginia. George Freeman Pollock, owner of the Skyland resort and with management control of some 5,000 acres of the surrounding mountaintop, successfully promoted the northern Blue Ridge site.

After Congress, in 1926, designated the Blue Ridge as the site of a park, the principal remaining obstacle was money. The Virginia site consisted of private land, and no precedent existed for the appropriation of federal funds to buy such land from its owners. But more than 24,000 Virginians contributed a total of $1.3 million to the project, and the Virginia legislature allocated $1 million more and arranged for acquisition of the land through procedures of eminent domain.

A decade was spent tracing and clearing titles, establishing boundaries, and litigating. When the park was established, more than 2,000 people were living within its boundaries. All were given the opportunity to relocate in one of the seven new communities that were established to receive them. Although paid and moved to more comfortable houses on more productive land, many mountain people resented having to leave the ridge. For one thing, the Depression-era prices paid to them were far below what their properties had been worth a few years earlier. Several decades later, one could still hear a visitor from a nearby town ask a park employee, "Why did you make my granddaddy move off the mountain?"

In December 1935, the Commonwealth of Virginia conveyed 176,429 acres of the Blue Ridge to the federal government, and Shenandoah National Park was established. On July 3, 1936, President Franklin Roosevelt dedicated the park in a ceremony at Big Meadows. The park now contains 195,363 acres.

The construction of Skyline Drive had begun in 1931, and the central section, between Swift Run Gap and Thornton Gap, was opened in 1934. In 1933, workers of the Civilian Conservation Corps began to serve in the proposed park, reducing the fire hazard, controlling erosion, and landscaping the 100-foot-wide right of way for the drive. One thousand strong by 1934, they also repaired and constructed trails and built shelters, picnic areas, and accommodations. The CCC worked in the park until the outbreak of World War II.

Preceding overleaf: Looking north at sunrise from Stony Man overlook, elevation 3,000 feet.

Skyline Drive was completed in 1939, and many facilities for visitors have since been added. But the most significant development of the ensuing decades has been the self-restoration of the forest—the gradual, natural obliteration of holdover signs of the area's former use and misuse. Shenandoah is not yet the Blue Ridge of precolonial days, but year by year, the likeness grows.

Erosion of volcanic flow has reexposed Old Rag Mountain's billion-year-old granite summit.

GEOLOGY

The Blue Ridge lies on the southeastern edge of the 300-mile-wide band of ridges forming the Appalachian Mountains, which extend from Alabama to Newfoundland. The Appalachians arose over a period of 50 million years, beginning 300 million years ago.

It is generally accepted that the crumpling of terrain that produced the many parallel ridges and valleys of the Appalachians was caused by a collision between two of the gigantic plates that compose the earth's crust. Although these plates move very slowly—only inches a year—they are so massive that the force with which they meet is powerful enough to fold vast beds of solid rock.

Granite and Basalt

Before the beginning of the long series of events known as the Appalachian Orogeny, much geologic activity had taken place at the site of the present Blue Ridge. More than 1 billion years ago, granitic rock completed its slow process of crystallization and solidification many miles beneath this part of the earth's surface. During the next 500 million years, many thousands of feet of overlying rock eroded, exposing the granite as rolling hills and stream-cut valleys.

About 750 million years ago, the granite split, creating miles-long fissures that overflowed with basaltic lava. The fissuring and volcanic outpourings continued at long intervals for centuries. The gravelly floors of the valleys were covered first. Successive eruptions filled the valleys and eventually covered even the granite hills. At Big Meadows can be seen evidence of twelve distinct flows, their thickness exceeding 1,800 feet. Erosion has removed the upper layers; the actual number of flows and the original thickness of the lava beds may have been much greater. When the eruptions stopped, the landscape was a flat, featureless plain of basalt.

The entire deposit of basalt has been named the Catoctin Formation. The original rock was metamorphosed into greenstone, which currently covers most of the central section of Shenandoah. The greenstone, although chemically different, retains many physical characteristics of the original basalt. It is fine grained and displays the columnar jointing typical of surface-cooled lava. Greenstone showing these characteristics may be seen at several places in the park, including Franklin Cliffs, Crescent Rock, and Little Devil Stairs, as well as along the Whiteoak Canyon Trail in the Limberlost. Greenstone weathers to shades of gray, but broken surfaces reveal the gray-green coloration from which it derives its name.

The cracks through which the lava reached the surface were left plugged with lava when each flow ceased; these plugs cooled into dikes of basalt that also metamorphosed into greenstone. An example of a fissure in granite now plugged with greenstone can be seen at the northern end of Marys Rock Tunnel. Although quite hard, greenstone is less durable than granite and erodes faster. A section of the Ridge Trail to the summit of Old Rag Mountain passes along the top of a greenstone dike that has worn considerably lower than the surrounding granite, through which it was squeezed millions of years ago. The trail resembles a corridor with granite walls and a greenstone floor.

Opposite: Six waterfalls add sparkle to the Whiteoak Canyon Trail.

At the time of the Catoctin eruptions, North America, Europe, Africa, and South America were probably joined as one huge continent. About 600 million years ago, the supercontinent split into two continents that slowly drifted apart. Shallow seas spread across much of what is now eastern North America as the crust topped by the Catoctin Formation slowly subsided. Most of the area where the Appalachian Mountains now stand was sea bottom for the next 300 million years. During that time, ocean-floor sediment collected and compacted into more than 30,000 feet of sedimentary rock.

About 300 million years ago, crustal movements reversed themselves. The parts of the divided supercontinent began to move back toward each other, and the ocean floor was reelevated and then compressed and folded into mountains. The Appalachians and the Blue Ridge appeared.

The mountains may once have been as high as the Rocky Mountains or the Sierra Nevada—or they may never have been much higher than they are today. If the rate of general uplift in the area during the period of compressive folding was almost matched by the rate of erosion, the Appalachians at their zenith may have been no more than 1,000 feet or so higher than they are now. But if the rate of uplift for perhaps 1 million years of that period was much greater than the rate of erosion, the range may have been very impressive indeed. In any case, between 300 million years ago and today some 30,000 feet of sedimentary rock and an unknown depth of metamorphosed basalt have been worn away from the crest of the Blue Ridge.

Limestone, formed under pressure out of algal mats and the shells of sea animals, erodes somewhat faster than sedimentary shale and sandstone and much faster than metamorphic greenstone and quartzite. Thus the valleys of the Blue Ridge usually are cut in limestone, shale, and sandstone formations, and the ridges usually are capped by quartzite or greenstone. Several high points in the central section of the park, however, do not have such caps. These are reexposed granite hills of the landscape antedating the lava flows. The lava covered them relatively thinly and has worn away, along with whatever sedimentary rock formed from oceanic debris. Old Rag Mountain, Hazel Mountain, Robertson Mountain, and Doubletop are composed of this 1-billion-year-old granite. Marys Rock Tunnel, along the Skyline Drive, is also cut through granitic rock.

Today, the only geologic activity in Shenandoah is the slow but inexorable leveling of the land by erosion. Deposition and uplift no longer play an active part in the drama of the Blue Ridge; the surviving rock serves merely as backdrop and underpinning for the kinetic life of the forest.

Distinctive Habitats

The deciduous forest is an ecosystem of great diversity because the climatic conditions suitable for temperate-zone broadleaf trees are also suitable for many other life forms. The diversity of the deciduous forest at Shenandoah is even greater because the mountains comprise a variety of elevations, exposures, and soil conditions. The Blue Ridge follows a sinuous course along its northeast–southwest orientation. Its western side is generally steeper than its eastern side. The park thus contains steep-sided hollows that may face in any direction and long, gentle slopes that may have either a northern or a southern exposure.

Shenandoah hosts hemlock groves, gray birches, and balsam firs normally found much farther north. At the same time, its well drained, south-facing slopes support expanses of the pine–oak climax forest usually seen farther south. In each distinct habitat, the shrubs, wildflowers, and birds are also distinctive. Among the

Frost crystals from a winter fog cover vegetation in a Hawksbill Mountain clearing.

hemlocks, visitors may find mapleleaf viburnum, Canada mayflower, veery, and various warblers. In the pine–oak forest, they may find azaleas, dwarf iris, wood anemone, scarlet tanager, and rose-breasted grosbeak.

Most Shenandoah mammals may be seen at one time or another anywhere in the park, but they, too, have their favorite habitats. Gray squirrels favor oaks and hickories; red squirrels linger around clearings and roadsides, where the seeds of herbaceous plants are more abundant. Red foxes inhabit the lower elevations, in proximity to the farmlands they prefer; the fox of the forest and mountains is the gray fox. Raccoons stay near water; bobcats frequent rocky outcroppings. Black bears range throughout the park but spend most of their time in secluded hollows. White-tailed deer also can be seen anywhere, but they prefer fringe areas where forest succession provides an abundance of shrubs for browsing.

The Four Seasons

The Blue Ridge has four distinct seasons of about equal length, and each brings dramatic changes. The gray and white of winter, the pastels of spring, the pervading green of summer, and the flamboyant reds and yellows of autumn segue gradually into one another and yet afford startling contrasts.

The dogtooth violet's name refers to the shape of its white, underground bulb.

Winter. Shenandoah's winters are a time of trial and testing for the forest life and of challenge to people. Visitors unprepared for cold may find winter here even a time of danger. Three feet or more of snow can be expected each year, and temperatures below 0° F are not unusual.

The most outstanding aspect of Shenandoah in winter is the quiet. Although more than 200 bird species have been sighted in the park and although more than 100 of them nest here, only about 25 species stay all year. They are mostly silent during winter—no territorial challenges or mating songs, only occasional calls. The bears sleep, and the ground hogs and chipmunks hibernate. Deer, in the furry gray coats that replace their reddish tan summer hair, move languidly through the snow or over frozen or muddy ground as they browse twigs and buds. The rustle of leaves, pervasive at other seasons, cannot be heard: the trees are bare. The streams are smaller and less noisy because their water supply is mostly locked in frozen ground. Snow falls far more quietly than does rain. Even the few human visitors seem less exuberant than they would be in summer.

Another noticeable feature of winter is that the views are longer through the bare trees. And because the leaves are gone and no longer transpiring moisture, the air is drier and clearer. Visitors can see farther from high places.

The red pigments of a sugar maple in autumn are suppressed during spring and summer.

Spring. The Blue Ridge spring advances not only with the days, but also with the elevation. It can be seen moving by degrees up the mountainsides. Any particular stage in the progress of spring reaches Skyline Drive two weeks after it occurs in the Shenandoah Valley or in the Piedmont, and it reaches the summits of Hawksbill and Stony Man mountains a week after that.

The developing leaves are the principal source of the pastels of the spring forest. Even as they burst from the bud scales that protected them through the cold weather, the leaves of each tree and shrub already contain the carotenoids—red, orange, or yellow pigments—characteristic of the species. Only gradually do these colors become masked by chlorophyll as the leaves grow to full size. The new leaves of spring display in subdued tones the same colors that show so brilliantly in the autumn.

Even though something is in bloom in Shenandoah from the first hepatica in February or March to the witch hazel in September or October, spring is the season during which wildflowers are most noticed. Perhaps the forest is more open, and visitors can see more; perhaps people are emotionally more attuned at springtime to signs of returning life; perhaps more plants really do bloom in the spring. Whatever the reason, new leaves and flowers are the stars of the spring production.

Spring unquestionably is the time when most flowering trees and shrubs bloom. Long before leaves are fully grown, the pink azalea is in flower, providing splashes of vivid color against an otherwise winterlike background. Hawthorn, chokecherry, redbud, and dogwood bloom in April and May. Although the mountain laurel blooms through late June, it, too, begins flowering in spring.

The waterfalls reach their most dramatic intensity in spring, as well. The snow melts, the ground thaws, and warm rains fall. Small mountain watercourses are extended to their limits in carrying off the excess water. Although trails are often muddy and slippery, traveling them to the waterfalls is worth the effort.

Because the Blue Ridge is steep on its western side, most of the streams on that side drain smaller areas and are therefore smaller than those that flow toward the east. Because the area of greatest steepness is just under the crest of the ridge, where streams do not have a chance to develop, few waterfalls can be found on the western side. Two of them, however—Overall Run Falls and Lewis Run Falls—are among the highest in the park. No Shenandoah waterfall is as high as 100 feet, and most consist of a series of falls or are cascades down angled slopes. Nonetheless, in the intimacy of the Blue Ridge forest, they provide dramatic and stimulating accents.

In spring, the rate of change seems startling. Black bears are moving about again; buck deer are growing new antlers; migratory birds have returned and fill the air with their songs; spring peepers trill from small puddles of melted snow; woodcocks perform their courtship flights; gray foxes bark to their mates. Shenandoah prepares for another summer of invigorating growth.

Summer. Animal activity seems to slow during the summer because it consists mostly of the growing and rearing of new generations. Most of that process is hidden from human eyes by the dense greenery. But summer is the season when the full diversity of the forest can best be observed. Because trees with leaves and fruit display their differences more clearly than do trees with bare branches, the presence in the ecosystem of more than 100 species can best be appreciated in summer. The full community of animal life, from monarch butterflies and red-backed salamanders to towhees, ravens, deer, and bears, is present—each species in its preferred habitat and following its own survival program.

At such a time, the curious visitor can collect fascinating information by observation.

—The spiral web of the garden spider is spun counterclockwise from the center outward.

At birth, white-tailed deer fawns weigh 4 1/2 to 5 1/2 pounds.

—The towhee makes so much noise as it seeks grubs among dead leaves because both its feet scratch backward at the same time.

—The favorite plant of the monarch butterfly (the orange and black butterfly that migrates as the birds do) is milkweed.

—Perhaps because the crest of the Blue Ridge has little in the way of streams or standing water, it seems to serve as a divide between two subspecies of frogs. The sleek, spotted one on the east side is the southern leopard frog, *Rana pipiens sphenocephala*; the similar one on the west side is the northern leopard frog, *Rana pipiens pipiens*.

—The large black bird that performs tumbling aerobatics in the updraft above the western slope is the common raven. Shenandoah is one of the places in the eastern United States where the raven is increasing its range.

—The giant puffball, a fungus that is all white and varies between the size of a fist and the size of a human head, is delicious sliced and sautéed in butter. It has the texture of pound cake and a slight flavor of anise.

Autumn. The days of summer slip past; the forest grows and regenerates; nesting birds rear their broods; young mammals outgrow dependence on their parents; 1 million or so visitors accumulate miles on the trails and hours in the woods. And then it is autumn.

Deciduous trees and shrubs put on a good show while preparing for winter. In their hundreds of thousands, they present a spectacular sight as they change. Because the first step toward winterizing is the breaking down and absorbing of chlorophyll, the result is the unmasking of the nongreen pigments that the leaves have contained all along. For a few weeks, centered usually on the middle of October, the Blue Ridge is a rolling swath of red, orange, and yellow. Although the process of chlorophyll breakdown is triggered primarily by the shortening of the days, weather affects the intensity of the carotenoid display. The best shows occur when a wet September is followed by a clear, cool October. Color peaks a couple of weeks after the black-locust leaves turn yellow and the barn swallows leave for South America. Then it fades slowly, and the leaves turn brown and drop off to add another layer of duff to the forest compost. Shenandoah relaxes for the start of a new cycle.

Shenandoah contains more than 500 miles of trails in an interlocking network that allows almost infinite variation. Some are moderately difficult—that is, they are for hikers, not walkers or strollers. Many are shorter, almost level trails; several are self-guiding. Most trail heads are situated along Skyline Drive, but many trails lead to the base of the Blue Ridge on one side or the other. Trails are well marked and well maintained, but a hiker can get lost by taking a wrong turn at an intersection.

Skyline Drive

Skyline Drive is a paved, winding, two-lane, 35-mile-per-hour scenic roadway that covers the 70-mile length of the park in 105 miles. Except for U.S. 211, which crosses the Blue Ridge at Thornton Gap, and U.S. 33, which crosses it at Swift Run Gap, Skyline Drive is the only public roadway in Shenandoah. It can be entered at either of those two highway intersections or from U.S. 340 near Front Royal or from interstate 64 at Rockfish Gap, near Waynesboro. Skyline Drive connects directly with the Blue Ridge Parkway at its southern end.

All visitor facilities and park entrances are situated along the drive. Scattered along its length are more than fifty scenic overlooks and some thirty trail-head parking areas. Skyline Drive is the outstanding constructed feature of the park, and for many visitors, it is the park. During the early years of Shenandoah, it was not unusual to meet people familiar with Skyline Drive but ignorant of the location of Shenandoah National Park.

Skyland and the Limberlost

The Skyland resort was established in the 1890s by George Freeman Pollock, who later was instrumental in having the Blue Ridge selected as a national-park site. The resort is now a concession-operated visitor facility that offers dining and overnight accommodations. Little remains of the original structures.

One of the nearby trails is an easy walk to and through a grove of very old hemlock trees, the Limberlost. Legend has it that the trees were saved from the loggers by Pollock, who, as they were scheduled to be cut, bought them from the mountaineers for $10 apiece.

Overleaf: The slight variations found in Shenandoah's different types of deciduous forests support diverse life forms.

Trails of Shenandoah National Park

Skyline Drive runs the full 70-mile length of the park in 105 miles; mileages given are measured from the Front Royal Entrance Station.

Fox Hollow Trail: Mile 4.6 Starts and ends at trail head across from Dickey Ridge Visitor Center; 1.3 miles round trip; 1 hour; self-guiding trail leaflet on sale at Visitor Center; Fox Hollow holds some of the secrets of the mountain families that once lived in this area.

Lands Run Falls Trail: Mile 9.2. Starts at trail head off Skyline Drive; ends at Lands Run Falls; 1.3 miles round trip; 1.5 hours; short walk down a fire road to a small series of cascades that are especially lovely in spring and summer; caution is required around falls, because hillside is steep and slippery.

Compton Peak Trail: Mile 10.4. Starts at Appalachian Trail on Skyline Drive; ends at Compton Peak; 2.4 miles round trip; 2.75 hours; use Appalachian Trail for short distance to trail head; rocky and steep in places; excellent for geology students.

Little Devil Stairs Trail: Mile 19.4. Starts and ends at trail head off Skyline Drive; 7.7-mile loop; 6–7 hours; take Keyser Run Road for 1 mile to a four-way intersection; from there, turn left onto Little Devil Stairs Trail, which leads down into a beautiful canyon for about 2 miles; turn right, upward on fire road, to starting point; return route climbs steeply.

Overall Run Falls Trail: Mile 22.2. Starts at Mathews Arm; ends at largest falls in park; 3.8 miles round trip; 3.75 hours; from the Mathews Arm Amphitheatre parking area, follow the Traces Nature Trail to the trail junction; turn right, then continue to next left turn, following markers to the Big Blue Overall Run; continue to falls; .5-mile steep descent to falls.

Little Stony Man Cliffs Trail: Mile 39.1. Starts at trail head on main road; ends at Little Stony Man Cliffs; .9 mile round trip; 1 hour; short hike to sheer cliffs and valley viewpoint; take Appalachian Trail from parking area .3 mile south of Stony Man overlook; turn onto Stony Man Trail; trail climbs steadily; rewarding view.

Stony Man Nature Trail: Mile 41.7. Starts and ends at parking area off north entrance road into Skyland Lodge; 1.6-mile loop; 1.5 hours; panorama of mountains fully revealed from viewpoints at summit.

Whiteoak Canyon Trail: Mile 42.6. Starts at parking area off Skyline Drive; ends at horse trail junction; 4.6 miles round trip; 4.5 hours; leads through section of hemlock forest; descends more than 1,000 feet to an 86-foot waterfall, first of six falls along canyon trail.

Hawksbill Mountain Trail: *Mile 45.6.* Starts at Hawksbill Gap parking area; ends at summit of Hawksbill Mountain; 1.7 miles round trip; 2 hours; short, steep hike to top of mountain for excellent views of Shenandoah Valley, the Blue Ridge, and the Appalachian ranges.

DARK HOLLOW FALLS TRAIL: *Mile 50.7.* Starts at Dark Hollow Falls parking area off Skyline Drive; ends at Dark Hollow Falls; 1.5 miles round trip; 1.5 hours; descends 440 feet, along excellent example of stream habitat, to falls; one of closest falls to main road; heavily used.

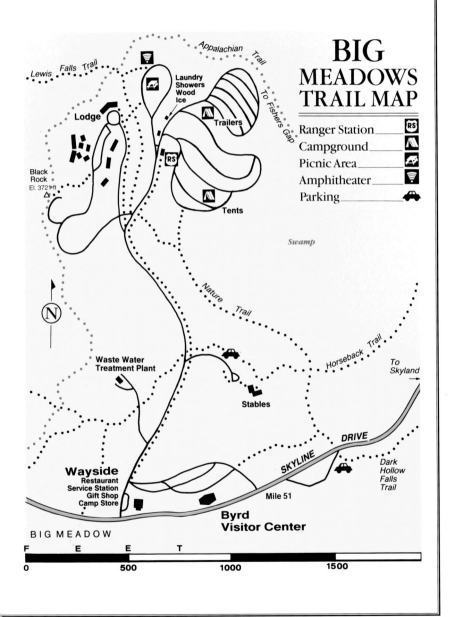

BIG MEADOWS TRAIL MAP

Ranger Station _____ **RS**
Campground _____ ⛺
Picnic Area _____ 🏞
Amphitheater _____ 📢
Parking _____ 🚗

295
SHENANDOAH

Big Meadows

Archeological evidence shows that Big Meadows was cleared in precolonial times, probably originally by fire, either natural or deliberately set. Arrowheads have been unearthed in the area, suggesting that it was used frequently by Native American hunters. Early settlers kept it open as a summer pasture for cattle. Today, by mowing and controlled burning, the National Park Service keeps it from reverting to forest. Big Meadows was the site of one of the CCC camps of the 1930s; the park dedication ceremony took place here in 1936.

Big Meadows is now a visitor-service area equipped with lodging and dining facilities, a campground, a picnic area, riding stables, a wayside shop, and the Byrd Visitor Center.

The several short trails at Big Meadows include the self-guiding *Story of the Forest Nature Trail*. The 300-acre mowed area has no trails, but visitors may wander at will.

Camp Hoover

While in office, President Herbert Hoover bought land and built a retreat at the eastern foot of the Blue Ridge where two mountain streams, Laurel Prong and Mill Prong, join to form the Rapidan River. It served Hoover much as Camp David in Maryland has served more recent presidents; he could escape the heat and formality of Washington and hold uninterrupted discussions with government officials and foreign dignitaries.

After Hoover left office, his Rapidan Camp was used by Boy Scouts for several years and renamed Camp Hoover. Still later, when maintenance became too expensive for the scouting organization, the camp and the surrounding Hoover land were deeded to the National Park Service. The terms of the transfer stipulated that the facility be available for use by government officials, but otherwise it was to be at the disposal of the park.

The Appalachian Trail

The Appalachian Trail is the longest continuous foot trail in North America, extending through the Appalachian Mountains from Springer Mountain in Georgia to Mount Katahdin in Maine. Ninety-five miles of the A.T., roughly paralleling Skyline Drive, are in Shenandoah National Park.

The trail is well graded, rarely becoming rough or steep despite

Opposite: Skyline Drive runs the full 70-mile length of the park in 105 miles.

going up and down as it follows the rolling terrain of the Blue Ridge. It is lowest, about 1,300 feet, at its northern end and is highest, about 3,300 feet, as it crosses The Pinnacle.

Trails to High Places

Among the many walking routes in Shenandoah are several that lead to the higher peaks of the park.

Marys Rock. The summit of Marys Rock, at 3,514 feet, is reached from the Panorama complex at Thornton Gap, at 31.6 miles on Skyline Drive, by way of the *Appalachian Trail* southbound and a .1-mile spur branching off to the right. Total round-trip distance is 3.7 miles, and the total climb is 1,210 feet. The summit is one of four places in Shenandoah that allow an unobstructed 360-degree view.

Marys Rock also can be reached by way of the *Meadow Spring Trail*, from the parking area at 33.5 miles. After .7 mile, the trail intersects the A.T.; hikers must turn right (northbound) on the A.T. to reach the spur trail to the summit. Total round-trip distance is 2.9 miles, and the climb is 830 feet.

Old Rag Mountain. Old Rag Mountain, an ancient granite hill, is separate from the Blue Ridge. The two routes to its summit begin at the eastern park boundary and are reached by way of obscure secondary roads that lie outside the park. One route is the *Ridge Trail*, which starts near the small settlement of Nethers in Weakley Hollow. The other is the *Saddle Trail*, up from the head of Berry Hollow. The beginning of the Saddle Trail also can be reached on foot from Skyline Drive at 43 miles via the Old Rag Fire Road.

The Ridge Trail is a 5.6-mile round trip with a climb of 2,380 feet. It can be made into a 7.2-mile circuit hike by returning from the top on the Saddle Trail and the *Weakley Hollow Fire Road.* The Saddle Trail is a 5.4-mile round trip with a climb of 1,760 feet. The route that starts from the drive is a 14.4-mile round trip that requires a climb of 1,510 feet up Old Rag from the low point on the saddle and, on the return, a climb back to the drive of 1,350 feet, for a total of 2,860 feet.

Stony Man Mountain. At 4,011 feet, Stony Man Mountain is the second highest peak in Shenandoah. It can be reached by way of a self-guiding nature trail from the Skyland complex, at 41.7 miles.

Hawksbill Mountain. Hawksbill Mountain is 4,049 feet high, the highest peak in Shenandoah. Its summit can be reached by three routes, two from Hawksbill Gap, at 45.6 miles, and one from Upper Hawksbill parking area, at 46.7 miles. The shortest way is 1.7 miles and 690 feet directly up from the Hawksbill Gap parking area. The second route from this parking area is a circuit hike leading to the crest via a 1.1-mile southward trek on the *Appalachian Trail,* followed by a left turn onto a side trail that winds upward to the summit. Hikers return to the parking area on the direct trail of the first route.

The third route up Hawksbill is a 2.1-mile round trip that climbs 520 feet. The trail is well graded and fairly easy. The views from the top of Hawksbill are worth the effort required on any of the routes.

Bearfence Mountain. Starting at 56.4 miles, the Bearfence Mountain Trail is one of the shortest of the park's "up" trails. Over a distance of .8 mile, hikers must climb only about 275 feet; the reward is a 360-degree view of the world. Part of the trail is a somewhat difficult rock scramble that requires the use of both hands and both feet. The rocks being traversed are part of a pal-

The cardinal, unlike many other songsters, may be heard at any time of the year.
Overleaf: 4,049-foot-high Hawksbill Mountain is the highest peak in the park.

isadelike outcropping that surrounds the summit and that probably gave the mountain its name.

Hightop. The route up Hightop begins at a parking area at 66.7 miles on Skyline Drive. It is a 3-mile round trip and a 935-foot climb. Except for a 120-yard spur trail at the top, the route follows the *Appalachian Trail.* The summit is the former site of a fire tower; fragments of the tower's foundation remain but are overgrown as the forest regenerates itself. About 100 yards before the summit spur, on the A.T., a short side path leads to a rocky ledge that provides good views to the south and west. Here, rather than on the crest of Hawksbill, may be the spot on which John Lederer stood in March 1669.

Trails Downward

Because there are no roadways along the boundaries of Shenandoah, most trails connect with Skyline Drive. Because the drive is high on the Blue Ridge, most trails lead downward—to waterfalls, into hollows, along stream courses. When setting out on these trails, hikers should bear in mind that who goes down must come up and that coming up takes twice as long and uses much more energy than going down. Only a small selection of the park's downward-leading trails are described here.

Big Devils Stairs. From Gravel Springs Gap, at 17.6 miles, the route to Big Devils Stairs runs a short distance south on the *Appalachian Trail* to the *Bluff Trail,* and then 1.4 miles to the left past the Gravel Springs Shelter. *Big Devils Stairs Trail* is on the right. From this point down to the park boundary, the way proceeds through a steep-walled canyon. There is little or no trail most of the way. A scramble is required over and around huge boulders and past waterfalls, cascades, and some very old trees that were too inaccessible for loggers to cut. The trail is not easy going down and is worse climbing back up, but it presents a dramatic spectacle. Round-trip distance is 4.5 miles, and the change in elevation is 1,850 feet.

Overall Run Falls. Overall Run Falls may be reached from Mathews Arm (entrance road at 22.2 miles). The 3.8-mile round trip has a 1,140-foot descent and return. *Mathews Arm Fire Road* leads downhill 1.4 miles before meeting the *Overall Run Trail;* after only 1 mile on this trail, hikers reach a short spur to the left

Opposite: A short walk from Skyline Drive takes visitors to Dark Hollow Falls.

Few open fields remain in Shenandoah; of note are Patterson's Field and Big Meadows.

that leads to a viewpoint above the upper falls, a 29-foot cascade. Farther along the main trail, several other spur trails lead to views of the lower falls, a 93-foot cascade—often only a trickle during dry weather, but impressive in wet seasons.

Whiteoak Canyon. The Whiteoak Canyon Trail begins at a parking area at 42.6 miles. It follows the course and development of Whiteoak Run from its source, in a small marshy area in the Limberlost, down to its junction with the Berry Hollow drainage, just beyond the park boundary, the beginning of the Robinson River. En route, it passes six waterfalls, several hemlocks that are 300 to 400 years old, and a number of large white oaks growing among boulders of greenstone. The hike to and from the first falls, which has an 86-foot drop (second highest in Shenandoah), is a 4.6-mile round trip that descends 1,040 feet. The route encompassing all six falls is 7.3 miles round trip and passes through 2,150 feet of elevation.

Dark Hollow Falls. The route to Dark Hollow Falls is the shortest and involves the least change in elevation of any trail to a major waterfall in Shenandoah. From the parking area at 50.7 miles, the falls lie .7 mile distant and 440 feet lower along the *Dark*

Hollow Falls Trail. Optionally, hikers may start at the Big Meadows Campground, travel half of the *Story of the Forest Nature Trail* in either direction to a junction with an extension of the Dark Hollow Falls Trail, turn off onto the extension, cross Skyline Drive at the parking area, and continue downward. At the lower end of the falls trail, hikers may extend the route into a circuit hike by continuing down Hog Camp Branch another 50 yards to the former Gordonsville Turnpike, now a fire road, and walking to the left on it up to Skyline Drive at Fishers Gap. Depending on their point of origin, hikers may either return to the parking area along the drive or cross the drive to join the Appalachian Trail and then follow it south to its intersection with the Story of the Forest Nature Trail near the Big Meadows Campground. Pedestrians walking along the drive should remember that motorists do not see all the sights, and what they miss with their eyes, they may not miss with their vehicles. The Dark Hollow Falls Trail also continues across the fire road as the *Rose River Loop Trail*, which runs down to the Rose River Falls and back to Fishers Gap.

Lewis Run Falls. The Lewis Run Falls Trail begins at a service road at 51.4 miles. It is a 2.5-mile round trip with a descent of about 800 feet. The falls are a twin stream with a double drop that totals 91 feet.

Camp Hoover. From Milam Gap, at 52.8 miles, two routes lead down to Camp Hoover. One is the *Mill Prong Trail*, a 4.1-mile round trip with an 870-foot descent. The second involves taking the Appalachian Trail south to its junction with the *Laurel Prong Trail*, and then following the latter down the mountain. The two routes may be used in combination to make a circuit hike. Camp Hoover also may be reached by taking the *Rapidan Fire Road* down from its junction with Skyline Drive, across from the Big Meadows Wayside. The fire-road route is considerably longer than the other two, but it allows easier walking.

South River Falls. The South River Falls Trail begins at the edge of the South River picnic area, at 62.8 miles. It is a 2.6-mile round trip. The journey to the falls can be made into a 3.3-mile circuit hike by crossing South River below the falls, climbing to a railed overlook on the north side, taking the marked trail from there to the South River Fire Road, and returning to the picnic grounds on the fire road and the Appalachian Trail. In either case, the elevation change on the climb back is about 900 feet. The railed overlook

Overleaf: Flowering dogwoods blossom in early spring.

is recommended for its view of the falls.

Doyles River Falls and Jones Run Falls. The Falls Trail may be entered at either 81.1 miles or 84.1 miles. From the first entry point, a 2.7-mile round trip with a drop of 850 feet reaches the Doyles River Falls, small but pretty. From the second, a 3.6-mile round trip with a drop of 915 feet reaches the Jones Run Falls, which plummet 42 feet down an almost vertical cliff. Part of the route to Jones Run Falls passes through young forest on land that was a pasture when the park was established. A circuit hike of 7.8 miles may be made by doing the full 4.8 miles of the Falls Trail and returning to the starting point on the Appalachian Trail.

Big Run. The Big Run Trail leads through the Big Run Valley, the largest watershed in the park. The Big Run itself is one of the most interesting streams in the park, even though it boasts only one very small waterfall. It includes several pools large enough to swim in, probably contains more fish than any other park stream, and is bordered by an extensive variety of wildflowers. When backcountry-camping regulations permit, it is a good place to spend a couple of days. The trail leads only to the head of the stream, from Big Run Overlook, at 81.2 miles, or (via the Madison Run Fire Road part of the way) from 83 miles. By using the Appalachian Trail to return to whichever end of the trail they started from, hikers can turn the route into a 5.8-mile circuit hike with a change of elevation of 1,385 feet. From the low point of the trail at the head of Big Run, a fire road accompanies the stream, crossing it several times, all the way to the park boundary and beyond to U.S. 340 about halfway between the towns of Elkton and Grottoes.

Calvary Rocks and Riprap Run. By entering the *Riprap Trail* at the Riprap Trail parking area, at 90 miles, or the *Wildcat Ridge Trail* at its parking area, at 92.1 miles, and by using the Appalachian Trail as a connecting link, hikers can make a 9.8-mile circuit trip that entails a descent (and subsequent climb) of about 2,400 feet. The several good viewpoints include Calvary Rocks, from which a 360-degree view is only slightly obstructed by trees. At its lower portion, the trail parallels Riprap Run through a picturesque hollow. At one point along the stream, a waterfall drops into a large, deep pool.

Opposite: The omnivorous raccoon eats nestling birds, baby muskrats, stream creatures, and seeds, nuts, and berries.

VIRGIN ISLANDS ISLANDS NATIONAL PARK

Virgin Islands was named an International Biosphere Reserve by UNESCO in 1983.

Virgin Islands National Park
Box 7789, Saint Thomas
U.S. Virgin Islands 00801
Tel.: (809) 775-6238

HIGHLIGHTS: Trunk Bay • Cinnamon Bay • Caneel Bay • Marine Life • Annaberg Sugar Plantation Ruins • Catherineberg • Louisenhoj Tuff Formation • Waterlemon Cay • Peace Hill • Centerline Road • Reef Fish • Reef Bay • Reef Bay Valley Petroglyphs

ACCESS: By passenger boat or commercial airline direct to St. Thomas. Ferry and water taxi services operate daily from St. Thomas to St. John.

HOURS: Open year-round, 24 hours daily.

FEES: Charged at concessionaire-run campground.

PARKING: Ample parking throughout park.

GAS, FOOD, LODGING: Housekeeping cottages at Cinnamon Bay Campground. Camp store with groceries, charcoal, and stove fuel. Gas for rental vehicles at Cruz Bay.

VISITOR CENTER: Cruz Bay Visitor Center on St. John offers exhibits and sells publications.

MUSEUM: Displays on history of St. John at Cinnamon Bay.

GIFT SHOP: At Cruz Bay and Cinnamon Bay.

PETS: Permitted when under physical restraint, but prohibited on public-use beaches, picnic areas, and campgrounds.

PICNICKING: At various locations in park.

HIKING: Self-guiding trails at Annaberg, Cinnamon Bay, and Reef Bay. Avoid private property. Carry water.

BACKPACKING: Not permitted.

CAMPGROUNDS: At concessionaire-run Cinnamon Bay and Maho Bay campgrounds. 14-day stay limit at Cinnamon Bay year-round.

TOURS: Auto tour of St. John via guided taxi or rental vehicle; boat-and-auto tour out of St. Thomas waterfront. Self-guiding underwater trail at Trunk Bay. Ranger-led bus tour of historic sites on park and island.

OTHER ACTIVITIES: Swimming and snorkeling; rod and reel fishing, with no license necessary; charter fishing trips; boating.

FACILITIES FOR DISABLED: Restrooms and showers at Trunk and Cinnamon bays accessible. Cinnamon Bay campground has accessible tent sites.

For additional information, see also Sites, Trails, and Trips on pages 340–353 and the map on pages 314–315.

The call of the black-necked stilt is a very sharp kip-kip-kip-kip.

THE VIRGIN ISLANDS. THEIR VERY NAME conjures images of paradise: white coral-sand beaches fringed by swaying palms; clear, turquoise waters inlaid with coral and ornamented with multihued fish; lush, verdant slopes footed by crescent bays and rugged promontories; and warm subtropical days cooled by trade winds. Nowhere else are such images more accurate than in Virgin Islands National Park on the island of St. John.

Lured to the park by visions of warmth and beauty, visitors find a far more varied environment than they had anticipated. Five centuries of multicultural history rich with pirates, planters, slaves, and revolution may be traced through the numerous historical sites. Along trails that wend down forested hillsides, many fruits unknown to most mainlanders—such as the soursop, sugar apple, genip, and hog plum—may be sampled in season. Bright splashes of bougainvillaea, frangipani, flamboyant, hibiscus, and oleander delight both the eye and the soul. Diurnal harmonies of mockingbirds, pearly-eyed thrashers, Zenaida doves, mangrove cuckoos, and smooth-billed anis give way to nocturnal choruses of donkeys, crickets, and frogs. Battalions of hermit crabs, condominiums of land crabs, ball-shaped nests of tree-dwelling termites, and the antics of mongooses, lizards, and sugarbirds intrigue and entertain the curious mind. Vendors offer rentals and instruction for snorkeling, diving, sailing, and wind surfing to entice the active body. Only the insensate could fail to respond to the charms of Virgin Islands National Park.

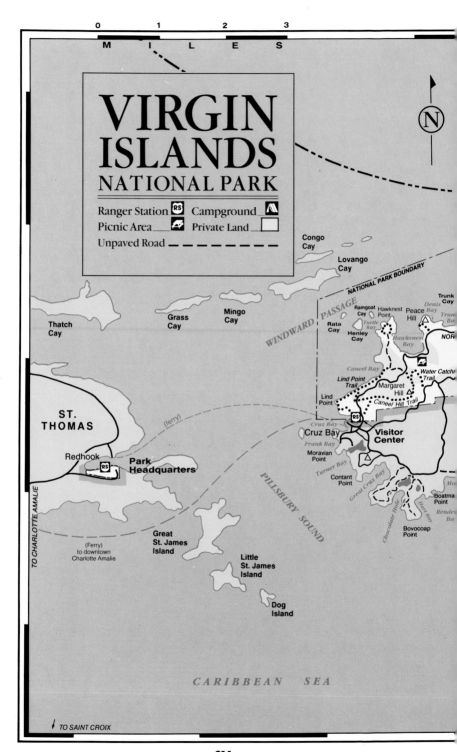

MILES

0 1 2 3

VIRGIN ISLANDS
NATIONAL PARK

Ranger Station **RS** Campground **▲**
Picnic Area **◢** Private Land **☐**
Unpaved Road – – – – – –

N

Congo Cay

Lovango Cay

NATIONAL PARK BOUNDARY

Trunk Cay

Denis Bay

Ramgoat Cay   Hawknest Point   Peace Hill   Trunk Ba

Grass Cay

Mingo Cay

WINDWARD PASSAGE

Rata Cay

Turtle Bay

Henley Cay

NOR

Thatch Cay

Hawksnest Bay

Caneel Bay

Water Catchr Trail

Lind Point Trail

Margaret Hill △

Lind Point

Caneel Hill Trail

ST. THOMAS

(ferry)

Cruz Bay

RS

Cruz Bay

Frank Bay

Visitor Center

Redhook

Park Headquarters

RS

Moravian Point

Contant Point

Turner Bay

Great Cruz Bay

Chocolate Hole

Hart Bay

Mo

Boatma Point

Bovocoap Point

Rende Ba

PILLSBURY SOUND

TO CHARLOTTE AMALIE

(Ferry) to downtown Charlotte Amalie

Great St. James Island

Little St. James Island

Dog Island

CARIBBEAN SEA

↓ TO SAINT CROIX

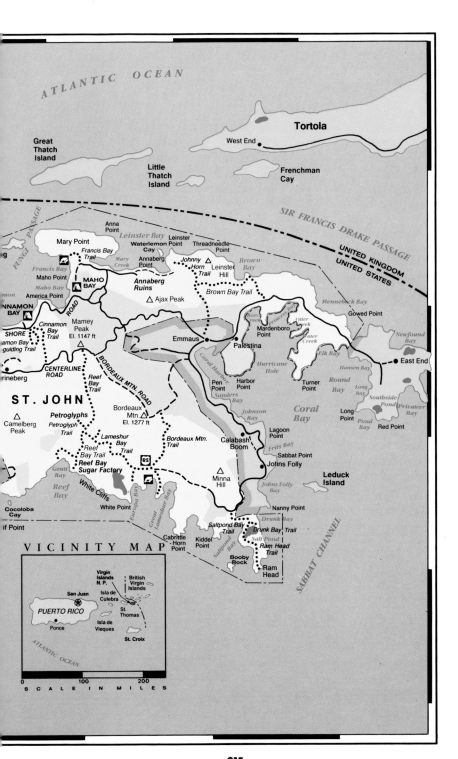

ATLANTIC OCEAN

Tortola

West End

Great
Thatch
Island

Little
Thatch
Island

Frenchman
Cay

FUNGI PASSAGE

SIR FRANCIS DRAKE PASSAGE

UNITED KINGDOM
UNITED STATES

Anna
Point

Leinster Bay

Mary Point

*Francis Bay
Trail*

Waterlemon
Cay

Leinster
Point

Threadneedle
Point

Johnny
Horn
Trail

Leinster
Hill

*Brown
Bay*

Francis Bay

Maho Point

*Mary
Creek*

Annaberg
Point

**MAHO
BAY**

Maho Bay

America Point

**Annaberg
Ruins**

△ Ajax Peak

Brown Bay Trail

Mennebeck Bay

Gowed Point

**CINNAMON
BAY**

SHORE

*Cinnamon
Bay
Trail*

*mon Bay
guiding Trail*

ROAD

Mamey
Peak
El. 1147 ft

Emmaus

Coral Harbor

Palestina

Borc   Creek

Princess Bay

*Otter
Creek*

Mardenboro
Point

*ater
Creek*

Elk Bay

*Newfound
Bay*

East End

rineberg

**CENTERLINE
ROAD**

*Reef
Bay
Trail*

BORDEAUX MTN. ROAD

*Hurricane
Hole*

Pen
Point

Harbor
Point

*Sanders
Bay*

Turner
Point

Hansen Bay

*Round
Bay*

*Long
Bay*

Southside

Privateer
Bay

ST. JOHN

△
Camelberg
Peak

Petroglyphs

*Petroglyph
Trail*

Bordeaux
Mtn. △
El. 1277 ft

*Bordeaux Mtn.
Trail*

*Lameshur
Bay
Trail*

*Reef
Bay Trail*

**Reef Bay
Sugar Factory**

RS

△
Minna
Hill

Calabash
Boom

*Johnson
Bay*

*Coral
Bay*

Lagoon
Point

Frits Bay

Sabbat Point

Johns Folly

**Leduck
Island**

Long
Point

*Pond
Bay*

Red Point

White Cliffs

*Genti
Bay*

*Reef
Bay*

White Point

Europa Bay

Great Lameshur Bay

*Johns Folly
Bay*

Nanny Point

*Cocoloba
Cay*

if Point

Cabritte
-Horn
Point

Kiddel
Point

Saltpond Bay
Trail

*Saltpond
Bay*

Drunk Bay

Booby
Rock

Salt
Pond

Drunk Bay Trail

Ram Head
Trail

Ram
Head

SABBAT CHANNEL

VICINITY MAP

Virgin
Islands
N. P.

British
Virgin
Islands

San Juan

Isla de
Culebra

PUERTO RICO

Ponce

St.
Thomas

Isla de
Vieques

St. Croix

ATLANTIC OCEAN

0   100   200

S C A L E   I N   M I L E S

Arawaks and Caribs

Goaded by tribal warfare in their homelands along the northern coast of South America, peace-seeking Indians launched canoes and used the favorable winds and currents to travel northward along the island arc of the Lesser Antilles. Although excavations on St. Thomas indicate human occupation since the fifth century B.C., the earliest sites on St. John have been related to the Arawak people who probably arrived between about A.D. 100 and 300. The Arawaks settled the Coral Bay area and the northwestern shore from Cinnamon Bay to Cruz Bay; sufficient rainfall here allowed them to conduct slash-and-burn farming, and they grew manioc as their staple crop. The Arawaks may have introduced to the Virgin Islands some South American plants, including the kapok tree (which was used for building canoes and, more recently, for filling pillows and life jackets) and the vanilla-scented genip tree (which produces a popular fruit). The iguana also may have been introduced here by the Arawaks. They certainly hunted iguanas, but generally, they seem to have preferred fishing over hunting and to have favored the meat of the queen conch (a large, pink marine snail). The conchs were collected by divers in shallow waters.

Supplementing their farming by collecting the bounty of the sea and shore, Arawaks lived peaceably for almost 1,000 years until faced with the onslaught of a warlike people whom they called *Caribs* (cannibals). Using their excellent canoes and sails, the Caribs proceeded up the island chain, enslaving or destroying other peoples as they went. After killing, absorbing, or displacing the Virgin Island Arawaks, the Caribs continued northward. By the time Christopher Columbus arrived in the West Indies in 1493, the Caribs had extended their territory from their base in the present-day

Petroglyph in Reef Bay Valley.

border area between Brazil and Bolivia to include most of Venezuela, the Guianas, and the area south to the Amazon, as well as the Lesser Antilles. Columbus skirmished with Caribs on St. Croix, but he did not stop at St. Thomas or St. John.

Sugar and Slaves

Smitten by the beauty and purity of the islands, Columbus named them after Saint Ursula and her 11,000 virgins and claimed them for Spain. The claim subsequently was contested by English, Dutch, French, and Danish adventurers and buccaneers, all of whom contributed to the islands' legacy of place names and lore. In 1595, Sir Francis Drake and Sir John Hawkins sailed through the passage separating Tortola and St. John, which now bears Drake's name, and they also entered Coral Bay. Robert Louis Stevenson immortalized the era and the area in *Treasure Island*; some locals believe that he used Norman Island, which lies off the eastern end of St. John, as the model for his novel's setting.

Although Danish sovereignty over the Virgin Islands was not recognized in Europe until 1754, the Danish West India and Guinea Company received a royal charter to establish a colony on St. Thomas in 1671. Extensive sugar plantations were soon developed. Wishing to thwart the expansion of independent operations, the company took control of St. John in 1694. Independent operations, although allowed to continue, were made subject to taxation and regulations established by the company. One regulation required each independent sugar planter to construct a mill and sugar refinery within eight years, a costly proposition. Less wealthy operators turned to growing cotton, indigo, and tobacco. The first company-operated plantation on St. John was established in 1716 at Estate Carolina in Coral Bay, the early locus of St. Johnian activity. Within twenty years, St. John hosted eighty-eight working estates.

At first, planters relied on the labor of indentured servants—poor people or prisoners who earned their freedom in America by working the cane fields. Unaccustomed to hard labor on steep slopes under a subtropical sun, many died or produced very little. Plantation owners' attention then turned to the slave barracoons of the Gold and Ivory coasts of West Africa. Initially, the importation of African slaves seemed advantageous for the planters. The first blacks obtained by slave traders and sent to the West Indies were members of conquered tribes; already reduced to slavery in Africa and to some extent accustomed to it, they were relatively docile. But as the demand for laborers remained insatiable, slave-

Ruins of sugar refinery at Annaberg.

trading tribes began delivering nobles, the royalty and aristocracy of their foes, to the slave markets. Having lived lives of luxury and authority, these new slaves fought the whip and fomented rebellion.

Nobles from the Amina, Adampe, and Aquambo tribes led a well-organized slave revolt on St. John. Communicating by means of drums and stealing away at night to meet in the bush, the leaders encouraged more slaves to leave their masters. Although hampered by a lack of food and water and by a reluctance to place full trust in members of other tribes, the slaves attacked estate owners in Coral Bay in November 1733. Many planters and their families were killed, but some slaves, through loyalty or fear, refused to join the rebels and even assisted in the counterrebellion directed from the Durloe Estate in Caneel Bay. The revolution continued until April 1734, when French mercenaries from Martinique methodically hunted the rebels. Refusing to return to a life of slavery or face execution, rebel leaders are said to have jumped from the cliffs at Ram Head and Mary Point to their deaths on the rocks below. In 1848, fearing another revolt, the Danes freed their slaves.

During the Napoleonic Wars, the British twice seized the Danish Virgin Islands to prevent the French from using the islands' resources. The strife damaged the sugar trade, and emancipation dealt it a crippling blow. A few plantations continued to operate—the Adrian and Reef Bay estates converted to steam-powered mills in the 1860s—until the emergence of sugar-beet production in the United States forced them out of the market.

The last refinery, at Reef Bay, closed after a devastating hurricane in 1916. The islands' population diminished; the people who stayed turned to subsistence farming; and the forest began reclaiming the once-extensive sugar estates. Today, park visitors may examine the remaining ruins, especially those that have been partially stabilized at Annaberg, Catherineberg, Reef Bay, Caneel Bay, and Cinnamon Bay, and envision the life that dominated the island for almost two centuries.

Establishment of the Park

Concerned about protecting the Panama Canal during World War I, the United States purchased the Virgin Islands—St. Thomas, St. John, St. Croix, and some fifty smaller isles—from Denmark on March 31, 1917, for $25 million. The United States Navy administered the islands and operated a naval station on Hassel Island in Charlotte Amalie harbor of St. Thomas until 1931. Congress then created the Territory of the Virgin Islands, granted considerable self-government to the islanders, and transferred general administration to the Department of the Interior. Virgin Islanders are United States citizens, but they may not vote in national elections.

The National Park Service considered St. John for park status in the 1930s, but the small population (700 people at that time) and the absence of economic pressure led authorities to believe that the beauty of the island would remain unimpaired without park protection. As a result, the government took little interest in the area until the tourist boom of the 1950s. At that time, Laurance Rockefeller and the Jackson Hole Preserve Corporation acquired and donated land for the park; Congress enacted legislation, and on August 2, 1956, President Dwight Eisenhower signed the bill creating Virgin Islands National Park.

The original legislation authorized the inclusion of up to 9,485 acres of land on St. John—omitting the population centers of Cruz Bay, Coral Bay, and East End—and the acquisition of 15 acres in Redhook on St. Thomas to serve as an administrative site. Additional legislation in 1962 added 5,650 offshore acres to preserve the marine environment. In 1978, Congress authorized inclusion of 135 acres of land on Hassel Island. The National Park Service does not own all the land within park boundaries; many private in-holdings, territorial-government properties, and easements exist.

Hassel Island was used for agriculture in the 1600s, when the land was a peninsula rather than an island, but attention shifted to Maritime concerns in the 1800s and 1900s. Coaling stations, marine railways (on which boats were hauled from the water for repairs), and a dry dock were constructed. The Danish and the British built fortifications to protect the harbor, and the United States constructed a naval base there. More recently, a resort flourished on the island. The park's general management plan calls for construction of trails, picnicking and camping sites, and the rehabilitation of docking facilities and Creque's Marine Railway. Because buildings and docks are crumbling, visitation is not advised until efforts have been undertaken to stabilize the area.

In 1983, the park was dedicated as an International Biosphere Reserve by UNESCO's Man and the Biosphere program. The program sponsors the study of unique cultural and natural sites in an effort to develop ways to balance the use and protection of the environment.

Hardening of volcanic flow into basalt produced the rocky headlands at Drunk Bay.

GEOLOGY

The story of geology in Virgin Islands National Park is tied to the theory of plate tectonics. The theory posits that the earth's crustal material is divided into a series of plates that float on a molten substrate. In regions where these plates meet, tremendous friction is generated. This builds up massive stresses that produce earthquakes, folding, faulting, and volcanism. The arc of the islands of the Antilles and the accompanying deep trenches mark the contact zone between two of these plates.

From a deep hole drilled in the ancient rock near Ram Head on St. John, geologists have extracted a sticky, clay-rich mud that they believe is typical of the prevolcanic ocean bottom. Beginning about 100 million years ago, volcanic material passed slowly upward through that mud and then flowed over its surface, beneath a sea at least 12,000 feet deep. The volcanic material became the Water Island Formation—the primal rock that underlies the entire island and is visible in largely unaltered form throughout its southeastern end. Over perhaps millions of years, a series of volcanic flows solidified and thickened the island base.

The first period of volcanism was followed by a significant uplift, involving several thousand feet of rise, as the crust continued to react to underlying stresses. A second period of volcanism, characterized by explosive shallow-water and subaerial (above-water) eruptions, ensued. The result was deposition of a bed of volcanic materials, including andesite and tuff (solidified ash). Because the thickest deposits of this material, the Louisenhoj Formation, are found on the western end of St. John and the eastern end of St. Thomas, the volcanic center was probably situated in Pillsbury Sound, the channel that separates the two islands.

Examples of the Louisenhoj Formation may be observed at the western end of the beach at Trunk Bay and at both ends of the beach at Cinnamon Bay. The Louisenhoj provides the beautiful blue beach rock prized as construction material for houses and buildings on St. John. So violent were the Louisenhoj eruptions that huge chunks of rock from the earlier Water Island Formation were tossed skyward and scattered over the hills. House-size Easter Rock, which lies near the road on the slope above the beach at Hawksnest Bay, is a relic of this activity.

Following the explosive Louisenhoj era, the land subsided somewhat and slopes became blanketed by organic material—the remains of planktonic algae and coral formations. Over thousands of years, a thin-bedded, dark-colored, impure limestone developed; it contains a few poorly preserved fossils of radiolaria (marine protozoans). Uplifting and tilting exposed the bed in cliffs on Outer Brass Island, north of St. Thomas, from which the entire formation derives its name. On St. John, the Outer Brass Formation is visible in the Leinster Bay area, especially at Mary Creek, Annaberg, and Leinster Hill. The original rock was metamorphosed by later intrusions.

The marine environment played yet a greater role in the development of the overlying Tutu Formation, named after a bay on St.

Thomas where it is exposed. Turbidity currents and submarine landslides, probably fostered by earthquakes, carried relatively unweathered debris from the Louisenhoj and Outer Brass formations and deposited it in a thick layer visible near Leinster and Mary points.

All the earlier formations on the northeastern shore of St. John were affected by the intrusion of the Virgin Islands Pluton, a mass of magma (molten rock) that was forced up through older materials but cooled before it reached the surface. Underlying the Sir Francis Drake Passage, between Tortola and St. John, the dark, dioritic rock of the pluton crops out on the cliffs of Mary and Threadneedle points on St. John. Heat and pressure generated by the pluton metamorphosed the contact rocks. The effects of this metamorphosis on the Water Island Formation may be seen in road cuts from Bordeaux Mountain east to Emmaus; near the eastern end, metamorphosed Louisenhoj rocks have been mixed in through faulting. Metamorphosed rocks of the Outer Brass and Tutu formations are visible in the Leinster Bay area.

The island's major rock formations have existed for the past 60 million years, but faulting, erosion, and variations in water level have rearranged them. Three fault systems cut the island, offsetting large blocks of rock and creating the major valleys. The most prominent fault runs from Cinnamon Bay to Fish Bay. Valley slopes channel the water from heavy rains into guts (drainages) that send surging, roiling, sediment-filled torrents to the sea, whose level was probably 200 feet lower during the last ice age. Although wave action eroded sediments from St. John's shores during glacial periods, enough depositional material accumulated to form an insular shelf. As the ice melted, waters warmed and rose, and corals found conditions favorable for reef formation on the submerged shelf. Rising waters overran the gradually sloping shorelines and invaded valleys, leaving arms of rock as headlands isolating each small bay. This phenomenon is known as a drowned coast.

Erosion and reef building continue today. Scientists are concerned about the increased erosion and sedimentation caused by construction projects on privately owned lands that lie both within and adjacent to the park. Coral polyps, which feed by filtering sea water for plankton, can tolerate only a certain degree of sedimentation and turbidity. Park biologists monitor the health of the coral in areas of heavy sedimentation as well as in areas recovering from 1989's Hurricane Hugo.

A stone crab is able to regenerate a lost pincer within two molts.
Overleaf: Colonizing mangroves slowly produce an island in shallow Leinster Bay.

Climate

Lying only 18 degrees north of the equator, the Virgin Islands bask in warmth and sunshine twelve months a year. During the day, summer temperatures range from the high 80s to the low 90s, and winter temperatures range from the high 70s to the low 80s. During some winter evenings, temperatures may dip into the high 60s. Rains occur throughout the year, but October and November are generally the wettest months, while February and March are the driest. Rain usually falls in brief showers, but heavy rains do occur and may wash out roads. Trade winds prevail during the winter. During early summer, winds may be light and variable to nonexistent, providing flat calm water that is excellent for snorkeling. Late summer and autumn may bring storm warnings. On Hurricane Supplication Day, in late July, islanders pray that the season's hurricanes will pass them by; on Hurricane Thanksgiving Day, in mid-October, they give thanks for having been spared. Most visitors consider January through April to be prime vacation time.

Vegetation

Only 9 miles long and 5 miles wide, St. John supports an incredible variety of plant life. Eight hundred or more species find niches in diverse habitats from the dry, cactus-pimpled eastern end to the moist, subtropical tangles of the island's northwestern slope. No virgin forest remains, but in some areas, the current vegetation may be similar to pre-Columbian growth. During the plantation period, land not being cultivated for cane was cleared for livestock, harvested for lumber and charcoal, or planted with cotton, tobacco, or indigo. Only the driest, rockiest, and steepest slopes escaped human impact. Second- or third-growth forest, a mixture of indigenous and imported plants, has regained 65 percent of St. John. Although the National Park Service generally tries to approximate original conditions in natural areas, several factors render such a goal impossible on St. John: rainfall has declined; some introduced plants have deeper root systems than do native plants and may have contributed to lowering the water table; and no one knows exactly what constituted the original forest.

Visitors to the Cinnamon Bay–Trunk Bay–Caneel Bay area and to upper Reef Bay find themselves in quasi-jungle. Philodendrons, which most mainlanders know as tame house plants, snake 30 feet up the trunks of palms, clothing them in rich cascades of spade-shaped leaves. Canopies of cinnamon bay rum, mango, genip, trumpet tree, and almost 100 other species block the sunlight. Both Cinnamon Bay and Caneel Bay take their names from the fragrant cinnamon bay rum tree, *kaneel* being the Dutch and German word for "cinnamon." Cinnamon bay is related to the myrtle and is not synonymous with the bay laurel, whose leaves are sold as a seasoning in mainland grocery stores. Islanders add the leaves of cinnamon bay rum to hot chocolate, breakfast cereals, soups, and stews. Oil extracted from the tree's crushed leaves was bottled and sold until the 1930s. St. John's leaves were to bay rum as sterling is to silver. Although the St. John label is still used, the leaves are now imported, and the product is manufactured on St. Thomas.

The fan-shaped fronds of the Teyer palm, the only indigenous palm on the island, have been used for fans, roofs, brooms, and fish traps. Many fruit trees, most of them introduced by plantation owners, thrive in moist areas, but visitors are cautioned to try only the fruits that are familiar or have been approved by a guide or naturalist. The starvation fruit, which resembles a mushy, white potato, is evident throughout the Cinnamon Bay

The roots of a large kapok tree are a highlight at Cinnamon Bay Campground.

Campground area; however, as its name implies, it should be eaten only during times of duress. The "pain-killer" leaves of the same plant may be heated and applied with Vaseline to relieve sore muscles. Roadways in moist areas are lined with vibrant hibiscus blossoms that bloom for only a day.

Drier slopes are covered by a shorter forest of gumbo-limbo trees, wild tamarinds, wild frangipanis, and a host of others. The showy yellow flowers of the Ginger Thomas tree, the official tree of the islands, are evident throughout the area, as is the thorny acacia. Lime trees, whose fruits are yellow when ripe, thrive in this environment.

The still drier, exposed, southeastern slope of St. John is cactus country, a surprise for most visitors. Rain clouds sweep westward over the flat eastern end of the island, retaining all their moisture until caught by Bordeaux and Mamey peaks. Prickly pear and barrel cacti are perfectly suited for the thin soil and and arid conditions of the southeastern slope; they may be typical of the original vegetation. Joining them is the century plant, or agave, which usually blooms every ten years or so, not the legendary hundred. Some islanders decorate the dried stalks of century-plant blooms as Christmas trees.

The sea grape, maho tree, and manchineel tree of the shoreline may have greeted Columbus as he sailed by. Early sailors who ate of the manchineel apple died, a warning to those who walk the shores today. Every part of the tree is toxic; raindrops falling through manchineel leaves onto unprotected skin can raise painful blisters. In shallow bays well-protected by reefs and headlands—such as at Leinster and Lameshur bays and in the fingers of Hurricane Hole—red mangroves are extending their branching prop roots seaward, slowly increasing St. John's acreage. The lagoons created by the water-footed mangroves harbor small fish, crustaceans, delicate nudibranchs (sea slugs), mangrove oysters, worms, and insects; these, in turn, draw myriad birds, including the colorful mangrove cuckoo. Behind the red mangroves, where sediment has accumulated and become muddy, the roots of black mangroves send up pencil-like shoots (pneumatophores) in search of oxygen. Black mangroves help prepare the soil for the buttonwood mangroves, which prefer drier footing.

Bats, Lizards, and Crabs

Although the land-based animals of the park rarely generate as much excitement as their counterparts of the sea and shores, they fill interesting niches in the island ecosystem. Bats are the only mammals indigenous to the island. While cave bats pollinate kapok

The bar-eyed hermit crab is found from the low-tide line into moderately deep water.

and calabash trees, fruit bats compete with humans for mangoes, avocados, bananas, and other fruits, concurrently helping disperse the seeds. Free-tail and house bats devour insects, a boon for visitors and residents; and fish-eating bats swoop around anchored boats in search of fry (small, young fish) that rise to the surface.

Imported animals have substantially affected the natural balance. The mongoose, introduced in the late nineteenth century to combat rats brought in by ships, eradicated some species of ground-nesting birds; seriously depleted the ranks of lizards, especially the large, scaly ground lizard; and reduced the turtle population by preying on eggs. With no natural enemies on the island, mongooses have taken over. Donkeys, commonly used for transportation until the mid-1950s, now roam freely, munching their favorite grasses and flowers. Goats have browsed much of the park and may have eliminated some species of plants.

Lizards seem to peer from every leaf, limb, wall, and table on the island. Most of them belong to the genus *Anolis*, the most common member being the man lizard. Male anoles inflate their brightly colored dewlaps (sacs under the chin) and do push-ups to proclaim their territories. Two species of eyelidless lizards called geckos; the burrowing blind snake, or footless lizard; and a few iguanas round out the reptile population. The reptiles, along with certain birds and bats, keep the insect population at a tolerable level, but reptiles must be wary of mongooses and feral cats.

Battalions of hermit crabs (crabs that live in discarded snail

A great egret hatchling resembles the proverbial ugly duckling.
Opposite: The oystercatcher uses its sharp bill to vivisect its bivalve prey.

and whelk shells) marching along the trails surprise many visitors who had imagined that all crabs live in the sea. Both marine and land varieties of the hermit crab live in the Virgin Islands, the latter returning to sea only to reproduce. Other land crabs live among mangrove roots where sand and debris have built up and in large holes arranged condominium-style in drier ground, such as those near the foot of the Reef Bay Trail.

Birds

More than thirty species of birds nest on St. John, and more than one hundred transit the island. As development of the Caribbean proceeds, the park is increasingly important as an area which preserves relatively large tracts of undisturbed land that provide winter habitat for migrants.

Swimmers and boaters delight in watching the brown pelican plunge into the sea beside them, fill its pendulous throat pouch, tilt back its head, and gulp its fish dinner. Endangered in most other areas where it breeds (the fish that it eats retain insecticides), the pelican flourishes in the Virgin Islands and nests in secluded rookeries such as the cliff face at Mary Point. Pelicans often are accompanied by brown boobies—brown-backed, white-breasted birds that also feed on schools of fish and nest in offshore-island rookeries. High over the water soars the scissortailed frigate bird, searching for a meal that it may steal from another bird. During the breeding season in the autumn, the male displays an inflated, red, heart-shaped throat pouch.

Solitary and spotted sandpipers teeter along sandy stretches, while oystercatchers crack whelks on rocky beaches. Greater and lesser yellowlegs, black-necked stilts, and green and blue herons step gingerly along swamp and pond margins. Gallinules gabble along the shore or join teal, Bahama ducks, and widgeons on pond waters. The pond behind the beach at Francis Bay is a good place to find them during winter months. Little blue herons and kingfishers do not mind human activity and are often seen around the Visitor Center.

The most conspicuous birds of the campgrounds and well-traveled areas of the western end are the pearly-eyed thrasher, locally known as the trushee, which plays camp robber quite shamelessly; the cooing, cinnamon-colored Zenaida dove, which sounds like the mourning dove of the mainland; the sugar-loving, black and yellow bananaquit, or sugarbird; and the gray kingbird, which roosts in large flocks and fills the woods with cheerful morning songs.

Two of the park's most interesting birds are the diminutive Antillean crested hummingbird and the large, raucous, glossy-black cuckoo—also known as the smooth-billed ani or the black witch. Easily recognized by its distinctive green crest, the little hummingbird often gathers nectar from hibiscus flowers along park roads. A fortunate visitor might find a tiny, gossamer nest on the very end of a genip-tree branch. In contrast, the ani often can be heard before it is seen, as visitors to the Reef Bay Trail and the Annaberg–Francis Bay area will attest. Typically, several anis share a nest high in the treetops, laying almost thirty eggs (not all of which hatch) in layers.

Reef Colonies

Reefs, whether fringing the island mass or growing in separate patches, form fascinating, colorful colonies of marine life. They are composed primarily of stony, or hard, corals, such as the branching staghorn and elkhorn corals and the round heads of brain and star corals. Each branch or head of these corals is really an entire neighborhood of tiny animals called coral polyps (relatives of sea anemones). Algae grow within each polyp, giving the coral its distinctive color. The algae and polyps maintain a symbiotic relationship, each helping the other. While receiving structure and protection from the coral, the algae provide the polyps with oxygen and organic nutrients produced by photosynthesis; some of these nutrients enable the polyps to form skeletal material. Because they are dependent on light, corals thrive only in relatively shallow waters. The size and distribution of polyps create the characteristic growth patterns of each coral species, and the hard skeletons ensure that the forms remain after the polyps die. The relatively soft brain coral was cut and used with bricks and stones in early plantation buildings.

Living alongside hard corals are soft corals, including the willowy sea whips, latticework sea fans, and feathery sea plumes. Lacking the calcium carbonate necessary to form hard skeletons, they fasten themselves securely to the sea floor and sway with the currents, capturing planktonic foods by means of tentacled polyps. More graceful and delicate than their hard relatives, the soft corals often are mistaken for plants.

A coral-like growth that stands alone or grows over true corals is the fire coral, named for the sting it gives unwary snorkelers. Instead of protruding from basal cups, fire-coral polyps extend as filaments through tiny pores in a relatively smooth, mustard-colored growth.

A host of creatures bore into or affix themselves to corals. Perhaps the most intriguing of these are the tube worms and the sponges. The tentacles (feeding parts) of tube worms look like tiny, brightly colored Christmas trees or feather dusters emerging atop the convoluted brain corals. A quick swish of water past these "trees," however, causes them to disappear immediately into protective tubes. Sponges abound in a variety of hues, shapes, and sizes. Two of the most easily spotted are the tube sponge, which looks like a series of tubes protruding from a common base, and the vase sponge, which may grow large enough to hold a person. A sponge is neither a true colony nor a well-defined individual, but it is a very successful organism with a primitive anatomy that has changed little in 500 million years.

Spiny lobsters, crabs, sea urchins, eels, and even shy octopuses lodge in reef crannies. Starfishes, black long-spined sea urchins, and sea cucumbers move slowly along the reef flats. The prickly sea urchins are the snorkeler's nemesis; the long spines can cause extreme discomfort if they break off in a finger or toe. Tiny fish, however, love sea urchins and seek protection in their forest of spines. In 1984, a sea-urchin disease swept the islands and decimated the population of long-spined sea urchins.

Fish

Perhaps the highlight of an island vacation is watching the dazzling fishes that sparkle like gemstones set in coral. Aside from the

Cinnamon Bay sea anemone.

clouds of fry that breeze through the waters, the most frequently encountered fishes of the reefs off park beaches are brightly colored parrot fishes, snappers, grunts, surgeonfishes, and wrasses. A quiet snorkeler may hear the rasping noise of a parrot fish as it gnaws the reef to harvest its dinner of encrusting algae. Surgeonfishes, like the brown doctorfish and the brilliant blue tang, swim slowly in search of algae and use the barbs at the base of their tails for defense. Schools of carnivorous snappers and grunts, which really do make grunting sounds, swim by in search of small fish and crustaceans. Wrasses vary in size but are frequently small, colorful fishes that swarm about the reef in search of invertebrates. Both males and females of one species, the bluehead wrasse, begin life as small yellow fish; but from among these youngsters, supermales develop, changing their head color to blue, their aft-section and tail color to green, and their mid-body color to bands of black and white or light blue and growing to several times the size of the other blueheads. Early-morning or evening snorkelers may see sizable numbers of large-eyed, spiny squirrelfish as they emerge from the protection of the reef for nocturnal forays after crustaceans.

Although not as numerous as parrot fishes and schooling fishes, the trunkfishes, trumpetfish, angelfishes, and triggerfishes are distinctive reef dwellers. Lacking speed to escape predators, the

The long-spined sea urchin is equipped with 10 sets of gills.

trunkfish relies on its bony carapace and the toxin in its skin as defenses. Seen face-on, this odd-looking fish has the shape of an isosceles triangle, with its stomach as the triangle's base. The equally odd-looking, long, narrow trumpetfish frequently hangs vertically in the water, head down, in an attempt to blend with sea whips and grasses. Elusive by nature, the graceful and delicate angelfishes hide in reef cavities, emerging when danger has passed to feed on sponges. The boldly patterned triggerfishes also stay close to the reef labyrinth; when danger approaches, they wedge themselves into reef crannies, using their first dorsal spines to hold themselves in place.

Southern stingrays, barracudas, sharks, and moray eels have bad reputations, but they rarely bother snorkelers and divers unless provoked. The shy rays generally lie on the bottom, partially covered by sand. If provoked or stepped on, a ray uses the barb at the base of its tail for defense; otherwise, it flees at the sight of human beings. With their long, toothy jaws moving menacingly as they glide through the water, barracudas have an intimidating mien. Visitors are warned against wearing jewelry in the water because it may flash like the scales of small fish and tempt barracudas, whose grainy eyesight is incapable of sharp daytime vision. Most snorkelers off St. John never see a shark; if they do, it is most likely to be the relatively harmless nurse shark. The best policy is to take a long look and then swim quietly away. Moray eels, shy and difficult to find, peer out of holes in the reef; to avoid them, swimmers should keep their hands and fingers out of reef cavities.

Beaches and Shorelines

The underwater realm of the park is a world unto itself, yet it is closely involved with the health and welfare of the beach and shoreline communities. The coral reefs constantly replenish and maintain St. John's famous white sand beaches. The sand is composed of minute particles of hard-coral skeletons and calcareous algae that have been broken down by the crushing waves of tropical storms and by the persistent nibblings of algae-browsing parrot fishes. The reefs also protect the beaches from the power of incoming winter waves that would wash the sand out to sea. The width of the beach affects the composition of the shoreline community. Each year, hawksbill turtles traipse across the narrow beaches to nest at the vegetation line or in the woody margin beyond. Green and leatherback turtles nest in sand, but generally prefer wider beaches than those that skirt St. John.

Preceding overleaf: Squirrelfishes' lidless eyes are as sensitive as a cat's.

View of St. John's north shoreline, looking west, from Cinnamon Bay overlook.

In some protected areas, such as Leinster Bay, reef growth aids more noticeably in the construction of new land. As a reef rises in shallow waters, the advancing front moves its living colony of coral farther from shore. Red mangroves step out onto the dead, older portions of the reef, and sand, mud, and debris fill in among their roots. The reef flat that extends seaward from the mangroves becomes covered with sand and turtle grass or, where the wave action is greater, with larger rubble consisting of stones and broken coral.

Each kind of flat supports a distinctive marine community. The algae-covered turtle grass forms protective nurseries for fish of many species, including the puffers, which expand to several times their normal size when frightened. Biologists have found that 133 creatures besides fish inhabit sea-grass beds, among them the queen conchs that graze the algae and deposit their slimy strands of eggs. Algae of many colors cover the rocks of rubble-strewn areas. One rock may host various algae and such tiny animals as conical limpets; a rock urchin; chitons, with their characteristic segmented plates; and a decorator crab, which covers its shell with bits of whatever materials it can find. Small, brittle starfishes hide beneath the rocks.

Two peninsular reefs growing toward each other may unite, fill in with sand, become colonized by salt-tolerant vegetation, and isolate the inner body of water—which then becomes a salt pond. Because of repeated sea-water flooding and evaporation, the salinity of the pond increases, and its inhabitants change. Brine shrimp and red algae are frequently found in salt ponds.

SITES, TRAILS, AND TRIPS

A trip to Virgin Islands National Park is best begun with a stop at the Visitor Center in the town of Cruz Bay on St. John. Detailed information about historical sites, trails, boating, snorkeling, and naturalist-led trips is available.

Light, casual clothing is appropriate, but visitors should consider themselves guests in another culture and respect the local preference for covering up, especially in towns. The law forbids the wearing of bathing suits in town. Short shorts on women sometimes meet with disapproval, and men should always wear shirts. On the trails, hikers prefer tennis shoes to hiking boots; those who seek out less frequented trails wear long-sleeved shirts and long pants to protect themselves from acacia thorns and from the shrub appropriately named catch-and-keep. Sun-tan lotion, a sun-block cream for the first few days, and insect repellent are recommended. The islands host far fewer bugs than might be expected, but insidious sandflies dine on sunbathers' flesh during the late afternoons, and mosquitoes thrive after rains.

Camping and Lodging

Camping is limited to two designated campgrounds. The Cinnamon Bay Campground is operated by a concessionaire on

The upper portion of the Reef Bay Trail descends through a moist forest habitat.

park land. The Maho Bay Campground is privately owned. Both are considerably different from what mainland campers might expect. Although Cinnamon Bay offers a few bare sites on which guests may pitch their own tents, most sites feature screened, canvas tents or concrete and screen cottages. Maho Bay's tent cottages, which seem more like tree houses, are connected by boardwalks designed to reduce impact on the environment.

Programs conducted by park naturalists are available at Cinnamon Bay. Both campgrounds are equipped with small grocery stores and outdoor cafeterias. Because all food must be imported, prices are higher than on the mainland. The Cinnamon Bay Campground also includes a museum in an old Danish warehouse, a dive shop, and shower facilities for visitors who wish to use the beach but not stay in the campground. Both campgrounds are open year-round. Reservations are necessary for the winter and are advisable during the rest of the year.

Visitors who wish more luxurious accommodations might select the elite Caneel Bay, an elegant resort situated on beautifully maintained grounds that were once the site of the Durloe Estate. Guesthouses and condominium rentals are available at or near Cruz Bay, and private homes scattered about the island may be rented for weeks or months at a time. Arrangements for lodging during high season (Christmas through April) must be made well in advance.

Roads

St. John's roads provide an excellent overview of the park and some incredible Caribbean vistas. Visitors may rent a vehicle or arrange for tours or transportation in the open-air island buses.

Drivers leaving Cruz Bay may take *Centerline Road*, Highway 10, which was constructed in Danish times and called King's Way. Centerline Road traverses the high ridges of the island's spine, affording tantalizing views of eastern St. John and the British Virgin Islands before descending to Coral Bay and East End. In Coral Bay, a spur road leads to Salt Pond, Ram Head, and Lameshur Bay, providing good views of the cactus country. Most vehicle-rental policies prohibit driving to Lameshur until road improvements have been completed, but visitors who park and walk the steep, rocky route generally find themselves sharing the uncrowded beaches with a few locals and a donkey or two. A ranger residence, historical ruins, and a marine-biology research laboratory sponsored by the College of the Virgin Islands terminate various forks in the Lameshur road.

TRAILS OF VIRGIN ISLANDS NATIONAL PARK

NORTH SHORE TRAILS

LIND POINT TRAIL: Starts at Visitor Center; ends at the Caneel Bay resort; 1.5 miles one way; 1 hour; trail ascends to scenic Lind Point overlook, then descends to Caneel Bay; open dry forest with cactus scrub environment.

CANEEL HILL TRAIL: Starts at Cruz Bay village; ends at North Shore Road entrance to Caneel Bay; 2.1 miles one way; 2 hours; a steep climb from Cruz Bay leads to scenic overlook atop Caneel Hill (.7 mile); trail continues to Margaret Hill (elev. 848 feet), then descends steeply through forest to North Shore Road.

CANEEL HILL SPUR TRAIL: Connects Caneel Hill Trail with Lind Point Trail; .9 mile one way; .75 hour; crosses North Shore Road at point overlooking Cruz Bay and Caneel Bay.

WATER CATCHMENT TRAIL: Starts along Centerline Road; joins Caneel Hill Trail; .8 mile one way; .5 hour; forest trail, leads from Centerline Road to North Shore Road via short connection with Caneel Hill Trail.

CINNAMON BAY SELF-GUIDING TRAIL: Starts and ends a few yards east of entrance road into Cinnamon Bay Campground; 1-mile loop; 1 hour; shady trail passes through old sugar-factory site and native tropical trees; illustrated direction markers.

FRANCIS BAY TRAIL: Starts at west end of Mary Creek paved road; ends at Francis Bay; .3 mile one way; .25 hour; passes through dry scrub forest, by the historic Francis Bay Estate House, and onto the beach; mangrove forest and brackish pond provide good birdwatching; swimming and snorkeling are popular beach activities at Francis Bay, but no lifeguards are on duty.

JOHNNY HORN TRAIL: Starts at Waterlemon Bay; ends at Emmaus Moravian Church at Coral Bay; 1.5 mile one way; 2 hours; passes through sunny, upland dry forest and scrub; follows ridges southward across island.

BROWN BAY TRAIL: Starts from ridge saddle on Johnny Horn Trail, .6 mile southeast of Waterlemon Bay; ends at Centerline Road, 1.3 miles east of Emmaus Moravian Church; 1.2 miles one way; 2 hours; unmaintained trail branches east from Johnny Horn Trail and descends through dry thorn scrub and open, hot valley; for a short distance trail borders Brown Bay, then ascends ridge overlooking Hurricane Hole.

SOUTH SHORE TRAILS

REEF BAY TRAIL: Starts 5 miles east of Cruz Bay on Centerline Road; ends at Reef Bay sugar factory; 2.5 miles one way; 2 hours; trail descends through a shady, moist forest and a dry forest, both of which contain a wide variety of plant life; visible remains of four sugar estates and more recently abandoned farming communities along way; guided tours available; check Visitor Center for schedules; no lifeguards at beach.

PETROGLYPH TRAIL: Starts 1.7 miles down Reef Bay Trail; ends at petroglyphs; .3 mile one way; .25 hour; petroglyphs are attributed to early Arawak Indians or to Christian slaves from Africa.

LAMESHUR BAY TRAIL: Starts along Reef Bay Trail near the trail head of the Petroglyph Trail; ends at Lameshur Bay; 1.8 miles one way; 1.25 hours; open dry forest; 1.4 miles from the trail head, a spur trail to the south leads .5 mile to a salt pond and to a beach covered with coral rubble at Europa Bay.

BORDEAUX MOUNTAIN TRAIL: Connects Bordeaux Mountain Road, at a point 1.7 miles southeast of Centerline Road, with Lameshur Bay 1,000 feet below; 1.2 miles one way; 1.5 hours; steep and sunny.

SALTPOND BAY TRAIL: Starts at parking area 3.6 miles south of Coral Bay; ends at Saltpond Beach; .2 mile one way; .25 hour; graded trail through dry cactus scrubland; good swimming and snorkeling at bay; no lifeguards; hat and extra drinking water are recommended.

DRUNK BAY TRAIL: Connects Saltpond Bay Trail with Drunk Bay Beach; .3 mile one way; .3 hour; windswept, stunted plant growth is conspicuous on the approach to rocky Drunk Bay Beach; swimming is hazardous.

RAM HEAD TRAIL: Starts at south end of Saltpond Bay Beach or junction of Saltpond Bay and Drunk Bay trails; ends at Ram Head; .9 mile one way; 1 hour; rocky, sunny trail leads to unique blue-cobble beach, then zigzags up the hillside to a point 200 feet above Caribbean Sea; magnificent windswept scenery; caution is required when walking near cliff edge.

Hikers on the Saltpond Bay Trail may come across a Turk's cap cactus.

The waters surrounding Trunk Cay, in Trunk Bay, are perfect for snorkeling.

The *North Shore Road,* highway 20, makes its roller-coaster, corkscrew passage from Cruz Bay past Caneel, Hawksnest, Trunk, Cinnamon, and Maho bays to Leinster Bay and Annaberg. The crests of the roller coaster afford scenic views of bays, beaches, cays (small, low islands), and the British Virgin Islands. The steep hills and hairpin turns remind drivers to obey the speed limit of 20 miles per hour and to stay on the left side of the road. Between Maho Bay and Annaberg, the road passes ruins of several plantations and at times parallels a Danish road built in the eighteenth century.

Snorkeling and Swimming

Visiting the Virgin Islands and not entering the water would be like going to Yellowstone National Park and not seeing the geysers. Snorkeling is easy, and the area's warm, clear waters and sandy bottoms assure the timid that there is no better place to learn. Park naturalists and dive shops provide instruction. Using the buddy system and trying just a small section of reef at a time are advisable. During the summer, north-shore waters are usually flat calm and viewing is excellent. When winter storms send breakers crashing onto north-shore beaches, stirring up the bottom sediments and making viewing difficult, the south-shore beaches at Saltpond Bay and Lameshur Bay are generally calm and much more suitable for snorkeling and swimming.

Trunk Bay. Acclaimed as one of the ten most beautiful beaches in the world, Trunk Bay offers a postcard-perfect beach, limpid waters, and a small cay surrounded by coral heads and fish. It is advantageous to avoid visiting between 10:00 A.M. and 2:00 P.M., when cruise ships bring crowds. Signs mark an underwater nature trail, but winter storms and careless snorkelers have damaged much of the coral. Visitors can protect reefs by remembering that coral consists of polyps, living animals, that find it difficult to survive the thrashing of a snorkeler's flippered foot. Coral growth is surprisingly slow: a brain-coral head the size of a basketball may be fifty years old. Swimmers should not touch, sit on, or stand on coral heads. A snorkeler who leaves the trail and encircles the cay will pass blue tangs, damselfishes, and sergeant majors that flit among the palms of the shallow-water elkhorn coral. In deeper waters away from the sides of the cay and around its outermost end, brain and star corals, sea plumes, sea whips, and sea fans take over. A lucky visitor may share a swim with a hawksbill turtle (but *not* by hanging on!).

Strong swimmers in search of more extensive reef formations may wish to swim westward to a crescent-shaped reef that spans the entrance to Jumbie Beach, a tiny beach normally visited only by locals. In the relative privacy of Jumbie's reef, a snorkeler may encounter a school of timid squid, while a sunbather may watch a sandpiper bob along the water's edge. Jumbie has no facilities, but Trunk Bay has rest rooms, changing rooms, showers, a rental shop

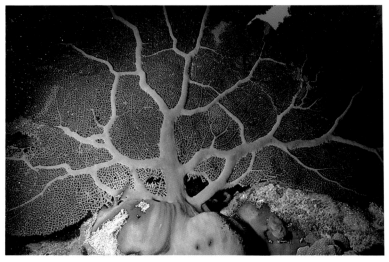

Sea fans are found in southern Florida, Bermuda, the Bahamas, and the West Indies. Overleaf: Red-backed cleaning shrimp feed on parasites they find on host fishes' skin.

for snorkeling equipment, a refreshment stand, and lifeguards.

Hawksnest Bay. A quiet beach and a shallow reef system in shallow water make Hawksnest a good bet for beginning snorkelers. Although the reef is not as varied as some, branches of elkhorn still harbor darting damselfishes, and parrot fishes still nibble along its edges. Without having to dive below the surface, the novice snorkeler can command good views while floating beside the fingers of reef. Rest rooms and changing rooms are available.

Cinnamon Bay: The campground at Cinnamon Bay makes the beach a logical starting point for many visitors. Interesting snorkeling is possible on the reef at the eastern end of the beach and around Cinnamon Cay, in the middle of the bay. Full facilities are available.

Francis Bay. One of the best places for seeing and swimming with green turtles is Francis Bay, but swimmers should give the turtles plenty of leeway. A longtime favorite with overnight boaters, Francis Bay is also easily reached from the Maho Bay Campground and from the road system, but shuttle buses do not travel the Francis Bay Road. The North Shore Road divides at Leinster Bay: the right fork leads to Annaberg; the left, to Francis Bay. Where the pavement ends, an open, low gravel road goes directly to the beach. The trail to Mary Point passes some plantation ruins and a pond and provides a good walk for bird-watching.

Waterlemon Cay. Some of the best snorkeling in the park can be found around little Waterlemon Cay in Leinster Bay. The biggest obstacle lies in getting there. Because the cay is a long swim from any road access, most visitors prefer to go by boat. Chartered snorkel trips or sailing trips with breaks for snorkeling and lunch may be arranged with local vendors. No facilities are available on the cay.

South-Shore Beaches. Traditionally, the snorkeling has been good off the eastern headland and central rocks of Saltpond Bay and in the western arm of Great Lameshur Bay. The turtle grass and sand flats in the center of the bays are homes for rays and queen conchs. Unfortunately, the savory conchs, in their captivating flared pink shells, have appealed to too many divers, and their numbers have seriously declined. Catch limits have been established to protect the species. Limits have also been imposed for spiny lobsters. Toilets are available at some south-shore beaches.

Most of Maho Bay's shoreline is private, but its waters make a good anchorage.

Smooth Sailing

Many sailors who have roamed international waters agree that the Virgin Islands offer some of the best sailing in the world. Consistent winter winds, delightful temperatures, well-marked charts, 1- to 2-foot tidal changes, and ample sunshine combine to make island sailing a dream. Crewed boats or bareboats (boats without captain and crew) may be chartered on St. John and nearby islands. Arrangements must be made well in advance. St. John's bays are a favored destination of yachts traveling Virgin Island waters. Leinster Bay and Francis Bay are especially good overnight anchorages when the trade winds are blowing, and Leinster offers the added bonus of excellent snorkeling around Waterlemon Cay. Wherever they stop, boaters should check charts and survey the clear waters to avoid dropping anchor on easily damaged coral formations.

Mooring buoys have been installed in many popular anchorages. Anchoring is prohibited in south-shore locations; however, moorings have been placed there as well. Vessels longer than 125 feet must anchor in Francis Bay in 30-foot depths or greater. Vessels longer than 210 feet are prohibited from anchoring in park waters.

Walking and Hiking

Annaberg. The Annaberg sugar refinery near Leinster Bay on St. John is the focus for historical interpretation in the park. A brochure describing the .25-mile self-guided trail is available at the Visitor Center. The trail passes stone remnants of the cramped slave quarters and proceeds past the windmill, the horse mill, and the boiling bench, with its five coppers (large boiling vats). Visitors are reminded of the tremendous amount of hard labor required to build and run the sugar refineries. Gathering materials and constructing the massive walls, which consist of blocks of stone and coral alternating with Danish ballast bricks, was a backbreaking task. (The Danes put the bricks in the holds of their ships to serve as ballast as they sailed to the West Indies.) Packing the cane from the steep-sided slopes, firing the ovens, and working over the boiling vats were no less arduous. The resulting sugar, molasses, and rum provided plantation owners a lucrative business for decades.

The National Park Service arranges guided walks and cultural demonstrations on certain days. St. Johnians deftly weave the island's traditional hoop-vine baskets and explain why hoop vine may be gathered only during the dark of the moon. They make charcoal as their ancestors did and discuss why the woods of acacia, genip, and wild tamarind trees are best. In the old cookhouse

Top: Green heron. Above: Hibiscus blooms year-round at Virgin Islands.

atop the horse mill, they prepare West Indian dishes over a charcoal fire and relate how forebears used dried sea fans as flour sifters, brewed a tea from black wattle leaves that could cure coughs and colds, and kept liquids cool in heavy, earthen jars.

Additional Historical Stops. Other points of historical interest include the ruins across the street from the Cinnamon Bay Campground, which can be visited on a self-guided trail, and the beautifully restored vaulted windmill at Catherineberg, about 3 miles up Centerline Road from Cruz Bay. The small park museum in Cinnamon Bay and the Historical Society Museum in Cruz Bay exhibit relics from times past.

Seashore Walk. Although visitors may walk in and along the waters of any bay, the shallow reef flats of Leinster Bay are especially rewarding. From the parking area at the end of the road, it is easiest to walk back up the road for about .3 mile to a trail that leads through mangroves to the beach. Along the road, visitors may look for the red love bugs, so named because they always seem to be joined as pairs. Green and blue herons, lesser yellowlegs, gallinules, and black-necked stilts stalk the mangrove swamps. Signs and red markers warn of the deadly manchineel tree, which hikers should assiduously avoid as they proceed to the beach. Tennis shoes protect feet as hikers wade into knee-deep waters along the turtle-grass flats and mosey across the rock and coral rubble that front the parking area. A diving mask held on the water's surface serves as a window to the bottom. Along the way, keen eyes can distinguish diverse algae and may spot conchs, turtles, a small stingray, assorted fishes, corals, sponges, brittle stars, shrimp, chitons, crabs, and a tiny octopus. Gently picking up rocks and turning them over can reveal new surprises. Rocks should be returned to their original positions; underrock organisms often cannot survive on top.

Ram Head Hike. The lack of shade and the slight incline may make the 1.8-mile round-trip hike to Ram Head seem longer. Hikers should start early, carry water, and choose a breezy day if possible. The trail drops through low, brushy catch-and-keep, century plants, and cacti to the white sands of Saltpond Bay beach. A slight detour to the white-foamed salt pond takes only a few minutes. For years, islanders have gathered salt crystals here. During periods of heavy rains, the salt pond's salinity decreases temporarily, and salt fails to form. From the white sand beach, the trail winds through wild nutmeg, poison ash (with its hollylike leaves), and mampoo trees to cobble beaches, before ascending the headland. Orchids are entwined in the arms of pipe organ cacti, and epiphytes, or air plants, spring from joints in both cacti and trees. Partway up the hill, an overlook reveals a craggy, fractured gorge that falls away to the rocks of Trunk Bay, a scene reminiscent of the New England seacoast. The trail proceeds through Arizona-land, a field of prickly Turk's cap cacti, whose tart, pink fruits are relished by people and bullfinches alike. It ends atop Ram Head, volcanic cliffs of the Water Island Formation, 100 million or more years old.

Reef Bay Trail. The 2.5-mile Reef Bay Trail seems relatively short during the descent from Centerline Road to the beach at Reef Bay, but the return climb seems closer to 6 or 8 miles. It is wise to join a National Park Service tour, which is met at the beach by a boat that returns hikers in comfort to Cruz Bay. The tour takes most of the day and includes a bag-lunch stop at the petroglyph pools about two-thirds of the way down. The top of the trail descends through a moist forest filled with hog plum, genip, and other fruit trees and past the remains of plantations. The broad, rubbery leaves of the strangler fig often block the sunlight. Black milli-pedes known as gongolo worms, whose secretions have been used to cure toothaches, crawl along branches, while golden orb spiders spin webs among heart-shaped anthurium leaves. A .3-mile side trail leads to the petroglyphs, rock carvings of disputed origin. Some anthropologists have attributed the designs to the Arawaks, while others point to the sign of the Cross and to similarities with African symbols and assert that Christianized African slaves were the artists. The high canopies give way to dry acacia scrub and lime trees as the trail continues down to the Reef Bay sugar mill. The Reef Bay mill operated until 1916, and much of its equipment remains. The last few steps lead to the beach and a refreshing wade in Reef Bay waters.

Peace Hill. A 10-minute walk from the North Shore Road above the eastern end of the beach at Hawksnest Bay leads to the remains of a sugar mill and a large figure of Christ, called *The Christ of the Caribbean.* Lieutenant Colonel Julius Wadsworth raised the figure in 1953 and donated the land to the park in 1975. Peace Hill provides views of Trunk Bay, Hawksnest Bay, and part of Caneel Bay.

Additional Trails. Many trails crisscross the island. Some are short, well used, and in good shape. Others are infrequently trav-eled and fight a losing battle with the encroaching forest. A National Park Service brochure lists trails, and employees give information about trail conditions.

Overleaf: Brittle stars often live symbiotically with sponges and soft corals.

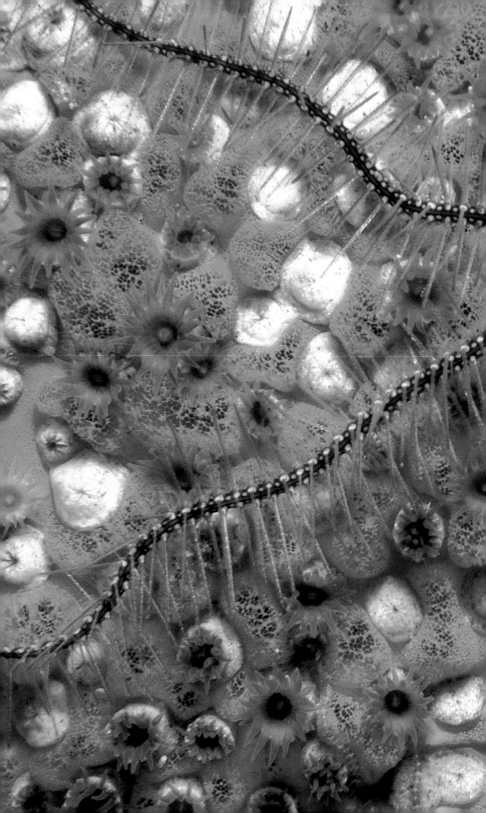

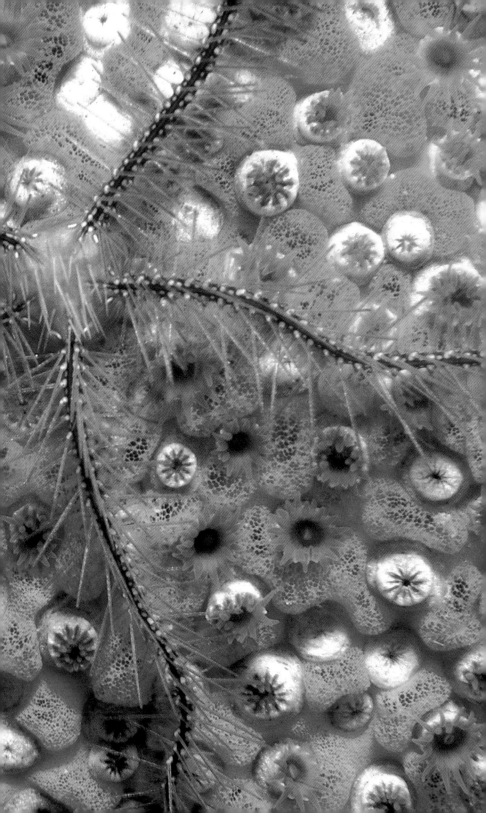

VOYAGEURS
NATIONAL PARK

The traditional canoe is yielding to the motorboat in Voyageurs' waters.

VOYAGEURS NATIONAL PARK
3131 HIGHWAY 53
INTERNATIONAL FALLS, MINNESOTA 56649
TEL.: (218) 283-9821

HIGHLIGHTS: Lakeside Resorts • Motorboat Camping • Voyageurs' Highway • Rainy Lake Ice Road • Cruiser Lake Trail System • Locator Lake Trail • Snowmobile Trails • Black Bay Ski Trail • Kettle Falls Hotel • Timber Wolves • Greenstone

ACCESS: From four resort communities approached by several spur roads from points along U.S. 53, which runs from Orr, at southern end of park, to International Falls, at northern end. Public boat-launching ramps provide boat access.

HOURS: Open year-round, 24 hours daily.

FEES: Charged at private boat-launching ramps; public ramps are free.

PARKING: Available for cars and RVs at all access points and at NPS facilities at Kabetogama Lake and Kabetogama Narrows.

GAS, FOOD, LODGING: Year-round, at concessionaire-operated facilities at Kettle Falls, accessible by water only, and in four resort communities adjacent to the park.

VISITOR CENTER: Rainy Lake Visitor Center, Kabetogama Lake Visitor Center, and Ash River Visitor Center offer an orientation movie, exhibits, maps, and publications.

GIFT SHOP: At visitor centers and in nearby resort communities.

PETS: Must be leashed; prohibited on trails and in backcountry.

PICNICKING: At Visitor Centers, Woodenfrog and Ash River campgrounds, and at backcountry sites accessible by water.

HIKING: 22-mile trail network, with trail heads accessible only by water; canoe and motorboat rentals and water-taxi service available at resorts.

BACKPACKING: No permit required; 130 backcountry campsites scattered throughout park, accessible only by water. Carry water.

CAMPGROUNDS: Camping at backcountry campsites in park, at Woodenfrog and Ash River campgrounds outside park, and in resort communities.

TOURS: Naturalist-guided interpretive tours; tour-boat concession trips on Rainy Lake and Kabetogama/Namakan/Sand Point lakes.

OTHER ACTIVITIES: Fishing, including ice fishing, with Minnesota state license; swimming, cross-country skiing, snowmobiling.

FACILITIES FOR DISABLED: Rainy Lake and Kabetogama Lake Visitor Centers, tour boats, Oberholtzer Nature Trail, one motorboat campsite accessible.

For additional information, see also Sites, Trails, and Trips on pages 378–383 and the map on pages 360–361.

VOYAGEURS NATIONAL PARK DOES NOT conform to many people's ideas of how a national park ought to look. Topographically, it is underwhelming: no spouting geysers, sawtooth mountains, painted deserts, or other spectacular oddities of nature are to be found here. Stretching along the United States–Canadian border in northern Minnesota, Voyageurs is an almost endless expanse of shallow blue lakes, low granite bluffs, and pine-covered islands sprinkled with glacial erratics. At least four times in the past 1 million years—the last time as recently as 11,000 years ago—ice sheets up to 2 miles thick scoured and bulldozed the region. The glaciers gouged out basins, kettles, and hollows that later filled with meltwater. They also exposed portions of the earth's crust nearly 3 billion years old.

The wilderness core of the park is the rugged Kabetogama (Kab-ah-TOE-ga-ma) Peninsula, a mass of land irregular in shape and surrounded by three large lakes: Rainy, Namakan, and Kabetogama. The smaller Sand Point and Crane lakes border the park on the southeast. The Boundary Waters Canoe Area and Quetico Provincial Park in Ontario are nearby. Waters in all five lakes flow toward Hudson Bay and the Arctic Ocean. The roadless peninsula, joined to mainland Minnesota by a narrow isthmus, is heavily forested and pockmarked with glacial lakes, beaver ponds, and muskegs.

Established in 1975, the park is named for the voyageurs (French for "travelers")—the French-Canadian canoemen who lit-

The irregular shores of the Kabetogama Peninsula border partly on Kabetogama Lake.

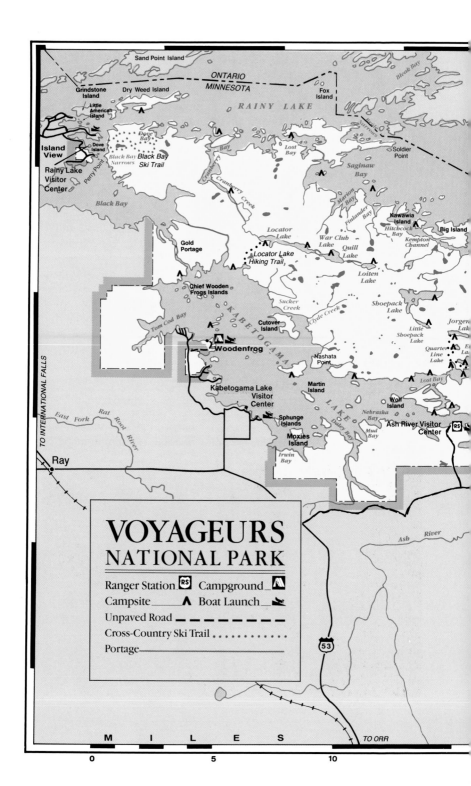

VOYAGEURS
NATIONAL PARK

Ranger Station 🆁🆂 Campground 🏕

Campsite ⋀ Boat Launch 🛥

Unpaved Road ▬ ▬ ▬ ▬

Cross-Country Ski Trail • • • • • • • •

Portage ▬▬▬▬▬▬▬

ONTARIO
MINNESOTA

Sand Point Island

Grindstone Island

Dry Weed Island

Little American Island

RAINY LAKE

Fox Island

Bleak Bay

Island View

Dove Island

Dove Bay

Black Bay Narrows

Black Bay Ski Trail

Lost Bay

Narrows

Soldier Point

Rainy Lake Visitor Center

Perry Point

Cranberry Bay

Saginaw Bay

Black Bay

Cranberry Creek

Marion Bay

Finlander Bay

Kawawia Island

Big Island

Locator Lake

Gold Portage

Locator Lake Hiking Trail

War Club Lake

Quill Lake

Hitchcock Bay

Kempton Channel

Loiten Lake

Chief Wooden Frogs Islands

Sucker Creek

Clyde Creek

Shoepack Lake

Little Shoepack Lake

Jorgen Lake

Tom Cod Bay

KABETOGAMA

Cutover Island

Woodenfrog

Nashata Point

Quarter Line Lake

En La

Lost Bay

Kabetogama Lake Visitor Center

Martin Island

Wolf Island

Ash River Visitor Center 🆁🆂

TO INTERNATIONAL FALLS

Sphunge Islands

Nebraska Bay

Moxies Island

Mud Bay

East Fork

Rat Root River

Irwin Bay

LAKE

Dairy Bay

Ray

Ash River

53

M   I   L   E   S

TO ORR

0   5   10

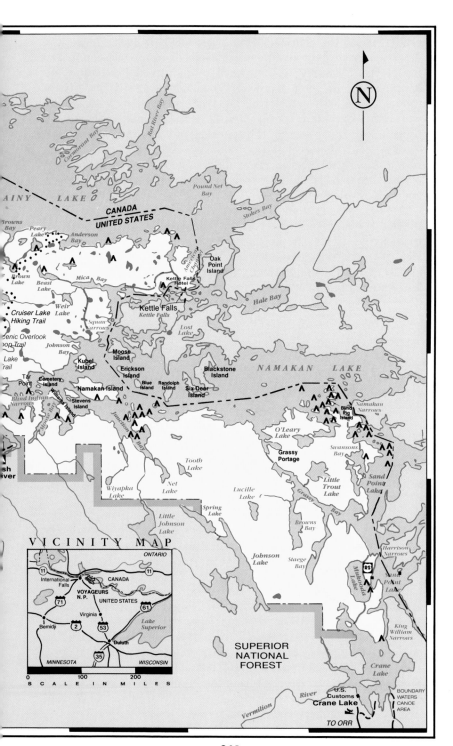

N

Cormorant Bay

Rat River Bay

RAINY LAKE

Pound Net Bay

Stokes Bay

CANADA
UNITED STATES

Browns Bay

Peary Lake

Anderson Bay

Oak Point Island

Brown Lake

Mica Bay

Beast Lake

Kettle Falls Hotel

American Channel

Hale Bay

Cruiser Lake Hiking Trail

Weir Lake

Kettle Falls
Kettle Falls

Lost Lake

Scenic Overlook Loop Trail

Squaw Narrows

Johnson Bay

Moose Island

Lake Trail

Kubel Island

Erickson Island

NAMAKAN LAKE

Tar Point

Cemetery Island

Namakan Island

Blue Island

Randolph Island

Blackstone Island

Blind Indian Narrows

Stevens Island

Six Deer Island

Namakan Narrows

Blind Pig Island

Namakan Narrows

Williams Island

Junction Bay

O'Leary Lake

Grassy Portage

Swansons Bay

Sand Point Lake

Tooth Lake

Net Lake

Lucille Lake

Little Trout Lake

Wiyapka Lake

Grassy Bay

Spring Lake

Browns Bay

Harrison Narrows

Little Johnson Lake

Mukooda Lake

Sand Point Lake

VICINITY MAP

Johnson Lake

Staege Bay

King William Narrows

ONTARIO

11

International Falls

11

CANADA

VOYAGEURS N.P.

71

UNITED STATES

61

Virginia

53

Bemidji

2

Lake Superior

Duluth

35

MINNESOTA

WISCONSIN

0   100   200
SCALE IN MILES

SUPERIOR
NATIONAL
FOREST

Crane Lake

U.S. Customs
Crane Lake

BOUNDARY WATERS CANOE AREA

Vermillion

River

TO ORR

erally carried the continent's fur trade on their backs during its heyday from the late seventeenth to the mid-nineteenth centuries. Every year, from spring thaw until autumn freeze, these rugged *hommes du nord* (men of the north) paddled king-size birch-bark canoes loaded with animal skins and trade goods along a 3,000-mile waterway extending from Montreal to remote outposts in Canada's subarctic interior. The park adjoins a 56-mile segment of the voyageurs' water highway. While satisfying a European (and North American) fashion craze for felt hats made from beaver pelts, these unheralded frontiersmen extended trade and Western civilization westward.

Voyageurs is first and foremost a water park. One-third of its 218,000 acres is covered by water. Because less than 6 miles of roadway lie within the park, visitors can hardly appreciate it by looking from the windows of a car. To experience Voyageurs properly, they must abandon their motor vehicles at one of the park's four gateways in favor of watercraft.

HISTORY

The First Minnesotans

The first human beings to populate the Voyageurs region were descended from people who had crossed from Asia to North America on the Bering Strait land bridge after the last major advance of glaciers had receded about 11,000 years ago. The first Minnesotans followed large migratory game, such as woolly mammoth and mastodon. Giant beaver, ground sloth, and caribou were also hunted. About 4,500 years ago, early inhabitants learned to grind stones and fashion tools from flint and chert. They also used fire and pounded copper into jewelry.

Hundreds of archeological sites in the park, most of them on lakeshores, date from 1000 B.C. to 300 B.C. Artifacts give evidence of a hunting and gathering people who lived in seasonal harmony with the land. By at least A.D. 800 the residents had established campsites near wild-rice beds to harvest the aquatic grain in the autumn; most likely they disbanded into small winter hunting groups, moved to sugar-maple groves following the ice breakup in the spring, and in the summer picked berries and fished. These early people buried their dead in elaborate mounds. The Dakota, or Sioux, may have been descended from these Mound Builders and were firmly established in northern Minnesota by A.D. 1500. They eventually were forced from the border-lakes region by the Ojibwa (also known as the Chippewa), however, who had moved west after being displaced by the Iroquois.

Dandies of the North Woods

A long-held conviction in Europe that a passage to the Orient lay somewhere in the American far northwest led European explorers to enter the region in the 1650s. The growing scarcity of fur-bearing animals in the St. Lawrence region also drew French traders westward. After the British incorporated the Hudson's Bay Company in 1670, thereby monopolizing the best fur-trade routes, the French undertook to obtain furs directly from the Ojibwa by sending in their own agents. Thus was the voyageur born.

The Native Americans traded beaver pelts and wild rice to the agents in return for tools, blankets, kettles, firearms, and whiskey; in addition, they schooled voyageurs in the building and repairing of birchbark canoes. These vessels, consisting of birch bark fastened to a cedar frame with spruce rootlets and sealed with pine pitch, enabled the voyageurs to penetrate far into the continent's interior. Lightweight and durable, the canoes were capable of transporting tremendous loads. The 35-foot *canot de maitre*, used on the Great Lakes, was manned by a crew of twelve and could carry more than 3 tons of cargo. The 26-foot North Canoe was used in the interior, including the park region.

The voyageurs were among the most colorful of the continent's explorers. These dandies lit up the north woods in their calico shirts, woven sashes (worn to prevent hernias caused by carrying heavy loads during portages), blue hooded cloaks, red stocking caps, and beaded pouches packed with clay pipes and tobacco. They may have been overlooked by historians because of their size: as a rule, voyageurs were short (5 feet, 6 inches was average), and they did not occupy much room in the canoe. Wiry and strong, they typically had overdeveloped upper bodies, short stocky legs, and a happy-go-lucky attitude.

Daniel Harmon, a partner in the North West Company, wrote of them in 1819:

> The Canadian Voyageurs possess lively and fickle dispositions; and they are rarely subject to depression of spirits of long continuance, even when in circumstances the most adverse. Although what they consider good eating and drinking constitutes their chief good, yet when necessity compels them to it, they submit to great privation and hardship, not only without complaining, but even with cheerfullness and gaiety.

Their daily routine was arduous. After rising at dawn, they paddled awhile and then gulped down a hurried breakfast of thick pea soup or pemmican (dried buffalo meat). They then paddled and portaged until late evening, pausing only once an hour to smoke their pipes. The voyageurs sang *chansons* (songs) to boost morale and to give rhythm to their strokes. They paddled at up to fifty strokes a minute, often covering 70 miles in a single day. Each portage required the carrying of the canoe as well as of several thousand pounds of trade goods or animal skins packed into 90-pound bales. Two or more of these "pieces" often were carried at the same time. The bales were supported by a tumpline—a broad leather strap that passed around the voyageur's forehead. The men trotted with these great loads and often competed to see who could carry the heaviest loads farthest and fastest.

To avoid portaging and to save time and energy, the voyageurs often ran dangerous rapids. Recent underwater discoveries reveal that despite their skill in maneuvering canoes, they paid a terrible toll in capsized vessels and lost lives.

Although the voyageur thumbed his nose at difficult tasks and life-threatening situations, trading-company records indicate that he commonly suffered from rheumatism, arthritis, strained muscles, and torn ligaments. He was often old at forty. His chief occupational hazard was not drowning, freezing, or starving, but strangulated hernia sustained from carrying heavy loads.

As fashions changed in the 1840s from fur to silk hats and as intense trapping and hunting in the north woods decimated the affected animals' populations, the fur trade—and with it the voyageurs—eventually disappeared.

Nevertheless, these men did more than provide the blood and sweat for a vast commercial empire held together by nothing stronger than birch bark. Many of the voyageurs married Native Americans and raised families that formed the backbone of early settlements in the north woods.

Boom Times in the Lakes Region

The young and growing nation required lumber, and northern Minnesota provided much of it beginning in the 1880s. Prized white pine and red (Norway) pine were cut first, followed by stands of spruce. The logs were floated to the mill, or were hauled by "alligator boats," steam-powered craft that traveled on land and water. Later, railroads were built to transport the logs. In its peak year, 1904, the lumber industry cut about 85 million board feet of timber in the park region, but the industry, from its inception, had been beset with controversy. U.S. and Canadian lumber companies not only stole from each other, they also robbed Native

Voyageur traders are depicted in Frances Ann Hopkins's 1873 lithograph, "Lake Superior."

American lands of prime timber. When accessible stands of pine trees as well as spruce trees became depleted, and when large numbers of homesteaders began to arrive by 1910, logging activity in the region began to peak. It diminished after 1920, just as it began to increase on more remote lands farther to the west.

Midway through this period of forest decimation, a small amount of gold was discovered in 1893 on Little American Island on Rainy Lake. The discovery led to a Wild West-style rush. Rainy Lake City, on the eastern bank of the strait leading into Black Bay near Rainy Lake, was thrown up almost overnight as fortune seekers descended on the border-lakes region. By the following year, there were mining rigs, steamboats, and a town of 500, including many pistol-packing prospectors. The gold vein was shallow, however, and gave out quickly. The town was abandoned in 1901 as adventurers were drawn away by reports of gold strikes farther west.

Commercial fishing of whitefish and sturgeon on Rainy and Crane lakes began in the 1890s. Whitefish were boxed in ice, auctioned at Kettle Falls, and shipped to Chicago and other large cities. The sturgeon was of little commercial value once its eggs were removed for caviar. It often was dried and used as firewood on steamboats. Commercial fishing is no longer permitted in park waters.

The Kettle Falls Hotel, built in 1913 to accommodate itinerant lumberjacks, was acquired by the National Park Service in 1975 and is listed in the National Register of Historic Places. The twenty-room frame house was constructed on timber pilings and probably was intended to last only twenty years or so. The building began to settle in the 1950s as the silty soil beneath the rotted timbers washed out. The pliable tamarack floorboards have been gradually stressed over time and have conformed to the ground's undulations. Although the National Park Service is straightening the floors in the hotel's reception area and restaurant, the heaved floors in the bar have been left as they were. In some places, the floor is pitted with spike marks from loggers' boots. Antiques and mementos in the room include a nickelodeon, calendar girls etched in glass, sepia-tone prints of somber Native Americans, and trophies of northern pike and woodland caribou. The Kettle Falls area affords a geographical oddity: a visitor can stand on United States soil near the hotel and look south into Canada.

Establishment of the Park

Within twenty years after Yellowstone became the first national park in 1872, Minnesota's state legislature requested President Benjamin Harrison to establish a park on the Canadian border between Crane Lake, to the east, and Lake of the Woods, to the west. The motion to set aside a portion of the voyageurs' canoe country was not based solely on a conservationist ideal. The legislature believed that creating a park from former timberlands in the north that were not used for farming would encourage forestation that would, in turn, promote rainfall beneficial to agricultural regions to the south.

The bureaucratic wheels turned slowly, despite the testimony of historians, naturalists, and Minnesota's own Charles Lindbergh, who toured the area by seaplane and later wrote: "The area is so beautiful and extraordinary that it seems to me it would be a tragedy to miss the (probably never to return) opportunity of establishing it as a national park. It is one of the most beautiful and attractive areas I have ever seen." For years a political football, Voyageurs National Park finally was established in 1975. State lands had been deeded, national-forest lands transferred, and privately owned land purchased to form the park. At present, less than 2,000 acres of Voyageurs is in private hands.

Opposite: Dozens of lakes dot the subarctic taiga forest that covers the Voyageurs terrain.
Overleaf: White birches, the species whose bark was used to make the voyageurs' canoes.

Voyageurs owes its stark lake, forest, and island setting to the erosive effects of glaciation. The rocks themselves tell the story of repeated glacial advances and retreats; many are marked with striations where glaciers, with their embedded debris, tore and gnashed at them.

Great ice sheets formed in the Hudson Bay area beginning 1 million years ago, during the Pleistocene epoch, and moved through the park region in four major advances, each lasting about 100,000 years. The power of these gravity-driven tongues of ice was inexorable. Everything in their path was warped, crushed, or removed. They shaped the region not only by scraping the ground like a giant rasp, but also by depressing the surface of the earth. Belated updoming of the earth's crust has occurred since.

The planing and plucking action of the glaciers is visible throughout the park. Where the ice rode up onto and then over a rock ledge, the rock is polished smooth. Where the glacier froze to a ledge before advancing, the rock is broken. The irregular shorelines of Rainy and Kabetogama lakes were formed by glaciers plucking house-size boulders from the ground. Glacial erratics, chunks of granite deposited by a receding glacier, are found on many of the park's 900 islands.

Not only did glaciers rob the land of its fertile mantle, carrying it gradually to the Great Plains, they also exposed the very roots of former mountains that 1 billion years before had been peneplaned to a rolling upland by an inland sea. Lava spewing forth from fissures in the earth beneath this inland sea formed the greenstone bedrock north of the Kabetogama Peninsula. It is known to be the oldest rock outcropping on earth. The entire park region is part of the Canadian Shield, a dish of crystalline rock conservatively dated at 2.7 billion years.

Following the retreat of the ice sheets about 11,000 years ago, an enormous lake of glacial meltwater—larger than all the Great Lakes combined—covered much of Canada and the northern Midwest. Named after Louis Agassiz, the nineteenth-century zoologist and geologist who postulated the ice ages, the glacial lake gradually receded largely due to downcutting of glacial rivers draining the lake. The wetlands in the western portion of Voyageurs are remains of the bottom of Lake Agassiz.

Voyageurs National Park, laced with lakes, ponds, and streams, bears witness to the power of ice moving over rock.

Opposite: Granite intruded with dikes of quartz on the south shore of Kabetogama Lake.

Climate

Voyageurs lies in the taiga, the subarctic coniferous forest of North America and Eurasia. As such, it is beset by polar air masses during much of the year. Mild temperatures prevail in June, July, and August, however, when the park's lakes are warmed by 16 hours of intense sunshine. The stored heat in the lakes tempers the southward flow of cold air in September and October, producing excellent autumn weather. Bodies of water usually freeze by late November, but it is advisable to wait until January before venturing onto them. During December, January, and February, temperatures fall below 0° F on most days and occasionally fail to rise above the zero mark for a week or more. The average temperature in January is -3° F. The wind-chill factor in midwinter is sometimes -50° F.

The deep snow and thick ice brought on by winter require much heat for their melting. However, the transition to summer is rapid following the spring thaw. By early May, shrubs and flowers begin to revive, although freezing temperatures are a threat through mid-June.

Violent weather changes are precipitated by storms that intensify over the southern plateau or Plains states and suddenly move northward, drawing up moist air from the Gulf of Mexico along the way. Severe thunderstorms and windstorms can occur in late spring and early autumn, while blizzards are not uncommon in winter. The park region and nearby International Falls—the self-described "Icebox of the Nation"—are well-known for their winter storms. Nonetheless, hardy visitors rise to the challenge offered by the cold of winter.

Flowers and Trees

As the glaciers retreated northward, life returned to the park region when airborne lichen spores landed on the sun-warmed rocks and began to grow. The lichens—each of which consists of a fungus and an alga in symbiotic relationship—produced humus, the life stuff of soil that enables more advanced plant life to germinate. Lichens also helped to break down the weathered rock into finer particles. Gradually, a thin layer of soil accumulated atop the rocks. Mosses grew; fireweed took root; and wiry grasses, coarse sedges, and herbaceous plants began to reclothe the region.

Opposite: White spruces cut through early morning autumn fog near Kabetogama Lake.

Shrubs and trees came next. Birches, willows, and aspens flourished, while sugar maples grew in well-drained glacial moraines. Hardy jack pines appeared, followed by black spruce and white spruce. Red pines and white pines, the nobles of the boreal forest, eventually came to dominate the region until loggers arrived in the late nineteenth century. Logging encouraged the new growth of acres of aspen forest at the expense of coniferous trees, although the park contains a few virgin stands of pine and spruce. Logging within the boundaries of the present park ended in 1972.

One of the park's most distinctive trees is the white birch, without which there might never have been a fur trade or a voyageur. The bark of this tree is lightweight, yet tough enough to be used in fashioning the canoes that negotiated the northern waterways. Birch usually grows in clumps of two to four trees and can reach heights of 80 feet.

Dams built in the early twentieth century at the outlets of Rainy and Namakan lakes continue in operation. Unnaturally wide fluctuations in water level, caused by operation of the dams, occur on Kabetogama, Namakan, and Sand Point lakes—though not as much on Rainy Lake. As a result, wild rice has been replaced in many areas by other plants, although isolated fields of this aquatic grain can still be seen growing in the muck of shallow bays and torpid streams.

Berries abound at Voyageurs—blueberries, strawberries, juneberries, raspberries, and many others grow wild. Cranberry bogs can be found in low wetland areas.

When the last snows of May have melted, marsh marigold, wild

Blueberries are one of many species of wild berries found at Voyageurs.

ginger, and trailing arbutus burst forth. The showy, or pink and white, lady's-slipper (the state flower) grows in wet areas, as does the clintonia, with its distinctive lilylike leaves and yellow blossoms. Heather, honeysuckle, and red sphagnum moss inhabit the park's muskegs (bogs), lending them a distinctive fragrance.

Wildlife

Birds are especially abundant at Voyageurs, with almost 240 species of winged creatures in the park. Most regal of all is the bald eagle. In the mid-1990s, thirty-six pairs of these great birds were nesting within the park. The sight of a bald eagle soaring above the treetops as it scans the lakes for dead or struggling fish is not soon forgotten. Eagles usually build a large, bulky nest of sticks and branches high in a dead white or red pine. Nests large enough to sleep a human adult are not unusual.

To many longtime area residents, the common loon is the symbol of the border-lakes wilderness. These large, green-headed birds, whose black backs are flecked with snowy white spots, are resident breeders during the summer. They usually can be seen bobbing contentedly in the middle of a lake. Loons are capable of diving to 200 feet in pursuit of fish, although most of the lakes in the park are fairly shallow and do not require the birds to expend such effort in pursuit of a meal. Hearing the wild, querulous cry of a loon echoing off the shoreline of a remote island at dusk is one of the joys of camping in the park.

Other large-wingspread birds in the park include ospreys, double-crested cormorants, ravens, owls, and several types of hawks. Herring gulls and mergansers are common on the lakes. Great blue herons wade in the shallows on stiltlike legs in search of fish, frogs, and crayfish.

Hikers on the Kabetogama Peninsula may stir up a ruffed grouse. When surprised, it leaps into the air with a loud whirr and beats a hasty retreat through the trees. Songbirds are numerous at Voyageurs; warblers, finches, chickadees, and white-throated sparrows fill the woods with melodious sound.

Fishing is excellent throughout the park. The region's most popular game fish is the walleye, so named because of its opaque, glassy eyes. Many people consider the walleye to be the tastiest of all of the freshwater fishes. Found throughout the large lakes of the park, it usually travels in schools over sand bars and rocky drop-offs.

The voracious northern pike inhabits shallow weed beds and places where streams feed into a lake. Smallmouth bass are also

The white-tailed deer is Voyageurs' most prevalent mammal.

common in streams and lakes. The muskellunge, an elusive trophy fish, is found in Shoepack and Little Shoepack lakes on the Kabetogama Peninsula, while lake trout inhabit three of the park's cool, deep-water lakes.

Voyageurs and Isle Royale National Park in Michigan are among the few places in the contiguous forty-eight states where the endangered gray, or timber, wolf survives. The wolf is rarely seen by summer visitors, but its lonesome, chilling howl is sometimes heard on a moonlit night.

Next to the white-tailed deer, the park's most prevalent mammal is the beaver. Trapped to near extinction during the fur-trade era, the beaver has since reestablished itself. Its dams and domed lodges dot the lowland regions of the Kabetogama Peninsula. On discovering that it has been approached unawares, the beaver will slap the water loudly with its tail and dive to one of the underwater entrances of its lodge. The beaver is not a rodent of ordinary proportions; adults may weigh 50 pounds or more.

While only a few dozen moose inhabit the park, they can be viewed on occasion dipping their huge heads in the water to feed on aquatic plants in shallow bays. Far more common are red squirrels and chipmunks, which scamper across trails and campsites.

Opposite: Autumn color makes a red maple stand out against a background of white birch.

In sharp contrast to most national parks, Voyageurs is almost inaccessible except by water. Although hiking trails are few, a great variety of canoe routes and other boating opportunities are available in the park. More than 100 primitive campsites are scattered throughout Voyageurs on secluded islands, many of which have sandy beaches fronting sheltered bays. Facilities at each campsite are Spartan: a tent pad (a level, cleared site), a picnic table, a fire ring, and a privy. Food should be hung from trees so as not to tempt the park's bears. Insect repellent is a must during the summer.

More than sixty privately owned resorts and lodges line the boundaries of the park at Crane Lake, Ash River, Kabetogama, and Rainy Lake. Most resort owners will provide water-taxi service to trail heads and campsites.

Voyageurs is most frequently explored by motorboat. Motorboats and houseboats may be rented at the resorts. But those who yearn to follow the tradition of the Ojibwa and the voyageurs may paddle along the miles of established canoe routes, which range from extended trails with several portages to short trips that are just right for novices. Almost soundless in the water, the canoe is the ideal boat from which to view wildlife. Sailing is popular on the larger lakes, especially in light, swift sloops. Boaters must be alert to weather changes on the larger lakes. Canoeists, in particular, should travel close to the shore and seek shelter in protected coves and inlets when necessary.

Winter visitors to the park can ski cross country on the lakes. The Black Bay ski trail offers flat terrain for beginners as well as challenging loops for skiers who are more accomplished. The marked ski trail winds through dense brush and in many places intersects animal trails.

Hiking Trails

Cruiser Lake Trail. Accessible by water, the 9-mile Cruiser Lake Trail crosses the Kabetogama Peninsula from Anderson Bay, on Rainy Lake, to Lost Bay, on Kabetogama Lake. It is clearly marked by stone cairns, and at several points it follows a glacial ridge high above the trees and water. Hikers can view seven lakes along the trail and its spur routes. A variety of plants, from blueberries and strawberries to large toadstools and stunted maples, border the trail. Reindeer moss in hues of buff and peach cover the rocks above Anderson Bay. Single-plank bridges cross streams and boggy areas at the heads of beaver ponds. Seven backcountry campsites are situated along the trail system.

Locator Lake Trail. The short, attractive Locator Lake Trail is approached by water from Kabetogama Lake opposite the Woodenfrog Campground. Hikers follow wooded terrain for 2 miles into the peninsula to Locator Lake, at the head of Cranberry Creek. A campsite is available on the lake's northeastern shore. Anglers find northern pike and largemouth bass in the lake.

Ski Trail

Black Bay Ski Trail. The 8-mile Black Bay Ski Trail comprises a series of loops routed through the Kabetogama Peninsula lowlands and is designed to accommodate all levels of skiers. Whitetailed deer, pine grosbeaks, pileated woodpeckers, snowshoe hares, and other wildlife are occasionally seen along the way. The trail, in the northwestern section of the park, can be reached by driving east from International Falls for 12 miles to the Rainy Lake Visitor Center, and then driving on the "ice road" (Rainy Lake) 1 mile to the trail head.

Canoe Routes

Kabetogama Peninsula Loop. The 68-mile Kabetogama Peninsula Loop circles the peninsula by way of Namakan, Rainy, and Kabetogama lakes. The Ash River Visitor Center, West Kabetogama, or Black Bay may serve as a starting point. Side trips can be taken to smaller, secluded lakes within the peninsula, including Beast and Peary. Portages are required at the Kettle Falls dam (the National Park Service-operated Kettle Falls Hotel maintains a dock and portage service) and at Gold Portage, so named not because that precious metal was found there but because the .25-mile portage was used by gold miners on their way to Rainy Lake City. A circumnavigation of the Kabetogama Peninsula usually takes from 5 to 7 days. Good fishing and camping are available en route.

Voyageurs' Highway. The one-way Voyageurs' Highway follows the great river road of the voyageurs for 55 miles along the international boundary from Crane Lake westward to Black Bay. Only

Overleaf: 16-hour-long summer days at Voyageurs bring temperate warmth that is swept away by polar air masses moving southward in autumn.

one portage, at the Kettle Falls dam, is required on this 5- to 6-day trip; a motorized portage is available. Observant canoeists will see reddish brown Native American pictographs of moose, men in canoes, suns, moons, a pipe, and other subjects on the Canadian side of Namakan Narrows. Also visible on the rock cliff is a serpentlike vein of feldspar, which early inhabitants worshipped as a manitou, or god.

Sand Point–Namakan Lakes Loop. Like the Voyageurs Highway, the 32 -mile Sand Point–Namakan Lakes Loop begins at the public landing on the southern shore of Crane Lake. After passing through King William Narrows into Sand Point Lake, canoeists can duck into a small bay that leads to the group campsite at Mukooda Lake. A short portage leads to 2-mile-long Mukooda Lake, where fishing is good for northern pike and—for anglers willing to troll deep with large spoons—lake trout. Other side trips on the 2- to 3-day trip may be taken to Staege Bay or Browns Bay, both of which are accessible from Grassy Bay. A short portage also can be taken from Grassy Bay to beautiful Little Trout Lake. The loop reaches its northern apex at Blind Pig Island and returns through Namakan Narrows.

Crane Lake–Lac La Croix–Namakan Lake Loop. An ambitious (nine portages) and international 75-mile canoe tour, this route extends from Voyageurs to the Boundary Waters Canoe Area and sections of Quetico Provincial Park in Ontario. The trip may be made 13 miles shorter by using the Dawson Truck Portage to Lac La Croix. A travel permit is required to enter the Boundary Waters Canoe Area. Canoeists also must clear customs before entering Canada. The highlight of the trip is Lac La Croix (Lake of the Cross), so named by the French because of its shape. The lake is also known by two Ojibwa names: *Nequawkaun,* which denotes the spout used in collecting sugar-maple sap, and *Sheshibagumag sagaiigun,* which means "the lake where they go every which way to get through." The route bypasses a number of white-water rapids that may have been run by the voyageurs. At least one week should be allowed to canoe this route.

Vermilion River Route. Although it lies outside the boundaries of Voyageurs, this former fur-trade route is connected historically and geographically to the park. The Vermilion River flows from Lake Vermilion for 35 miles to Crane Lake, at the southern extremity of the park. A portion of the river is part of the western boundary of Superior National Forest. This demanding trip requires ten portages, one of which bypasses dramatic Vermilion Falls and its narrow, rocky gorge.

Moonrise over an isolated island, from approach over frozen Rainy Lake.

TRAILS OF VOYAGEURS NATIONAL PARK

CRUISER LAKE HIKING TRAIL: Traverses the Kabetogama Peninsula from Lost Bay on Kabetogama Lake to Anderson Bay on Rainy Lake; 9 miles one way; 5 hours; trail passes five lakes and several beaver ponds situated in a dense forest of aspen, birch, spruce, and fir, and follows bedrock ridge tops where stunted pines and oaks cling to shallow soil; watch for thick carpets of reindeer moss and blueberries in season; camping is available at crystal-clear Cruiser Lake.

CRUISER LAKE HIKING TRAIL SYSTEM: Short loops and spurs from the Cruiser Lake Hiking Trail provide a variety of opportunities for hiking. At Anderson Bay a 2-mile loop trail follows the rocky, pine-covered uplands, with fine views of Rainy Lake. From Lost Bay on Kabetogama Lake, the 2-mile Agnes Lake Loop Trail explores various forest types and passes a beaver pond. A third 2.5-mile trail winds past three inland lakes. Allow 1 hour for each 1.5 miles.

LOCATOR LAKE HIKING TRAIL: Starts on northwest shore of Kabetogama Lake; ends on southwest shore of Locator Lake; 2 miles one way; 1 hour; trail passes by base of active beaver dam, follows glacial ridge with scenic vistas of forested valley; watch for carpets of reindeer moss; deer occasionally seen; north shore of Locator Lake presents striking picture, with its steep south-facing cliffs.

Overleaf: Rime ice covers marsh plants following a foggy night of sub-0° F temperatures.

ANIMALS & PLANTS
OF THE EAST AND MIDDLE WEST

This appendix provides a sample of animals and plants commonly found in the national parks of the East and Middle West. The two-letter abbreviations indicate the parks in which these animals and plants are most often seen.

AC	Acadia	GS	Great Smoky Mountains	MC	Mammoth Cave
BS	Biscayne			SH	Shenandoah
DT	Dry Tortugas	HS	Hot Springs	VI	Virgin Islands
		IR	Isle Royale	VO	Voyageurs

MAMMALS

BEAVER
AC, GS, HS, IR, MC, VO

The beaver is North America's largest rodent; it generally is up to 4 ft. long, including a 1-ft., flat, scaly tail, and weighs 45–60 lbs., but can weigh up to 100. Mainly nocturnal, it is seldom seen; but there is evidence of its work in the dams of small streams. The beaver lives in lodges formed by logs; on major rivers, it lives in dens along the bank. The beaver's diet is mainly the bark of trees, although in summer it feeds on water vegetation.

BOBCAT
AC, EV, GS, HS, MC, SH

The bobcat is North America's most common wild cat; because it is nocturnal and secretive, it is seldom seen. It is tawny in color, with indistinct black spots, a pale or white belly, and a short, stubby tail with 2 or 3 black bars. It weighs 14–68 lbs. and measures 2.3–4 ft. long; the males are larger than the females. In the late winter, the male may be heard yowling at night, much like a domesticated cat. Kits are born in a den, usually in thickets or under rocks and logs. The bobcat feeds on rodents and, especially, ground-nesting birds.

EASTERN CHIPMUNK
AC, GS, HS, MC, SH, VO

The eastern chipmunk is stouter and brighter than its counterpart in the West, and it has a shorter tail (3.25–4.5 in.). Above it is reddish-brown with a dark stripe down the center of the back; a white stripe on each side is bordered by two black stripes; the belly is white. Nose-to-tail length is 8.5–11.75 in. Generally a ground species, this chipmunk climbs oak trees when acorns are ripe, storing up to a dozen quarts of nuts and seeds for consumption in winter. It is likely to be seen in Shenandoah, Great Smoky Mountains, and Hot Springs national parks.

GRAY FOX
EV, GS, HS, MC, SH, VO

Of the six species of foxes in North America, the gray fox is the most commonly found in national parks; yet, being nocturnal, it is seldom seen. It is gray, with a black stripe running down the top of its tail, stands 14–15 in. at the shoulder, and is 3–4 ft. long, including a 9–17 in. tail. It ranges throughout the East, into parts of the West and Southwest.

LITTLE BROWN BAT
AC, GS, HS, IR, MC, SH, VO

The little brown bat is the most common bat in North America. Above it is colored with varying shades of glossy brown; below it is buff-colored. It measures .25–3.75 in. long. In autumn, little brown bats may fly several hundred miles in search of a suitable cave or mine for winter hibernation; in summer they form smaller nursing colonies in buildings. This species ranges throughout much of North America, except Texas, southern California, and Florida, into Alaska and Nova Scotia.

MINK AC, EV, GS, HS, IR, MC, SH, VO

The 19.25–28.25 in.-long mink is easily recognized by its lustrous, uniformly chocolate brown to black coat, which is marked with white spotting on the chin and throat. Like other members of the weasel family, males fight viciously among themselves both in and out of breeding season, emitting an odor as pungent as a skunk's. Males are larger than females. The mink preys on a variety of small animals and birds, and takes easily to water when hunting. It ranges throughout most of North America, except the Southwest.

MUSKRAT
AC, GS, IR, MC, SH, VO

A large, volelike rodent with dense, glossy brown fur, the muskrat can be seen at any time, but especially at night. It measures 16–24.5 in. in length, including a 7–12 in. scaly tail, and weighs about 4 pounds. Muskrats live in multi-chambered structures made of plants, roots, and mud in marshy areas along streams and lakes, similar to those of the beaver. It eats nearby vegetation—cattails, sedges, water lilies, rushes—on a specially built eating platform.

RACCOON
AC, BS, EV, GS, HS, MC, SH

The notorious "black masked" raccoon raids garbage cans in national parks, just as it does in the suburbs; nocturnal, the raccoon can be seen around park campgrounds. It is reddish-brown with black above and gray below, and measures 2–3 ft., including a 7.5–16-in. bushy tail with alternating black and brown rings. Its diet includes grapes, nuts, insects, rodents, turtles, frogs, and birds' eggs; dens are usually in hollow trees, caves, rock clefts, or culverts.

RED BAT
AC, GS, HS, MC, SH, VO

The red bat is one of the few mammals whose colors vary between the male and female; males are bright red or orange-red; females are dull red; both are frosted white on back and breast, with a white patch on each shoulder. This species measures 3.75–5 in. long. By day the red bat hangs 4–10 ft. from the ground in dense foliage, but with an open avenue of flight downward and out into the open air; by night it feeds on insects. It ranges throughout the eastern United States into the Southwest and southern Canada.

RED FOX
AC, GS, HS, IR, MC, SH, VO

Although this fox goes through color phases—black and silver—it is primarily reddish with white underparts, chin, and throat. Its tail is 13–17 in. long, bushy with a white tip. Doglike in size, it measures 15–16 in. high and 15–40 in. long. Though common, the red fox is difficult to spot in the parks; it is shy and primarily nocturnal. Red foxes feed on whatever is available, from corn and apples to birds and mice, crickets and crayfish. Dens are usually "remodeled" or enlarged marmot or badger dens along stream banks, slopes, or rock piles, but are always high for a full view of the surrounding area.

SHORT-TAILED SHREW
AC, EV, GS, HS, MC, SH

The largest shrew in North America and one of the most common of North American mammals, the short-tailed shrew is ferocious, biting its prey—mice or smaller shrews—in the face and neck, paralyzing it almost instantly with venomous saliva; it may kill mammals of its own size or even larger, but its primary diet is insects and larvae. This species measures 3.75–5 in. long; its coloration is solid gray. The short-tailed shrew's range extends across southern Canada, south to Nebraska, West Virginia, and the southern Appalachian Mountains.

SOUTHERN FLYING SQUIRREL
EV, GS, HS, MC, SH

The southern and northern flying squirrels are the smallest of the tree squirrels, and the only nocturnal ones. They do not really fly, but rather glide downward from tree limb to tree limb moving the legs and tail to control direction and the wide flaps of skin on the sides as a parachute to slow descent. The southern flying squirrel has a very silky coat, grayish-brown above and white below, and measures 8.25–10 in. long. It feeds on nuts, seeds, berries, insects, and sometimes vertebrate flesh. This species ranges throughout the eastern United States except Maine and southern Florida.

STRIPED SKUNK
AC, EV, GS, HS, MC, SH

The striped skunk is the skunk that is found almost everywhere in the U.S., except Alaska. It has a narrow stripe of white down its nose, and a V-shaped, white configuration down its back; males weigh 6–14 lbs. and measure 20–31 in., including a 7–15 in. bushy tail. The striped skunk feeds on insects, small mammals, amphibians, and eggs of small ground-nesting birds.

WHITE-TAILED DEER
AC, EV, GS, HS, MC, SH, VO

The white-tailed deer was once hunted nearly to extermination throughout its original range, the Northeast and Midwest; hunting restrictions and a decline in its predators' populations have allowed resurgence and the extension of its range, which now extends nearly throughout the United States (except parts of California, Nevada, and Utah). In summer it is tan to reddish-brown above; in winter, it is grayish-brown. This deer measures 4.5–6.75 ft. long, and weighs up to 300 lbs.; males' antlers measure up to 3 ft. wide. Two dwarf subspecies inhabit the South.

WOODCHUCK
AC, GS, MC, SH, VO

Contrary to legend, the woodchuck, or groundhog, forecasts the arrival of spring only generally. It emerges from its burrow after hibernation in early spring, which sometimes arrives on or about February 2, "Groundhog Day"; in the northern parts of its range (central Alaska southeast through Canada and Maine, south in the East to the southern Appalachian Mountains) it emerges much later. It measures 16.5–32.25 in., and has a large bushy tail. Overall it is grayish-brown to reddish to blackish. The woodchuck feeds on green vegetation.

BIRDS

AMERICAN GOLDFINCH AC, EV, GS, HS, IR, MC, SH, VO

Often called the "wild canary," the American goldfinch is smaller than the sparrow; it measures 4.5–5 in. The male is bright yellow with a white rump, black forehead, and black wings and tail edged with white. In winter the male loses its bright color and resembles the female, which is a dull grayish black with black wings. The goldfinch nests in late summer when weed seeds are available.

AMERICAN REDSTART AC, DT, EV, GS, IR, MC, SH, VO

One of the most abundant birds in North America, the American redstart is about 4.5–5.5 in. in length. The male is black with bright orange patches on its wings and tail; the female is dull olive-brown above, white below, with yellow wing and tail patches. Its coloration may be seen as it drops down suddenly from the sky in pursuit of flying insects.

AMERICAN ROBIN AG, GS, HS, IR, MC, SH, VO

Best known of all North American birds, once called "robin," the American robin is gray-brown, with puffed-out, red or orange breast, white throat, and blackish head and tail. It measures 9–11 in. The robin feeds primarily on worms pulled from the ground. In cold weather, the nest is built of twigs and mud and lined with fine material in low, densely leafed or needled trees and bushes; in hot weather, the nest is high in maple or sycamore trees.

BLACK-AND-WHITE WARBLER AC, BS, DT, EV, GS, HS, IR, MC, SH, VI, VO

Once called the "black-and-white creeper" because of its method of searching for insects both upward and downward along the branches and trunks of trees, this warbler is about 5 in. long, with black-and-white stripes that extend over its crown. The male is distinguished by its black throat; the female's throat is white. The black-and-white warbler's return to the North may be noticed as early as mid-April.

BLUE JAY AC, EV, GS, HS, IR, MC, SH, VO

Although it is one of our most beautiful birds, this is the scoundrel that drives smaller competitors away from bird feeders. The blue jay is 12 in. long, with black and white stripes on the wing and tail; its face is ringed with black and capped by a prominent crest. It effectively plants trees by burying many of the seeds and acorns it gathers, then forgetting to retrieve them. The blue jay's raucous screams often signify the presence of a predator nearby.

CEDAR WAXWING AC, EV, GS, HS, IR, SH, VO

Cedar waxwings have the unusual habit of sitting in a row on a tree branch and passing berries from one beak to another until one of them eats. The cedar waxwing is a sleek brown bird about 6.5–8 in. in length, with red-tipped wing feathers, yellow-tipped tail feathers, and a black mask. It is almost always seen in flocks, and appears and disappears suddenly in an area in accordance with the availability of a berry crop.

CHIPPING SPARROW
AC, EV, GS, IR, MC, SH, VO

Also called the "hairbird" because it lines its nest with hair, the chipping sparrow has been known to pluck hair from a sleeping dog when horse hair is not available. It measures about 5–5.5 in., and is smaller than a sparrow. Above it is brown, streaked with black, with a chestnut crown; underparts, sides of the face, and rump are gray. The chipping sparrow usually feeds on seeds, but in summer adults and young also feed on insects.

COMMON CROW AC, EV, GS, HS, IR, MC, SH, VO

Despite its unseemly conduct and raucous cries, the familiar common crow, a stocky black bird with a stout bill and fan-shaped tail, is judged to be one of the most intelligent of birds. The common crow quickly learns to mimic the human voice and appears to utilize a complex language and well-developed social structure within its communities. It gathers in huge roosts that may number more than half a million, and is considered a menace to crops; however, it also consumes enormous amounts of grasshoppers and other plant-destroying insects.

COMMON FLICKER
AC, EV, GS, HS, IR, SH, VN

The common flicker is really a woodpecker, the only one in North America that feeds on insects at ground level; it may be seen on lawns, licking up ants with its long tongue. Its familiar pecking or hammering on deadwood or tin roofs is a display during courtship and a means of proclaiming territory. The common flicker measures about 12 in. and has a brown back and a white rump which is seen in flight; it has a black crescent on its breast and numerous dark spots and bars on its underparts and wings. The "yellow-shafted" strain found in the West and the "red-shafted" strain found in the East interbreed on the Great Plains, and are considered one species.

COMMON NIGHTHAWK AC, EV, GS, HS, IR, MC, SH, VO

A slim-winged gray-brown bird, with ample tail, large eyes, tiny bill, and short legs, the common nighthawk measures 8.5–10 in. from bill to tail. The male has a white throat patch and a white subterminal tail bar. It feeds on nocturnal insects, and by day sits on tree limbs in a "dead-leaf" camouflage.

COMMON YELLOW-THROAT AC, BS, DT, EV, GS, HS, MC, SH, VO

The common yellowthroat measures 4.5–6 in., and has olive-brown coloration above, with a bright yellow throat and upper breast. The male has a bold black face mask which is capped by a border of white; females and young males have no mask. The male's most notable breeding behavior consists of a sudden flight into the air and return to ground level while uttering high-pitched sounds. The yellowthroat lives in marshy areas and moist, weedy thickets.

EASTERN WOOD PEEWEE AC, DT
EV, GS, IR, MC, SH, VO

One is more likely to hear the eastern peewee than to see it, for its dull, olive-gray coloration blends into the dense foliage of the treetops where it is usually found. It has two whitish wing bars, and measures 6.5 in. The eastern wood peewee's nest may resemble a fungus growth or a knot of wood.

INDIGO BUNTING
AC, BS, DT, EV, GS, HS, IR, MC, SH, VI, VO

Indigo is a deep blue, but the indigo bunting's feathers are actually black; the diffraction of light through its feather structure gives the male a distinctly blue appearance. The female is a dull brown overall. The 5.5 in.-long indigo bunting is generally found in thickets alongside country roads, and in other areas where woodlands meet open areas. It eats insects and weed seeds.

OVENBIRD AC, BS, DT, EV, GS, IR, MC, SH, VI, VO

The ovenbird's name comes from its nest, which resembles a Dutch oven. Made of dead leaves and plant fiber and lined with grass, the nest has a side entrance and sits on the forest floor. The ovenbird measures about 6 in., the size of a sparrow, and is olive-brown above and white with dark streaks below. It has a bold eye-ring and an orange-brown crown bordered with black stripes. Ovenbird males often mate with more than one female; when the brood hatches, more than one male may assist with feeding.

RED-EYED VIREO AC, DT, EV, GS, IR, MC, SH, VO

The 5.5–6.5 in.-long red-eyed vireo can sing even while it attempts to seize and eat a large insect; it sings from sunup to sundown, even on the hottest summer days, and this habit has earned it the nickname "preacher." The red-eyed vireo is olive-green above, whitish below, and has a narrow white eyebrow that is bordered above with black; it has prominent reddish-brown eyes. It is one of the most abundant birds found in eastern North American deciduous forests.

RED-WINGED BLACKBIRD
AC, BS, EV, GS, IR, SH, VO

Measuring 7–9.5 in., the red-winged blackbird lives in marshes, swamps, and wet and dry meadows. The male is black with a yellow-bordered red shoulder patch; the female is brown, heavily streaked with dark brown. Mating red-winged blackbirds build a new nest for each of the two or three broods they raise in a season. After breeding, they join with other blackbirds into flocks which may number into the millions.

RUBY-THROATED HUMMINGBIRD AC, EV, GS, HS, IR, MC, SH, VO

The ruby-throated hummingbird is the only hummingbird that breeds east of the Mississippi River. It is very small, 3.5 in. long, with metallic green coloration above and white below. The male has a brilliant red throat. Like other hummers, the ruby-throated hummingbird can fly backward and straight up and down. Constantly in motion, it is able to feed on the nectar of the tubular red flowers to which it is attracted without landing on the blossoms themselves.

SONG SPARROW
AC, EV, GS, IR, MC, SH, VO

The song sparrow is found almost everywhere in North America, from Mexico to Alaska and Newfoundland. Over its vast geographical range its characteristics show some variation; the song sparrow of the eastern United States is about 5 in. long, while the same species may grow to 7 in. and possess a long bill in Alaska. The eastern strain is brown, with whitish, heavily streaked underparts.

SWAINSON'S THRUSH
AC, EV, GS, HS, IR, MC, SH

Named for the English naturalist William Swainson (1789-1855) and formerly called the "olive-backed thrush," this thrush is about 6.5-7.5 in. in length and has uniform dull olive-brown coloration with mottled, whitish underparts and a buff-colored eye-ring and cheek. This bird dwells on the floors of coniferous forests and willow thickets, from Alaska to northern New England, Michigan, and mountain areas south to Colorado and West Virginia; it winters in South America.

WHITE-THROATED SPARROW AC, EV, GS, HS, IR, MC, SH, VO

The white-throated sparrow breeds in Canada and is known in the United States as a winter resident. It measures 6-7 in. and has a black-and-white striped crown, white throat patch, and gray underparts; the back, wings, and tail are brown. The evening flocking call of migrating white-throated sparrows is particularly appealing.

YELLOW-RUMPED WARBLER AC, BS, DT, EV, GS, HS, IR, MC, SH, VO

Also called the myrtle warbler, the yellow-rumped warbler has dull bluish coloration above, with black streaks; underparts are blackish. The crown, rump, and sides of the breast are yellow; wings have two white bars. This warbler measures 5-6 in., and is found in abundance in winter throughout the eastern and southern parts of the United States, to which it migrates from northern coniferous forests.

AMPHIBIANS, REPTILES, AND FISHES

AMERICAN TOAD
AC, GS, HS, IR, MC, SH, VO

Found in suburban gardens as well as mountain forests, the American toad is 2-4.5 in. long. Its coloration is brown to rust to olive, with brownish spots on the belly; the male has a dark throat. Brown to orange-red warts may be present. Mostly nocturnal, it ranges over northeastern North America, south to the southern Appalachian Mountains, north to Wisconsin and Manitoba; it is found in a variety of habitats wherever moisture and insects are abundant.

BROAD-HEADED SKINK
GS, HS, MC, SH

The broad-headed skink is mistakenly called a scorpion in many of the localities of its range, the southeastern quarter of North America. It is a lizard, 6.5-12.75 in. long, with a wide head and 5 broad, light stripes which fade with age. Adults are brown, with a red-orange head; from June to August, when eggs hatch, black juveniles with blue tails may be seen. Diurnal, the broad-headed skink climbs trees to hunt insects more effectively.

BULLFROG
AC, GS, HS, MC

The bullfrog is the largest frog in North America. It is probably more often heard than seen; its booming voice may be heard for a quarter mile on quiet spring nights. It is 3.5-8 in. long, with mottled, green to yellow coloration above and a cream-colored belly. Bullfrogs eat insects, young frogs, and minnows; large specimens may eat small birds and snakes. Tadpoles may take up to two years to transform. Originally, the bullfrog ranged over the eastern and central states; it has now been extensively introduced in the West.

COMMON GRAY TREEFROG
AC, EV, GS, HS, MC, SH, VO,

The two species of gray treefrog, Cope's gray

treefrog and the common gray treefrog, cannot be distinguished from each other in the field; the Cope's gray treefrog has half the number of chromosomes that the common gray treefrog has. These rough-skinned, 1.25-2.5 in.-long frogs are greenish to brown to gray, with dark splotches above; they are nocturnal, occupying the upper reaches of trees in or near water, descending to breed. Both species range from southern Ontario to Maine, south to Texas and Florida.

EASTERN GARTER SNAKE
AC, EV, GS, HS, IR, MC, SH, VO

The eastern garter snake is one of the many subspecies of the common garter snake, the most widely distributed snake in North America. It measures 18-51.5 in. long, with overall brown-green coloration and yellow to brownish to bluish side and back stripes; some specimens may be all black, or lack stripes. Active during the day, it feeds on frogs, toads, salamanders, earthworms, and sometimes small fish or mice. It ranges throughout the United States, except in southwestern desert regions.

FOUR-TOED SALAMANDER
AC, GS, HS, SH

All salamanders have four toes on their front feet; this one has the same number on its hind feet. Measuring 2-4 in. long, this small species is reddish-brown above, with grayish sides and a white, spotted belly. Larvae mature in 2.5 years. When seized by a predator, its tail breaks off—a new one is then regenerated. Often found where sphagnum moss is present. The four-toed salamander's range is discontinuous, mostly east of the Mississippi (except the Florida peninsula).

GREEN FROG
AC, GS, IR, MC, SH, VO

Prevalent east of the Mississippi, north to southeastern Canada, the green frog is green, bronze, or brown, with a white belly, yellow throat, and prominent external eardrums. It measures 2.25-4 in. long, and lives near the edges of ponds and lakes, streams, and in swamps. It is primarily nocturnal.

GROUND SKINK
EV, GS, HS, MC

The ground skink is a brown, long-tailed lizard with a dark side stripe running from eye to tail. It has small legs, and a portion of its lower eyelid is transparent. It measures 3-5.25 in. long. Its diet consists of insects and spiders. This skink ranges throughout the southeastern quarter of the United States, and may be found in humid forests and forested grasslands.

MAP TURTLE
GS, HS, MC, SH

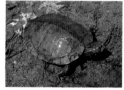

The map turtle's name comes from the designs on its head and shell. Males measure 4-6.25 in. long; females are 7 - 10.75 in., with an enlarged head. The shell is greenish to olive-brown, with a pattern of yellow-orange lines; skin is greenish with bright yellow stripes. The female's jaws are strong enough to break open freshwater clams and large snails; males and juveniles eat insects, crayfish, and smaller mollusks. The habitat of this species is the mud bottoms of slow-moving rivers and lakeshores; it ranges from Lake George west through the drainage areas of the Great Lakes, south to the Arkansas and Missouri River drainages.

PICKEREL FROG
AC, GS, HS, MC, SH

The pickerel frog hibernates from October to March; when active, it is nocturnal. It measures .75-3.5 in. long. Above, its coloration is light brown, with a parallel row of dark, squarish blotches; the belly and the bottoms of its hind legs are bright yellow. The pickerel frog lives in sloughs with dense, low vegetation, near streams and in swamps and meadows; it ranges throughout the eastern states, except the extreme Southeast. An unappetizing skin secretion protects this frog from some predators.

PUFFER
BS, DT, EV, VI

Some 100 species of puffer are distributed around the world, mostly in the tropics. When threatened, the puffer, as a defense mechanism, takes in water or air and inflates itself. Its teeth can crush the shells of the crustaceans, mollusks, and other invertebrates on which it feeds. This species, the porcupine fish, can be up to 3 ft. in length (or diameter, when inflated), though most are 1 ft. or less.

RED-SPOTTED NEWT
AC, GS, IR, MC, SH, VO

The red-spotted newt is a subspecies of the primarily aquatic eastern newt; western newts are primarily terrestrial. Adults are 2.5-5.5 in. long, with black-bordered orange-red spots along the back in adult and eft stages. Eggs are laid in water in late winter or early spring. Larvae hatch in summer and live on damp forest floors as subadults (in the West, terrestrial adults) called efts in early fall; in 1-3 years they assume adult characteristics and breed in water. The red-spotted newt ranges from Ontario to Nova Scotia, south to Alabama and North Carolina.

SNAPPING TURTLE
AC, GS, HS, MC, SH, VO

When teased or raised from the water, a snapping turtle may deliver a serious bite. It measures 8-18.5 in. long, and weighs up to 45 lbs. The shell is tan to dark brown, sometimes covered by algae, with three rows of armor-like plates; the tail is as long as the shell. The "snapper's" habitat is the warm shallows and mud bottoms of freshwater ponds and lakes. It ranges from southern Alberta to Nova Scotia, south to Texas and Florida.

SPOTTED SALAMANDER
AC, GS, HS, MC, SH

The spotted salamander spends most of its time underground, so it is seldom seen. Squat in appearance, it is 6-9.75 in. long. Above, its coloration is dark gray to black, with 2 irregular rows of orange or yellow spots down the back; the belly is slate gray. This species ranges from Nova Scotia to the drainage areas of the Great Lakes, south to Louisiana and Florida; acid rains have threatened its populations in the Northeast. Specimens may live as long as 20 years.

SPRING PEEPER
AC, GS, HS, IR, MC, SH, VO

A member of the treefrog family, with northern and southern subspecies, the spring peeper offers one of the first signs of spring with its familiar chorus. It measures .75-1.5 in. long, and is tan to brown to gray, with a dark "X" on the back; the southern subspecies is identified by its spotted belly. Mostly nocturnal, this frog hibernates below fallen limbs and in bark crevices. It lives in wooded areas near ponds and lakes, or in pools created by spring flood rains.

FLOWERS, SHRUBS, AND TREES

ALTERNATE-LEAF DOGWOOD
GS, IR, MC, SH, VO

A shrub or small tree with a short trunk and flat-topped crown, the alternate-leaf dogwood matures to a height of 25 ft. Unlike other native dogwoods, this species has alternate rather than opposite leaves, 2.5–4.5 in. long. White flowers, .25 in. wide, appear in late spring; berry-like blue-black fruit matures in late summer. This species ranges from Newfoundland to the southern Appalachian Mountains, west to Minnesota.

BALSAM FIR
AC, IR, SH, VO

The balsam fir is the traditional Christmas tree of the northeast, where it is also the only native fir. It grows 40–60 ft. high, with a trunk diameter of 1–1.5 ft.; needles are .5–1 in. long, flat, dark shiny green above and whitish below, at right angles to one another; cones are purple-green, 2–3.75 in. long, borne from the topmost branches. In winter, deer and moose browse the foliage.

BLACK CHERRY
AC, GS, HS, MC, SH

Wild cherry cough syrup from the dark gray bark, jellies and wine from the fruit, and fine furniture from the wood are some of the products made from the black cherry. This widespread species is the largest native cherry, and has 5 different varieties. It grows 50–60 ft. high; leaves are 2–5 in. long, elliptical, with a tapered tip and finely sawtoothed edges; autumn foliage is yellow or reddish. The black cherry's white flowers appear in late spring; fruit matures in late summer.

BLACK-EYED SUSAN
AC, IR, MC, SH

Black-eyed Susan is found nearly everywhere in North America, in fields, on prairies, and in open forests. Growing 1–3 ft. high, its flowers are golden yellow, 2–3 in. wide, with a central brown cone. This native prairie biennial produces a rosette of leaves in its first year, and flowers from June to October in its second year.

BLACK LOCUST
AC, GS, MC, SH

The black locust is a medium-sized tree with a forking, irregular trunk and crown of branches. It grows 40–80 ft. high; leaves "fold" at night, and are dark blue-green above, 6–12 in. long. Highly aromatic white flowers appear in late spring; the fruit (a flat, brown pod) appears in autumn and remains on the tree until it splits open in winter. This species is short-lived, and grows mainly in the southern Appalachian Mountains.

BLOODROOT
GS, HS, MC, SH, VO

Bloodroot stems were used as a source of red dye by Native Americans. Its flowers are white with a golden center, up to .5 in. wide, each on a stem enfolded by a blue-green basal leaf; flower stems grow to 10 in. high. Like other members of the poppy family, the bloodroot's flowers last only a short time; it is found along streams in woodlands, across Canada to Nova Scotia, south to Texas and Florida.

BLUETS
AC, GS, HS, MC, SH

More than two dozen species of bluets are found in North America. Its flowers are pale blue, .5 in. wide, with yellow centers. Bluets bloom from April to June on grassy slopes and in thickets and fields, from Ontario to Nova Scotia, south to Alabama and Georgia. This plant grows 3–6 in. high.

EASTERN REDBUD
GS, HS, MC, SH

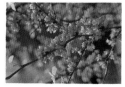

The eastern redbud is often planted as an ornamental tree. It has a short trunk and

grows to a mature height of 20 ft.; dull green leaves are long-stalked and heart-shaped. 2.5–4.5 in. long and wide. Pink (rarely white) pea-shaped flowers appear in early spring on stalks; fruit (pinkish, long, flat pods) matures in summer and splits open on one side in autumn or winter. The flowers of the eastern redbud can be eaten in a salad, or fried.

EASTERN WHITE PINE
AC, GS, IR, MC, SH, VO

The largest northeastern conifer and the state tree of Maine, the eastern white pine was once prized for its use as the mast of Colonial sailing ships. It is now harvested for construction and pulpwood purposes. As it grows to its mature height of up to 100 ft., 1 row of horizontal branches per year is added. The blue-green needles, 2.5–5 in. long, grow in tassels of 5; cones measure 4–8 in. This species ranges from southeast Manitoba to Newfoundland, south to Iowa and northern Georgia.

MOUNTAIN LAUREL
GS, MC, SH

Protected by most state laws, the mountain laurel is considered one of our most beautiful native flowering shrubs. An evergreen, it may grow 20 ft. high. Its narrow, elliptical leaves can be either opposite or alternate, or in threes, 2.5–4 in. long and 1.5 in. wide. Pink or white flowers in clusters of pointed buds open in spring; brown fruit splits open along 5 lines in winter. This species ranges from southern Maine to northwestern Florida, west to Louisiana.

RED MAPLE AC, EV, GS, HS, IR, MC, SH, VO

The red maple has the longest north–south range of all tree species that grow along the East Coast, from Newfoundland to Florida and Texas (west to Minnesota). This tree grows 60–90 ft. high. Lobed leaves (2.5–4 in. long and wide) show red coloration in both spring and autumn; red flowers appear in slender clusters before leaves in late winter or early spring. Winged fruit matures and falls in spring. Ink and brown and black dyes have traditionally been made from red maple bark.

SASSAFRAS
GS, HS, MC, SH

The sassafras grows in moist sandy clearings in uplands and valleys from Michigan to Maine, south to Texas and Florida. European colonists used the aromatic root bark to make a medicinal tea. This tree grows 30–60 ft. high; lobed leaves are long-stalked, elliptical, 3–5 in. long, turning yellow, orange, or red in autumn. Clusters of yellow-green flowers appear in early spring (male and female often on separate trees); fruit clusters of bluish-black berries in red cups on red stalks mature in autumn.

SUGAR MAPLE
AC, GS, IR, MC, SH

Birds-eye maple is a special grain pattern that sometimes develops in the sugar maple, whose wood is popular with furniture makers. Indians taught European colonists to use the sap of sugar maples to make maple syrup. This tree grows 70–100 ft. high, with a trunk diameter of 2–3 ft. Its bark has a rougher, darker appearance than that of red maples. Leaves are lobed, 3.5–5.5 in. long and wide; autumn foliage is multicolored. Bell-shaped yellowish flowers appear with new leaves in spring; winged fruit matures and falls in autumn.

UMBRELLA MAGNOLIA
GS, HS, MC

It is theorized that the first plant to bear seeds in a protective ovary was a magnolia, more than 70 million years ago. This tree grows 30–40 ft. high, in moist soils of mountain valleys, and may be seen in Great Smoky Mountains National Park. Leaves are ovate, 10–20 in. long, 5–10 in. wide. Flowers 7–10 in. wide appear in spring; cone-like fruit matures in autumn.

YARROW
AC, GS, HS, IR, MC, SH, VO

A member of the sunflower family, yarrow draws its Latin name, *Achillea millefolium,* from the Greek warrior Achilles, who allegedly discovered the plant's blood-clotting qualities. The stems of its flowers grow 8–40 in. high; white to pink flowers are .25–.5 in. wide, in flat-topped clusters. Yarrow blooms from June to November, in old fields and by roadsides. It ranges throughout North America.

PHOTO CREDITS

Page 10: ©Manuel Rodriguez
13: ©Lynn M. Stone
17: Acadia National Park
18: ©Alan D. Briere/Tom Stack & Assoc.
20: ©Ed Cooper
22: ©Bill West
24-25: ©Gwen Fidler/Tom Stack & Assoc.
26: ©Alan D. Briere/Tom Stack & Assoc.
27: ©Manuel Rodriguez
29: ©Steven C. Kaufman
32-33: ©David Muench
34-35: ©J. Robert Stottlemyer
39: ©Jeff Gnass
40: ©Manuel Rodriguez
41: ©Stephen J. Krasemann/DRK Photo
42-43: ©Bullaty–Lomeo
45: ©Manuel Rodriguez
46: ©Dave Woodward/Tom Stack & Assoc.
49: ©Robert Perron
54, 55: Florida State Archives
56-67: ©Robert Perron
59: ©Dave Parker
60-61: ©Al Grotell
62: ©Stephen Frink/Southern Stock Photos
63: ©Buddy Mays
64, top: ©Nancy Sefton/Seaphot Ltd.
64, bottom left: ©Dave Woodward/Tom Stack & Assoc.
64, bottom right: ©Dick Clarke/Seaphot Ltd.
67: ©Cindy Gray/National Stock Network
69: ©M. Timothy O'Keefe/Southern Stock Photos
70-71: ©Dave Woodward / Tom Stack & Assoc.
73: ©Hinke/Sacilotto
74, 77: © Matt Bradley
80: Office of the Chief of Engineers in the National Archives
83: © Matt Bradley
85: National Park Service photo by John Brooks
86, 87: © Chris Huss/The Wildlife Collection
89: © Ben Altman
90: ©John Netherton
93: ©David Muench
97, 100, 101: Florida State Archives
102: ©Raymond G. Barnes/Click, Chicago
104-105: ©Manuel Rodriguez
106-107: ©John Netherton
109: ©Robert Perron
111: ©Steven C. Kaufman
114-115, both: ©John Netherton
117: ©Jeff Foott
119: ©Brian Parker/Tom Stack & Assoc.
120-121: ©Fred Hirschmann
122-123: ©Marty Cordano
124: ©John Netherton
125: ©Kim Heacox
127: ©John Netherton
128, 129: ©Bullaty–Lomeo
130-131, 133: ©John Netherton
134-135: ©Marty Cordano
136: ©Bullaty–Lomeo
139: ©David Muench
143; 145, both: Great Smoky Mountains National Park Archive
147: ©John Netherton
148: ©David Muench
150-151: ©Bill Deane
153: ©Bullaty–Lomeo
154: ©Tom J. Ulrich
155: ©John Netherton
157: ©Karen Phillips/Click, Chicago
158-159: ©Tom Algire
161: ©John Netherton
163: ©Tom Algire
164: ©Lynn M. Stone
165: ©Manuel Rodriguez
167: ©Tom Algire
168: ©John Netherton
170-171: ©Bill Deane
172: ©Jeff Gnass
175: Hot Springs Advertising & Tourist Promotion
179, 180-181: Arkansas State University Museum
182, 185: Hot Springs Advertising & Tourist Promotion
186: ©Tom J. Ulrich
187: ©Craig Blacklock
188: ©John Shaw/Tom Stack & Assoc.
189: ©Connie Toops
190: ©Jeff Gnass
193, top: Hot Springs National Park

Appendix of Animals and Plants Photo Credits

388, col. 1, top: ©Larry Thorngren/Tom Stack & Assoc., **bottom:** ©Roy Murphy; **col. 2:** ©John Gerlach/Tom Stack & Assoc.; **col. 3, top:** ©Bob McKeever/Tom Stack & Assoc., **bottom:** ©Kerry T. Givens/Tom Stack & Assoc.

389, col. 1, top: ©Karl H. Maslowski, **bottom:** ©Keith H. Murakami/Tom Stack & Assoc.; **col. 2, top:** ©Roy Murphy, **bottom:** ©Robert C. Simpson/Tom Stack & Assoc.; **col. 3:** ©John Shaw/Tom Stack & Assoc.

390, col. 1, top: ©Rod Planck/Tom Stack & Assoc., **bottom:** ©Robert C. Simpson/Tom Stack & Assoc.; **col. 2, top:** ©Robert C. Gildart, **bottom:** ©W. D. Weber/Tom Stack & Assoc.; **col. 3:** ©E. P. I. Nancy Adams/Tom Stack & Assoc.

391, col. 1, top: ©Robert C. Simpson/Tom Stack & Assoc., **bottom:** ©John Gerlach/Tom Stack & Assoc.: **col. 2, top:** ©Stephen Trimble, **bottom:** ©Robert Villani, **col. 3, top:** ©Don & Pat Valenti/Tom Stack & Assoc., **bottom:** ©John Gerlach/Tom Stack & Assoc.

392, col. 1, top: ©John Shaw/Tom Stack & Assoc., **bottom:** ©Tom J. Ulrich; **col. 2:** ©Arthur Swoger; **col. 3, top:** ©John Shaw/Tom Stack & Assoc., **bottom:** ©Robert C. Simpson/Tom Stack & Assoc.

393, col. 1, top: ©Arthur Morris, **bottom:** ©Leonard Lee Rue III/Tom Stack & Assoc., **col. 2, both:** ©Robert C. Simpson/Tom Stack & Assoc.; **col. 3:** ©Larry R. Ditto/Tom Stack & Assoc.

394, col. 1, top: ©Robert C. Simpson/Tom Stack & Assoc., **bottom:** ©Tom J. Ulrich, **col. 2, top:** ©Robert C. Simpson/Tom Stack & Assoc., **bottom:** ©Tom J. Ulrich; **col. 3:** ©Mary Stibritz.

395, col. 1, top: ©Rod Planck/Tom Stack & Assoc., **bottom:** ©John C. Murphy/Tom Stack &

Assoc.; **col. 2, top:** ©John Shaw/Tom Stack & Assoc., **bottom:** ©Rod Planck/ Tom Stack & Assoc., **col. 3:** ©J. R. MacGregor.

396, col. 1, top: ©Robert C. Simpson/Tom Stack & Assoc., **bottom:** ©Rod Planck/Tom Stack & Assoc.; **col. 2, top:** ©J. R. MacGregor, **bottom:** ©Robert C. Simpson/Tom Stack & Assoc.; **col. 3, top:** ©David M. Dennis/ Tom Stack & Assoc., **bottom:** National Park Service photo by John Brooks.

397, col. 1, top: © John C. Murphy/Tom Stack & Assoc.; **bottom:** ©John Cancalosi/Tom Stack & Assoc.; **col 2, top:** ©Rod Planck/Tom Stack & Assoc., **bottom:** ©Bob McKeever/Tom Stack & Assoc.

398-400, all: ©John J. Smith.

INDEX
Numbers in italics indicate illustrations.